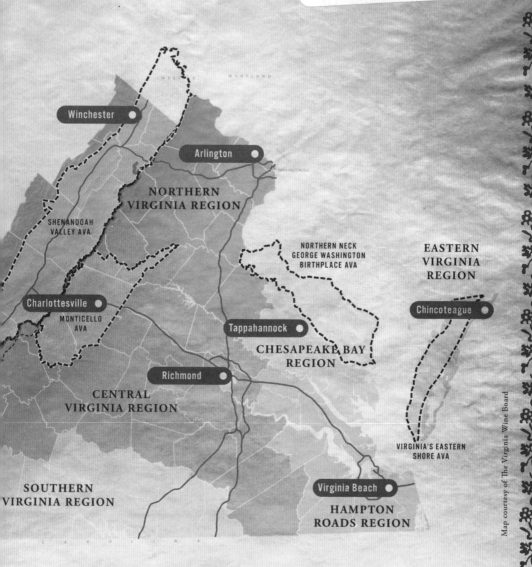

MARYLAND

WEST VA.

WASHINGTON D.C.

Winchester

Arlington

NORTHERN VIRGINIA REGION

SHENANDOAH VALLEY AVA

NORTHERN NECK GEORGE WASHINGTON BIRTHPLACE AVA

EASTERN VIRGINIA REGION

Charlottesville

MONTICELLO AVA

Tappahannock

Chincoteague

CHESAPEAKE BAY REGION

Richmond

CENTRAL VIRGINIA REGION

VIRGINIA'S EASTERN SHORE AVA

SOUTHERN VIRGINIA REGION

Virginia Beach

HAMPTON ROADS REGION

CAROLINA

BEYOND

Jefferson's Vines

THE EVOLUTION OF QUALITY WINE IN VIRGINIA

RICHARD G. LEAHY

STERLING EPICURE
New York

STERLING EPICURE
New York

An Imprint of Sterling Publishing
387 Park Avenue South
New York, NY 10016

ISBN 978-1-4027-9774-3 (hardcover)
ISBN 978-1-4027-9775-0 (ebook)

Distributed in Canada by Sterling Publishing
c/o Canadian Manda Group, 165 Dufferin Street
Toronto, Ontario, Canada M6K 3H6
Distributed in the United Kingdom by GMC Distribution Services
Castle Place, 166 High Street, Lewes, East Sussex, England BN7 1XU
Distributed in Australia by Capricorn Link (Australia) Pty. Ltd.
P.O. Box 704, Windsor, NSW 2756, Australia

For information about custom editions, special sales, and premium and
corporate purchases, please contact Sterling Special Sales at 800-805-5489
or specialsales@sterlingpublishing.com.

Manufactured in the United States of America

2 4 6 8 10 9 7 5 3 1

www.sterlingpublishing.com

For my family,
And in memory of Joseph P. Leahy,
Dan Neumeister
And George Hazen

"Kiss today good-bye,
And point me t'ward tomorrow.
We did what we had to do.
Won't forget, can't regret
What I did for love."

—A Chorus Line

Author's Note

There are roughly two hundred wineries in Virginia, and unfortunately it was not possible to include them all in this book. In an effort to create a coherent narrative, the wineries and regions are presented as a travelogue, which necessarily limits the wineries covered. There are certainly other, equally valid routes to be explored. The inclusion or omission of a particular winery, or the length of any individual winery entry, is not meant to be a reflection on a winery's merits or importance. I encourage readers to visit wineries not in the book as well as those I have written about here, and to consult additional resources such as the wine bloggers cited, the official Virginia wine industry website (virginiawine.org), and winery websites for more information.

CONTENTS

FOREWORD

It's time for Virginia to get over Thomas Jefferson.

"Mr. Jefferson," as he is still sometimes called around Charlottesville, was not only the author of the Declaration of Independence and the country's third president, but he ranks even today as Virginia's most famous vintner. His modern successors still celebrate his enthusiasm for viticulture and his confidence that Virginia, and America, would someday produce wines to rival the best of Europe.

The problem, of course, is that Jefferson was a failure as a vintner. He never produced a single bottle of wine from the seven attempts he made at Monticello to grow European grape varieties. There are many reasons for his failure, and Richard Leahy explores them. But the fact that Jefferson, accomplished in so many fields from politics to architecture and music, could not grow wine in Virginia has shaped the popular perception of the Old Dominion's modern wine industry.

That perception is finally changing. Just as Jefferson helped lead a political revolution, Virginia's vintners today are participating in a revolution of their own. Wine is now produced in all fifty U.S. states. Wine lovers across the country are discovering the joys of local wine from "the other 47"—those states not called California, Washington, or Oregon. New York ranks fourth in the number of wineries, while Virginia and Texas vie for fifth place. Strike up a conversation with a Virginia winemaker, and before long he or she will make the comparison with Napa Valley in the 1970s, when a young wine region began to realize its star potential.

Virginia's modern wine renaissance began about that time, when Gianni Zonin, the soft-spoken patriarch of an Italian wine family, decided to start a winery in the rolling hills north of Charlottesville. Today, Barboursville Vineyards is the state's most important commercial winery. Winemaker Luca Paschina, a native of Piemonte, has been at the helm since 1990 and has created Octagon, a merlot-based blend that many consider the first to fulfill Jefferson's dream.

Other pioneers followed, and their stories populate Leahy's vinous guidebook to the Old Dominion. We meet Dennis Horton, who thrust Virginia wine into the spotlight by entering his viognier in a California tasting competition. The publicity ignited a rash of viognier plantings, and today the variety is considered Virginia's "official" grape, even though there is no uniformity of style or quality. Horton also brought the Norton grape back to Virginia, and along with the affable Jennifer McCloud, the generous dreamer behind Chrysalis Vineyards in Middleburg, has spearheaded a Norton revival.

In the early 1980s, a quiet Ohio native and Peace Corps veteran named Jim Law founded Linden Vineyards in the Blue Ridge foothills just east of Front Royal. Law is a restless tinkerer who is never satisfied with his wines, but always looks for ways to improve them. And improve them he has, steadily gaining a reputation as one of Virginia's premier winemakers. Law is a leading advocate of the importance of choosing a suitable vineyard site, favoring steep slopes with poor soils as the best places for grape vines.

These were some of Virginia's leaders—many followed their example. A handful of wineries in 1980 grew to about seventy at the turn of the millenium. That number tripled to two hundred wineries by the end of 2011. Wine became a major contributor to Virginia's economy. A 2006 study estimated that the Commonwealth's then-120 wineries gave the state a $350 million economic stimulus. And the Virginia Tourism Corporation estimates that for every dollar spent driving someone to a Virginia winery, the state collects $5 in tax revenue within ninety days, from gas, food, lodging, and, of course, wine purchases.

As the number of wineries increased and the quality of wines improved, Virginia began to attract attention from France. Several wineries turned to Bordeaux rather than California as a model and began hiring French consultants. Patricia Kluge, a wealthy divorcee who transformed her enormous estate just around the hillside from Jefferson's

Monticello into Virginia's largest vineyard, hired the world-famous "flying winemaker" Michel Rolland to help fashion her red wines. When John Kent Cooke, former owner of the Washington Redskins football team, planted vines on his Boxwood estate near Middleburg, he hired Stephane Derenoncourt, one of Rolland's competitors as consultant.

While those headline grabbing names helped elevate awareness of Virginia's wine industry, the French invasion was actually more extensive as several fresh graduates from French enology schools came to hone their craft in a fledgling wine region where nature throws every challenge imaginable their way. But France's biggest contribution to Virginia wine, at least so far, is undoubtedly Claude Thibaut. A native of Champagne, Thibaut came to Virginia after working in Australia and California to make sparkling wines for Kluge Estate. There, and subsequently with his own Thibaut-Janisson label, he demonstrated Virginia's capability to produce excellent fizz.

Virginia's rise to prominence in wine has not always been smooth. To survive financially, many wineries must rely on income from their tasting rooms or events such as weddings or concerts. Some have become embroiled in legal troubles brought by neighbors resentful of the traffic; others have found their commitment to wine quality questioned by skeptics who don't seem to realize it's a business.

The recession took its toll when the spectacular bankruptcy of Kluge Estate played out in national headlines. That saga ended with real estate magnate Donald Trump purchasing the property at auction in April 2011. The renamed Trump Winery will have a natural distribution channel through Trump's hotels and casinos that may help raise Virginia's wine country profile. More quietly, Steve and Jean Case of America Online fame purchased another winery that fell victim to the recession, with hopes of bringing their Internet marketing savvy to play and get Virginia wine onto more dinner tables throughout the region.

It's popular to say Virginia wine is at a "tipping point," and there is indeed reason for excitement. The industry is maturing like a fine wine.

Many growers are still experimenting to see which grape varieties will thrive in the state's variable climate, but increasingly there is a preference for vineyard-designated blends of the traditional red Bordeaux varieties. After touting first cabernet franc and then petit verdot as Virginia's champion red, people are recognizing they go well together in the same glass. Viognier remains the most notable white wine, but petit manseng also does well here, in both dry and sweet versions. And you don't find that grape anywhere else in the United States.

Virginia wines can be hard to find. Ironically, it is easier to buy them in London today than in Washington, D.C. That's due to Christopher Parker, a British ex-pat who believed Virginia's European-styled wines would appeal to his countrymen's palate. Parker has shown Virginia's vintners that there is indeed a market beyond the tasting room or the festival booth.

Much of the excitement, however, comes from a sense among winemakers that Virginia is ready to rise to a new level of quality. Four decades of experience and experimentation have yielded a clearer understanding of what sites are most appropriate for vineyards. New viticultural practices, most notably dense spacing of vines and strict management of the leaf canopy, are helping vintners ripen grapes more consistently.

So it is fitting that Leahy begins his oenological travelogue of Virginia at RdV Vineyards, which Jim Law calls "the next generation of Virginia wine." RdV's charismatic vintner, Rutger de Vink, set out to make a wine that can stand proud among the world's best, sparing no expense in the vineyard or the winery and incorporating the lessons of Virginia as well as the world's greatest wine regions to his steep hillside vineyards in Fauquier County.

Mr. Jefferson would indeed be proud of Virginia's vintners today And he'd probably ask us to stop talking about him so much.

—DAVE McINTYRE, Washington Post wine columnist
and cofounder of DrinkLocalWine.com

INTRODUCTION

It was a beautiful, sunny day in early September 2010 in the orchard at Monticello, home of Thomas Jefferson. The heavy humidity usual for late summer was gone, and it felt more like early fall. In the shade of fruit trees, ten members of the prestigious Circle of Wine Writers sat at two cloth-covered picnic tables and served themselves salad and chicken with penne. The tables had been set up where the orchard meets a vineyard, and the table legs had to be leveled on the slope of the hill; but it provided a most charming, bucolic setting, and a very appropriate one for a talk about Thomas Jefferson and his vines.

The vines the writers could view from their tables had, like all the other plants mentioned in Jefferson's *Garden Book*, been painstakingly replanted in their original positions. Gabriele Rausse, assistant director of gardens and grounds, had researched the names of the eighteenth-century grape varieties Jefferson had imported through his friend, the patriot and native Italian Filippo Mazzei. The grapevines are trained as they would have been two hundred years ago, on split-rail fencing, but with an important difference: The vines are now grafted on American rootstock (standard practice in nearly all wine regions in the world today) to avoid the phylloxera vine louse that helped doom Jefferson's efforts at viticulture. Planting grapevines on phylloxera- and disease-resistant rootstocks is now a major part of viticultural success in Virginia.

Rausse has a small winery of his own, where he processes the grapes harvested from the Monticello vineyard and makes them into a traditional chianti-style blend dominated by the sangiovese grape but also containing the white trebbiano. I learned the practical reason why the Tuscans blended the two grapes together: "Sangiovese is a high-acid grape that also has high pH," explained Rausse, which makes it problematic to achieve stability in the finished wine. "Trebbiano has good acidity [with lower pH], so in blending them, it corrects the pH and makes a more stable wine."

The writers were able to enjoy this contemporary blend of the heirs of Jefferson's vines: a dark rosé–colored wine, fresh and lively, with bright, snappy cherry flavors and acidity and low tannin—a perfect wine for an alfresco Italian lunch on a gorgeous late-summer day.

Thomas Jefferson, who drafted the Declaration of Independence, founded the University of Virginia, and wrote the Statute of Virginia for Religious Freedom (and was also the third president of the United States), was the father of American wine. As he wrote to Thomas Appleton from Monticello in 1816, he considered wine "a necessary of life." Not content to merely import the best wines from Europe (he was one of the first to have them bottled at the château), he also believed in the potential of American viticulture for producing both quality wine and prosperity for the farmer.

In a letter to John Dortie in 1781, Jefferson wrote, "Wine being among the earliest luxuries in which we indulge ourselves, it is desirable it should be made here and we have every soil, aspect and climate of the best wine countries, and I have myself drank wines made in this state and in Maryland, of the quality of the best Burgundy."

Jefferson's first plantings of grapevines at Monticello were made in 1771. Arriving in 1773, Filippo Mazzei was happy to help Jefferson establish a European-style vineyard at Monticello, and another at a nearby farm called Colle (site of today's Jefferson Vineyards).

Unfortunately, Jefferson never harvested a crop from his vineyard. Conventional wisdom blames the phylloxera vine louse, fungal diseases, and winter injury for this failure. The Colle vineyard planted by Mazzei's vignerons, having survived several years, was leased by Mazzei to General Friedrich Adolf Riedesel, "whose horses in one week destroyed the whole labor of three or four years, and thus ended an experiment," Jefferson wrote to Senator Albert Gallatin, in 1793, "which, from every appearance, would in a year or two more have established the practicability of that branch of culture in America."

Jefferson by then believed it would "be well to push the culture" of native grapes, as it would "take centuries [for European grapes] to adapt to our soil and climate." "We could," he prophetically declared in an 1808 letter to Count C. P. de Lasteyrie, "in the United States, make as great a variety of wines as are made in Europe, not exactly of the same kinds, but doubtless as good."

Planting European grapevines on their own roots—as Jefferson and Mazzei did—proved to be unsustainable for commercial viticulture in Virginia, but how long did Jefferson's vines last? We know the vines planted at Jamestown and later in the eighteenth century survived long enough to produce accidental hybrids with American grapes, so phylloxera and fungal diseases might not have wiped them out for some time. A more intriguing question is, What happened to the grapes on Jefferson's vines?

Rausse has spent time reading the letters between Jefferson and his estate managers in an attempt to determine if grapes ever ripened in the vineyards Mazzei planted. Although Monticello officials tell us wine was never made from grapes on the estate (Jefferson was a meticulous record-keeper, and as an enthusiastic gardener and wine lover would certainly have documented the event), Rausse disputes the popular notion that the vines were destroyed by phylloxera, fungal diseases, or other threats before they could produce fruit.

"In one letter [of February 1786] answering Jefferson's inquiry on the progress of his vineyard, Antonio Giannini [the farm manager] at first says the vines are 'improving marvelously' but then explains that the reason no wine had been made is 'because each year the grapes are taken before they are ripe, which is very harmful to the vines,'" quotes Rausse. Taken by whom? Certainly correct picking instructions would be given by Mazzei, but what if the grapes were already gone before picking could begin? This tantalizing bit of evidence suggests that birds were the primary culprits, if not deer or other animals. And this makes sense. The European vinifera grapes are also sweeter and less bitter than the small, berry-size grapes from native varieties such as *Vitis riparia* that grow wild in the woods at Monticello today.

Giannini also seems to be shrewdly covering himself in case Jefferson returned to find devastation in the vineyard. "It was suggested that some people were stealing the grapes," says Rausse. "If they had, they would not have done it year after year, for fear of being caught."

The first vineyards were planted in 1771, and the letter from Giannini is dated 1786; the vines obviously survived and matured, but whether they produced a crop that was not preyed on by animals or fungal diseases is a different matter, as all grape growers today know. Deer fences—which have to be at least ten feet tall to discourage deer from jumping over them—are now common in commercial vineyards in the East, even though it can cost up to $10,000 to protect ten acres of vines.

If Jefferson hadn't spent so much time away from his beloved Monticello, he might have noticed his delectable ripening grape crop suddenly disappear, which to his rational mind would suggest their being eaten by wildlife. He then might have employed scarecrows or other tactics (including hunting) to increase the chances of the grapes reaching ripeness, being harvested, and being made into fine table wine.

Although Jefferson never lived to see a crop harvested from his own vines, his optimism about the future of American viticulture was not ill founded. About the time he died, Dr. Daniel Norton pioneered the Norton's Virginia Seedling grape (now simply known as norton, or cynthiana in Arkansas), upon which a successful commercial grape and wine industry was built in Virginia and Missouri in the nineteenth century. At the same time, American grapes such as concord and catawba created booming native wine industries from New York to the Ohio River Valley. Unfortunately, Prohibition all but killed the American wine industry—it was barely kept alive by the exemptions to the Volstead Act allowing home wine production and consumption, and the making of sacramental wine (leading to occasional scandals involving "rabbis" with non-Jewish surnames trying to claim a "sacramental" exemption).

Repeal occurred during the Depression, a bad time to invest in vineyards or wineries (those looking for a faster return on investment in alcoholic beverages made beer or liquor). While the California wine industry recovered, the loss of craft knowledge in the East was devastating. With the challenge of high humidity and fungal diseases (not to mention animal depredation), it would take decades for the industry to branch beyond industrial giants making branded wine out of native grapes for an unsophisticated market.

Other writers, from Leon Adams, Thomas Pinney, and Hudson Cattell to the wine bloggers in every state today, have told the story of the renaissance of the American wine industry beyond the West Coast. This book, however, tells the story of what has happened to Jefferson's vines in his native Virginia, focusing on the last thirty years but also shedding light on previously unexamined chapters of the eighteenth-century Virginia wine experiment, and demonstrating that Jefferson was following in the footsteps of many American colonists in trying to make fine wine in Virginia.

The story encompasses many people in many fields: university researchers, grape growers, winemakers and winery owners, politicians, marketing professionals, the media, and many others—all players in an industry persevering in the attempt to make not just wine, but fine wine that will restore Virginia's reputation as an important American wine region. Every one of them is striving to validate Jefferson's viticultural ambition by saying, in effect, "Mr. Jefferson, here are your vines and wines, and they are doing very well today."

RᴅV VINEYARDS,
DELAPLANE

Some Virginia wineries have hired famous consultants, issued press releases trumpeting their locality, charged exorbitant prices for their wines, and expected the world to clamor to buy them. Others have quietly but single-mindedly combined a passion for great wine with the goal and means of making it in Virginia, while keeping production and marketing very limited. The latter path is the one taken by RdV, whose founder and principal Rutger de Vink's goal is nothing less than to make world-class wine in Virginia. His resources, training, determined passion, and the discipline of his time in the Marine Corps (as well as the quality of his wine) sold me. Jim Law, a leading Virginia winegrower and de Vink's mentor, when asked about the new operation, told me, "I think it's the greatest thing to happen to Virginia wine ever. Rutger apprenticed here and understands the impact of soil and terroir on wine quality. They are in [this industry] for the right reasons, not to flash money but to focus on making great wine."

De Vink gave me a bottle of his 2008 Friends and Family wine, an easy-drinking, clean, and refreshing red Bordeaux blend.

I liked its elegant, understated style but it was clear the wine was made from superior fruit.

There are three major visual impressions you get as you approach RdV from the town of Delaplane. The first is the way the vineyard rises up on a steep knoll, with the rows trained to follow the flow of air down the hill. The second is the sparse but elegant winery: three rectangular spokes radiating from a central cylinder like an iconic farm silo. The third is the lack of visitors, or even a regular tasting room.

The winery entrance is a glass door framed by two of the radiating wings. On entering, you notice that the silo is a hollow skylight rising up; it also spirals down to the wine cellar by way of a circular staircase. The left-hand wing is a reception area, with windows looking onto the hill and vineyard beyond, but with no tasting bar. The right-hand wing is actually the sides and roof of the tank cellar below, and the third wing houses offices. The architecture and space, reminiscent of Frank Lloyd Wright, speak of elegant proportions and extremely adequate funding.

When I walked in, I heard voices coming up from the cellar. Cellar master Joshua Grainer—also a former Linden Vineyards apprentice—introduced me to soil and land use specialist Alex Blackburn, environmental teams manager for Loudoun County. They had been discussing land Grainer had been considering purchasing for a vineyard. Surface features can be deceiving, and despite a steep gradient, Blackburn explained, the subsoils were not favorable for drainage, so the site was rejected. On the wall nearby were a series of gray and brown cylinders; my first thought was *modern art*, but Grainer told me that these were a selection of soil cores taken from the vineyard. The series went from basement rock on the left to subsurface rock on the right. *These people are serious about their soils*, I thought to myself. And that was just the beginning.

I walked with Grainer into the cave where barrels and bottled wines are stored, laid out in an H shape, past French oak barrels and cages of bottled wine aging in the cool, dark quiet, waiting for enough maturity to be labeled and released. At the end of one of the long tunnels, the light shines on the naked rock; the wine aging in cages or casks has come back to its source.

Rutger de Vink met us in the tank room, where he explained that the vineyard has eleven "blocks" and that each block has a dedicated fermentation tank. They are conical in shape so that the cap of skins and seeds that forms during fermentation can be more easily submerged for optimal extraction of flavor and color compounds. This also avoids the extraction of harsh compounds when the common punch-down method is used to submerge the cap.

De Vink is tall, with tousled, wavy brown hair, a sense of energy and purpose, and a ready smile. With his brimmed hat, boots, and shorts, he looks like an Australian rancher, although his family is Dutch. He was in the Marines for four years, then enrolled in business school. He came to Washington, D.C., and worked for a venture capital company for three or four years, but found he didn't like the work. "I love farming and working outside; the Marine Corps was not just a job but also a way of life, which I missed."

He met with Virginia-based viticulturist Lucie Morton and asked her if he could make a world-class wine in Virginia. Morton recalls recommending three important things to de Vink: high-density planting, quality clones on low-vigor rootstocks (designed to curb a vine's vegetative growth), and that he go to work for Jim Law while he was preparing his own site. "It was clear to me that anything he did would be first class," she says. "By working with Jim, he would get a reality check on the physical nature and challenges of the work through each season, along with the seasoned perspective of an experienced local pro. The site he chose has excellent potential, and his choice of consultants is world-class."

"The main thing I learned at Linden," explains de Vink, "was that site matters." On his first day there, Law asked him to hedge heavy canes on a divided canopy vineyard row; he noticed another block was trained to vertical shoot positioning (and not divided) and was much less vigorous. "I asked Jim why that was, and he said it was all about soils."

Virginia Tech enologist Dr. Bruce Zoecklein led an industry trip to Bordeaux, where de Vink met Kees Van Leeuwen (also Dutch), an enologist at the University of Bordeaux and winemaker at Château Cheval Blanc in Saint-Emilion, and learned about the primacy of soil. We both remembered Van Leeuwen's presentation at the 2004 meeting of the American Society for Enology and Viticulture, Eastern Section, where he demonstrated the terroir effect in a tasting by pouring three different Saint-Emilion wines from the superior 2000 vintage. Soils in Saint-Emilion are mixed, with gravel, sand, limestone, and clay. Late in that vintage, the vineyards planted on well-drained soils dried out, and the resulting wines were a little thin from the drought stress on the vines. The châteaus making these wines were not of the top rank; Van Leeuwen explained that this was because soils and site determine the hierarchy of château ranking. The wine that tasted richest and fullest, neither coarse nor thin, was ranked premier grand cru classé, the top rank in Saint-Emilion.

Van Leeuwen explained that the winemaking regimen was identical in all three châteaus, the only variable being vineyard soil type. The premier grand cru classé château was planted on limestone soils, with a layer of clay beneath. In a hot vintage, the water was retained in the top limestone soil by the clay beneath, and the vines did not suffer drought stress, which led to completely ripe and balanced fruit, and that was expressed in the wine.

"I wanted to be in a place where people say 'you can't do it here' as a challenge," declares de Vink. Before deciding on Virginia, he looked at the Santa Rita Hills, Sonoma Coast, and Sierra Foothills regions of California. The process of narrowing the search down to the current site took three years. "There's something really special and beautiful about Virginia," he reflects, smiling.

Once focused on Virginia, he was looking for a site with good air and water drainage, and low vigor. "People say cabernet sauvignon can't ripen in Virginia, but it's about where the vine is planted. The key isn't heat summation [the Amerine/Winkler system describing wine regions by total heat units in the growing season], it's the change in vine metabolism. Vines in clay soil won't transition from vegetative growth to putting sugars into fruit ripening," he explains. Before planting, he brought in soil consultants including Drs. Alex Blackburn and Daniel Roberts's Integrated Winegrowing, a group of viticulture and soil consultants from Sonoma. "We worked for three months every day clearing the property. The local crew thought the soil was awful for farming, low vigor and rocky, but Dr. Alfred Cass, from Integrated Winegrowing, said it was great for vines." The vineyard was planted only after a year of digging two hundred soil pits and analyzing a range of data.

De Vink wrote a business plan and pooled several investors together with family backing. "Their role is supportive, but they enjoy wine," he says. "When I first started, I loved syrah (such as Côte-Rôtie). I considered planting it but leaned towards Bordeaux varietals because with Bordeaux you have the blending process, as well as a month between ripening of merlot to cabernet sauvignon. It mitigates the risk of rain during harvest, which is why they plant that way in Bordeaux."

The RdV vineyard is just under sixteen acres, planted 40 percent cabernet sauvignon, with 40 percent merlot, 12 percent petit verdot, and 8 percent cabernet franc, all Bordeaux ENTAV clones, on the very low-vigor *riparia* rootstock.

Vines are closely spaced in the rows to reduce vigor, and yields are about 2.5 tons per acre. "We're very selective," says de Vink. Walking the vineyard, you're impressed not only by the views, but by the meticulous order and precision of the rows trained to vertical shoot positioning; prior to harvest, bird netting is tightly wrapped in the fruiting zone.

The estate makes three wines: RdV, a Left Bank–style, cabernet sauvignon–dominated blend; Rendezvous, a Right Bank–style, merlot-dominated blend; and the Family and Friends blend of lots that don't make the cut for the two estate wines. Family and Friends is made in a fruit-forward style for everyday drinking, whereas the other two need time in the bottle to mature. Ratios of varietals vary with the vintage, but the cabernet-based RdV will be a more consistent blend, says de Vink. The RdV (when available) sells for $88, the Rendezvous for $55.

Production in 2008 was 600 cases, in 2009 it was 1,200 cases, and in 2010 they made 2,000 cases. "We want to be just 2,500 cases total capacity," says de Vink. "We have [investor] permission to cull out anything we want."

Eric Boissenot, from Bordeaux, blended the RdV's 2008 vintage and oversees the winemaking team. Jancis Robinson explained, in her column on "Virginia and RdV" in the *Financial Times*, September 17, 2011, that "the first samples [from RdV], from vines just three years old, so intrigued the Médoc's most famous oenologist Eric Boissenot that this highly respected Bordelais volunteered to become a consultant for RdV Vineyards, advising on the blends for the main wine, RdV, that is designed for long aging in the Bordeaux tradition and another rather more accessible expression of each vintage called, neatly for Francophones, Rendezvous. 'There is an atmosphere at RdV that attracted me,' Boissenot explained in an e-mail, 'an exceptional team spirit and a humble determination to get every detail right, in Rutger, his assistant Josh Grainer and the [six] Mexican vineyard workers.'"

De Vink wanted a Bordeaux consultant to help with the critical phase of shifting plants to ripen the fruit rather than put out foliage; he also prefers Bordeaux wines to California wines. Boissenot does his work from Bordeaux, receiving must (unfermented grape juice) samples shipped via two-day DHL express, analyzing them, and making recommendations via e-mail, while other Bordeaux-based enologists consulting at the winery assist on-site.

The fruit is double-sorted, first on a vibrating table and then at the destemmer, to eliminate underripe or damaged berries. One change made since the beginning is chilling the picked fruit down to 40° F; the fruit goes better through the sorting tables when cold, and also the chill restrains native yeast fermentation. In 2010, de Vink for the first time co-inoculated malolactic and primary fermentations, and he will experiment with a native fermentation tank in fall 2011. The reds will be aged in French oak for eighteen to twenty-four months. "If you get high-quality fruit, you shouldn't worry too much about the processing. If you bring it in, and don't mess it up, you'll get what you need." Block number 9 cabernet sauvignon will always be the lead for the RdV blend, but they'll vary it. In 2010, Boissenot said the petit verdot came in a blockbuster, but would overwhelm the blend. De Vink is finding the merlot and cabernet franc aren't what he expects; he wants to go to Bordeaux and ask them how they get the structure in their merlot. "Merlot is like a woman; you have to treat her just right."

De Vink believes Virginia is in a position similar to where Oregon was twenty-five years ago. "The challenge in Virginia is that it's too easy for us to sell our wine here [through proximity to the Metro D.C. market and with winery events]. Oregon was forced to improve quality as well as specialize and associate itself with pinot noir. Now, they're planting on the correct soils. My hope for Virginia is that it follows the same trend, going for a focus on site selection, not on what's best for tourism but for where the best grapes are grown."

The business model for RdV is to sell wine exclusively through a mailing list, and the marketing plan is basically not to do any marketing (they turned down an offer to be featured on the cover of the *Virginia Wine Gazette*). When wines are available, the winery will accept visitors by appointment, and will handle between thirty and sixty visitors per week. Wine prices are not mentioned on their website. "How do we take advantage of proximity to the D.C. market without becoming an event center?" asks de Vink, rhetorically, explaining their approach to sales.

In March 2011, Dave McIntyre, wine columnist for the *Washington Post*, came to RdV, and de Vink set up a comparison tasting with Château Montrose 2006 (Saint-Estèphc), Dominus Napa Valley 2007, and the 2008 RdV. The Montrose retailed for around $100 at the time, while Dominus went for around $150. While McIntyre wrote that he was impressed, he decided to get outside opinions and repeated the tasting blind for four experienced Washington, D.C., wine professionals. All four preferred the Montrose, but they also agreed that the RdV was in the same class, and most preferred it over the Dominus. "But," recalls McIntyre, "the four were also unanimous in their assessment that consumers will have a hard time swallowing a $90 Virginia wine that does not have a track record, especially when they can buy a classed-growth Bordeaux for about the same price."

"Fifty-five and eighty-eight dollars are expensive," agrees de Vink. "It's not flying out the door, and we're not doing the usual model, but we're going according to our plan, and we've never seen anyone say that we've missed the mark once they've tasted the wine." He says that McIntyre's column generated sufficient interest to sell through the spring allocation just from people on the mailing list.

"What if you take industry leaders' experience in Virginia, and put it on a better site?" de Vink asks. "We've taken Luca [Paschina, of Barboursville Vineyards near Charlottesville, founded in 1976] and Jim Law of Linden's [since 1985] thirty years of collective experience and have built on that, taking the next step." How will he know when he's succeeded in making world-class wine? "I want to reach full capacity and sell out just through the mailing list." When he sees skeptics understand the wine, that validates what they're doing. "We're ripe but not as ripe as California; we're kind of between Napa and Bordeaux, and we want to express the best potential of this site by making world-class Virginia wine, not ersatz Bordeaux or California wine." He acknowledges that it's hard to evaluate a wine as world-class when it's just two years old, or a site as world-class without a track record. "We need ten years to really show that the wines can age; then we can be considered a success."

TASTING THE 2010 VINTAGE: A GLIMPSE INTO THE FUTURE

Linden Vineyards

A cold July thunderstorm blasts into my windshield as I cross the gap between the Blue Ridge Mountains to the southwest and the Catoctin Mountains to the northeast, driving west on Rt. 55 then up Rt. 638, crossing the Appalachian Trail at a remarkably low elevation. The narrow road twists and turns, and I drive slowly, finally coming out of the trees to farmland on Freezeland Road, where I see the iconic round logo announcing Linden Vineyards on the right.

Despite the rain, a couple is tasting wine at the bar, and a number of regular club members relax on their members-only deck.

Down in the cellar, I taste a selection of recent wines with Jim Law and his latest apprentice, Jonathan Weber. The 2008 and 2009 Hardscrabble estate chardonnays are very different, showing distinct vintage character: The 2008 is richer, with full texture (some botrytis, a fungus that shrivels ripe grapes, concentrating the sugar in them) but still elegant and balanced, and the 2009, still tight and needing time, is racy and high in acid—very Burgundian (and highly praised by Jancis Robinson). "It needs another four years," says Law, explaining that he's trained his retail and restaurant customers to lay his estate wines down, since he makes them so reductively (in an anaerobic environment that requires bottle-age maturity for optimal pleasure).

Virginia has gained an international reputation for viognier, but with chardonnays such as these—one ripe yet balanced, the other lean and Burgundian—will Virginia become the next Burgundy? Law and others, especially in the cool, high-elevation vineyard sites, are showing excellent potential.

In the cellar, we taste the 2008, 2009, and 2010 barrel samples of the estate Hardscrabble red Bordeaux blend, from youngest to oldest. Again we see an impressive range of vintage character combined with consistent high quality and classic Old World character. The 2010 is bursting with fresh cassis on the nose, especially for a wine still in the barrel, with ripe black fruits on the palate and firm, crunchy tannins tapering to a mocha finish.

While the 2010 is very good, with classic cabernet sauvignon character, I'm astonished by the 2009 Hardscrabble, now in the tank and ready for bottling. The nose is a hedonistic blend of blackberries, spice, and cassis. The palate balances fresh and bright blackberry fruit with firm acidity; between the nose and palate, I think I'm hearing Bach's fifth Brandenburg Concerto. "I think it's sexy because it's so elegant and refreshing," remarks Law. The wine is fully ripe and concentrated, yet fresh and elegant, like the wines of Saint-Julien in the Haut-Médoc.

Could this be the flagship for future Virginia red wines, a re-creation of the classic Bordeaux model of blends from great estates based on grape ratios that work best for the site and the wine rather than 100-percent varietal cabernet or merlot, as so often found in California?

Horton Vineyards

Horton Vineyards, the catalyst for so much progressive innovation in Virginia wine, produces thirty labels, and though I like their malbec, rkatsiteli, and roussanne (among others), I'm most impressed with the viognier, the petit manseng, and a reserve cabernet franc. The 2010 viognier is as good as any in the state and represents (or maybe even, established) a Virginia style: ripe, fresh peach, apricot, and tropical fruits with some honeysuckle, but with fine balancing acidity and lack of new oak. The 2008 reserve cabernet franc, Dennis Horton tells me, is a selection of the best 10 percent from 180 barrels of cabernet franc in the cellar. The regular cabernet franc is good—no vegetal flavors or heavy oak—but the reserve is on a higher plane. The emphasis is not on extraction or oak but on finesse. The nose is spicy, with an integration of oak and red cherry. The palate is powerful and focused, with nice spice elements and an impressively long finish. The petit manseng has only a threshold level of sweetness, but the delicate yet racy pineapple fruit has a fine acid balance to match the flavor intensity.

Horton is still planting new grape varieties, but these three (along with norton) have revolutionized the Virginia wine industry since he introduced them as varietals over twenty years ago, and they continue to define the state both in regional style and wine quality.

Barboursville Vineyards

One hot midsummer afternoon, I pass the ruins of the James Barbour mansion, designed by Thomas Jefferson and built in 1814. Now surrounded by gargantuan boxwood trees, the historic octagonal brick mansion, which was a design trademark of Jefferson's, burned down in a kitchen fire in 1885, but the ruins still stand on the property of Barboursville Vineyards. I'm on my way to taste barrel samples from the excellent 2010 vintage with Barboursville general manager–winemaker

Luca Paschina, who's been here for twenty-two years. We taste a range of wines: smooth and succulent merlot, deeply rich petit verdot, firm but smoothly tannic nebbiolo, several variations of cabernet franc and cabernet sauvignon and, finally, the assembled Octagon blend, with typical proportions of roughly 60 percent merlot, 20 percent cabernet franc, and the balance mostly petit verdot with just a hint of cabernet sauvignon. I'm immediately struck by two things: the depth of fruit and the smoothness of the tannins compared to twenty years ago, when the top wine was a reserve cabernet sauvignon that always seemed to have a bit of an edge to it and didn't have this kind of opulent fruit. Paschina admits that the alcohol levels are unusually high in this California-like vintage, approaching 15 percent, but we agree that the balance of the wine (enough natural acid and lack of coarse new oak) leaves you with the impression that the alcohol isn't out of balance with the rest of the wine—another contrast from twenty years ago, when most Virginia red-wine grapes were lucky to reach 12.5 percent potential alcohol before the fruit rotted on the vine.

It's rare to taste a red Bordeaux blend such as Octagon only nine months from the harvest and find the wine to have such finesse and integration still in the barrel. The nose has red and black cherry, and some spice nuances, with a multilayered palate and juicy fruit, but it is firm and elegantly structured.

Paschina, like many of the Virginia winemakers who have persisted in the industry over the years, continues to change and innovate, listening to the vineyard and to the market. In August 2011, he released his first varietal petit verdot (2008 vintage), and he made his first bottled vermentino in the 2010 vintage. "It's a warm-climate grape from Liguria and Sardinia," he says, "so I planted an experimental lot because I thought it would do well in Virginia." The grape is, like most Italian whites, delicate and not very fruity, but with lemon and mineral nuances that make it a natural with seafood and many appetizers. Paschina's 2010 vermentino has a subtle bouquet with just a hint of citrus, is broad on the palate but has lovely, lively lemon flavors and tanginess that grow in the finish; a welcome step up from pinot grigio (although Barboursville's is one of Virginia's best).

Opposite the Barbour mansion ruins, below the winery, tight-spaced rows of merlot are planted. Visitors may be surprised by the rosebushes at the end of each row, but as fellow members of the vine family, the bushes act as botanical canaries in the viticultural coal mine, warning of diseases that would threaten the grapevines but are easier to see first on the roses.

Still, one can't help thinking Thomas Jefferson would be charmed, seeing both the rosebushes and his beloved European grapevines growing together in harmony within sight of the original boxwood bushes—now trees—across the lane by the ruins. He'd be proud of today's Virginia wine industry, with its roots in tradition but continuing to innovate, just as he did, remodeling Monticello, a metaphor for the dynamic new American republic, until the end of his life.

PIPPIN HILL FARM & VINEYARDS, NORTH GARDEN

T he story of this new Virginia winery illustrates how multifaceted the Virginia wine industry has become. Instead of being just another pretty building in the countryside selling local wine, this operation offers several kinds of worthwhile on-site experiences in addition to wine.

Pippin Hill Farm & Vineyards, which opened on June 17, 2011, is located on Bundoran Farm, a preservation development along Plank Road just west of Rt. 29 in North Garden. A gently winding road takes you through the newly planted vineyard, and the first building you see is the striking Granary event hall. The view is more than scenic; it's breathtaking. The rolling fields in the valley below contrast with the frozen waves of green hills to the southwest. A long-roofed patio with low, comfortable wooden chairs and tables lies under the extended eaves of the Granary, which you walk past to get to the tasting-room door. The view to High Top and Tom mountains to the west is framed by support beams holding antique rectangular lanterns.

What you see from inside the tasting room is no less striking: The walls facing the view are all paneled with windows, and as you stand tasting wine at the tasting bar, your view is of the mountains. Although the vista is classic Albemarle County, it takes me back to the hills of the Vienna Woods, where little villages offer *Heuriger*, or new wine, in uniquely local wine taverns of the same name. The new wine is served in twelve-ounce beer mugs; the food is cold cuts, fresh bread, and cheese; and guests are serenaded by a violin-and-accordion duo, or perhaps a zither. While Pippin Hill Farm is more elegant, it is just as relaxed and unpretentious.

Dean Andrews and Lynn Easton Andrews are the husband-and-wife owner-operators. Dean brings thirty years of professional hotel management experience to the operation; while Lynn, founder of Easton Events, brings event planning and design experience to Pippin Hill. She also directed the facility's design, to ensure it would be considered the premier event venue in Virginia.

Dean says that green design and construction were a high priority. All heating and cooling for the buildings is geothermal, and rain runoff is collected for vineyard irrigation (the water is pumped through fountains to keep it fresh). Cellulose is used for insulation, avoiding formaldehyde; it is a highly efficient insulator, with an R-value of 3.6 to 3.8 per inch (fiberglass insulation has an R-value of about 2.2 to 2.6). Pippin Hill has six inches of cellulose insulation, giving an R-value of approximately 24 to 25. Tasting-room materials are reclaimed wood, including a four-hundred-year-old Montezuma cypress from Mexico.

In his previous career, Dean says, he did a lot of construction and development work in countries such as Peru, Mexico, and Brazil, including four resorts with their own septic and water systems. Because of the remote locations and limited infrastructure, they really had to be sustainable to get the results they wanted. "This kind of construction (post/beam, cellulose insulation, high UV-resistance on windows) makes a very clean and well-functioning building. Geothermal has huge benefits from reductions on emissions, [and] uses a third less energy."

Other leading professionals on the team include: Chris Hill, vineyard consultant; Michael Shaps of Virginia Wineworks; Amalia Scatena, executive chef; Craig Hartman, consulting chef; Whitney Walker, director of marketing and sales; and Francois Goffinet, landscape architect.

There are six acres of vineyard planted to sauvignon blanc, viognier, and petit verdot. The wines show Shaps's versatility and talent. The whites are crisp and bright, the viognier offering delicate floral and peach nuances but with balanced acidity, and the Winemaker's Select White (a blend of chardonnay, viognier, and traminette) is lively and fruity, with more texture and dimension than either the chardonnays or the viognier, but just off-dry.

The dry Summer Farm rosé of cabernet franc has aromatic fresh strawberry notes, and the Winemaker's Select Red is a fun, fruity blend of 66 percent cabernet franc and 34 percent chambourcin. Barrel tastings of the reserve red components from the 2010 vintage are impressive and encouraging, with well-defined varietal aromas and flavors, balance, and finesse. It's worth watching for. Other wines include a blanc de blancs, a sparkling rosé, regular and reserve merlot and cabernet franc, cabernet sauvignon, and a Meritage (Bordeaux-style) reserve.

The wine is made at Virginia Wineworks' custom-crush facility, which, Dean says, "allows me to access a better winemaker than I could afford to get as a start-up. I spent a lot of time working with protocols with Michael on wine style. It's been a fascinating learning curve for me." They'll start doing some limited on-site production in the wine cellar when the vines mature, starting with sauvignon blanc, which requires little cellaring. When their red reserves from 2010 are bottled, they'll offer sixteen wines across a range of price points.

A major part of the branding of Pippin Hill Farm is its "vineyard-to-table" culinary program, featuring local and imported cheeses, charcuterie salads, and daily specials to accompany tastings or wine by the glass or bottle. Breads will be baked fresh daily in a brick oven. The winery will grow an herb garden, and in addition to sourcing ingredients from local farmers, Chef Scatena will make preserves from local fruit, balsamic vinegar from wine musts, and appetizers with the vineyard's pickled grape leaves and salamis hung on-site, all as part of the concept of using local ingredients that she experienced while training in Tuscany (80 percent of ingredients will be locally sourced).

Dean, who is thin and fit, with alert gray eyes and a calm voice, is enthusiastic about joining the Virginia wine industry. "For the East Coast of the US, I can't think of a better place to establish a winery than in central Virginia. We have the potential to make world-class wine here. This is also a terrific industry because it's noncompetitive; its collaborative nature appeals to me."

Dean and Lynn wanted to combine their professional skills in a synergistic enterprise, and thought about how to leverage events and wine-and-food destination tourism. Easton Events specializes in weddings, and the Granary can seat up to two hundred, with a bridal suite in a loft overhead, from which the bride can toss the bouquet to the crowd below. "We combine an event space of a working winery with everything the bride needs for great views and photo opportunities, and fine-tuning details on-site," says Lynn. Over thirty weddings have already been booked at Pippin Hill Farm through fall 2012.

Dean explains that the concept for combining professional skills with Lynn came together fairly quickly about two years ago. Dean had been head of operations for the Orient-Express hotel chain, which brought him to Keswick Hall in Charlottesville when it was acquired by the company. He oversaw the revamping of Keswick Hall and its sports club, and conceived and built Fossett's restaurant there. He helped take the company public in 2000, overseeing investor relations as Orient-Express grew from eleven to fifty properties.

"I was looking for something that would anchor us both in Charlottesville instead of commuting to New York," he recalls. "At that time, both of us decided that we wanted to move on to a new chapter in our careers and lives; we didn't want to travel as much. Pippin Hill Farm was the best way to do it." Part of the concept grew from Lynn's event business. "We know that Charlottesville has emerged as probably the top wedding destination [after Charleston, South Carolina] on the East Coast," he says. "Some of it is UVA, some of it is the professional community in Washington, D.C. Eight of the ten highest net income counties in the country are in and around Washington and northern Virginia."

But why a winery? "We were looking for an authentic concept," says Dean. "The reason that we called it 'farm' instead of just 'vineyard' or 'winery' is that we're doing the whole vineyard-to-table concept. We want to help define that concept that captures the link between food and wine." He explains that the inspirational model is Blue Hill at Stone Barns, in Westchester County, New York. It's a nonprofit agricultural research center and also a high-end private-event center and gourmet restaurant located on the original dairy farm owned by the Rockefeller family. The first Blue Hill restaurant opened in 2000, in Greenwich Village; its founders restored the farm at Blue Hill at Stone Barns and are pioneers in the locavore movement. "We're going to be planting our own fig trees," Dean continues, "using vine twigs to smoke our own sausage, a wood-burning brick oven to bake bread on-site, doing food and wine tastings to show the link between local food and wine." He is also eagerly anticipating the creation of a "dining in the vineyard" experience. He left a couple of rows unplanted in the center of the vineyard, where he will build trellises, tables, a stone grill, and a cooking oven. "You'll be able to have a wood-fired dinner in the vineyard. The sun will be setting; it will be a beautiful experience. It's about creating memories. We want to be part of their fond memories of wineries in Virginia."

"We want to have fun doing it," Lynn is quick to add. "There are other businesses, less complex, that make more money, but I think that the Monticello Viticultural Area has the emerging potential to become the Napa of twenty years ago. I think this is a golden time for Virginia wine. It's about creating memories."

THE HISTORIC ROOTS
OF VIRGINIA WINE

The history of the Virginia wine industry to date has five distinct phases: its beginnings in the seventeenth century; the eighteenth century and Thomas Jefferson's ultimately failed experiments at Monticello, with recent discoveries shedding new light on the period; the successful rise of a native wine industry based on the norton grape in the nineteenth century; the industry's very slow return to health in the twentieth century after its obliteration with the onset of Prohibition; and the rapid rise in wine quality, stylistic distinction, and international recognition in the first decade of the twenty-first century.

The Seventeenth Century:
Virginia Wine's Tentative Beginning

As the leading American wine historian Thomas Pinney explains in his seminal work *A History of Wine in America*, when the Jamestown Settlement was established by the Virginia Company in 1607, a primary motivation was to make profits for its shareholders through supplying what was unavailable to English merchants due to various wars: olive oil, silk, and wine. However, starvation and hostile relations with the natives stalled any commercial development of the colony until reinforcements and new administrators arrived in 1619 (it's hard to plant and tend a vineyard in a swamp, outside a protective stockade, under constant threat of attack). By 1619, the Virginia Company had been taken over by the Crown, which brought a number of changes, including the first elected assembly in the New World.

Although the Virginia Company had gone to some trouble to pay for European grapevines and vignerons to tend them, the colonists had discovered tobacco and the profits that addiction and fashion could bring to those who sold it, a reality that has continued to the present day. Tobacco is a native Virginian plant, whereas the imported *Vitis vinifera* is native to a semiarid Mediterranean climate, is very susceptible to fungal diseases, and has no resistance to the indigenous vine louse phylloxera, which other American grape species have adapted to. Even if the vines had been impervious to these threats, tobacco has other advantages: grapevines—unlike tobacco—require three years to yield their first small crop, and grapes are a favorite food of all manner of American fauna, from birds and bears to deer and raccoons.

The return on investment for colonists on annual tobacco seed cultivation, compared to the highly risky and delicate perennial grapevines, made it a no-brainer to favor tobacco and its far more certain profits. On top of this, since the cooling of the European climate in the fourteenth century, the English no longer had any culture of vine cultivation, unlike the Latin countries in warmer climates; it was far cheaper and more reliable to brew beer, and later to distill corn, wheat, rye, and barley into whisky.

Accordingly, despite stern remonstrations from London to focus solely on grapevine cultivation, colonists thousands of miles away did as they pleased, doing no favors for Virginia viticulture and setting a pattern for transatlantic relations that would result in war some 160 years later. Acte 12 of the Jamestown Assembly in 1619 (commemorated in a chardonnay of that name from Williamsburg Winery) shows both London's determination to yield wine from its colony and the fact that the colonists needed strong motivation if they were to plant vines. The law provided that every male household head should cultivate twenty imported vinifera (European) grapevines, adding that a punishment to be determined by the governor would be the penalty for failure to comply.

While documentary evidence exists for commercial vineyards having been established in the Tidewater, they soon vanished from the seventeenth-century record due to negligence, natural pests, and the lure of quick profits from tobacco cultivation.

The Eighteenth Century: Jefferson's Experiments and Recent Discoveries

Thomas Jefferson's viticultural efforts at Monticello and Colle have been well documented, as have the Virginia colonists' continued dogged attempts at viticulture through the eighteenth century. Interestingly, in the last few years some missing chapters of eighteenth-century Virginia history have come to light. While reading the first volume of Thomas Pinney's definitive history of American viticulture, Michael Bowles of Montdomaine Cellars in Carter's Bridge noticed a reference to a manuscript that piqued his interest: *A Sketch of Vine Culture for Pennsylvania, Maryland, Virginia, and the Carolinas*, written by Robert Bolling Jr. in 1774. At the time of the Revolution, the tobacco-based agrarian economy of colonial Virginia was in an economic slump. Bolling planted a vineyard in Buckingham County in central Virginia and, in the *Sketch*, urged his fellow Virginians to abandon tobacco and replace it with wine grapes.

Part of what made this work intriguing was what it might reveal on the subject of wine in the eighteenth century, but Bowles also knew that Bolling was a distant ancestor, so he took an interest in the work out of both personal and professional curiosity. He traced the manuscript to the Huntington Library in San Marino, California (part of the Brock Collection), bought a microfilm copy, and had it transcribed via software. He later used the *Sketch* as the basis for a class he taught at the University of Virginia (UVA).

Bowles's family has been farming in Albemarle County since the eighteenth century. The original Montdomaine Vineyard, south of Charlottesville near Carter's Bridge, was one of the early (and renowned) Virginia wineries that stood out in the 1980s, when only a handful of wineries were producing anything quality-driven. Its 1985 vintage chardonnay was served at a state dinner at the first Bush White House, and by the late 1980s his merlot and cabernet sauvignon reserve were consistently considered among the best in the state (the 1991 vintage cabernet won the 1992 Governor's Cup, an annual award given to the top red and white wines in the state following a competition). The frequent European travels of Michael Bowles, a retired airline pilot, gave him his appreciation for fine wine, and he can be energetic and animated while discussing his favorite topic. Bolling was very focused on the practicalities of viticulture, he explains over a glass of his own chardonnay, looking out on the vines from which it was made (the wine is now made at the adjacent Virginia Wineworks, a custom-crush winery). The first chapter is titled "Profits," and Bolling describes "certain diseases of the vine and some quackeries," as well as pruning and vine training at his own vineyard at Chellowe. "He anticipated the Umbrella-Kniffin system of training by a hundred years," Bowles says.

In early 1773, Bolling published an "Essay on the Utility of Vine Planting in Virginia," in which he refers to cultivation techniques used at the time in Madeira and Champagne as models. Unfortunately, Bolling died later the same year, but Bowles notes that Thomas Jefferson was his brother-in-law, and Bolling could therefore have had a major influence on Jefferson's vineyard experiments at Monticello and Colle. "His site selection was impeccable. . . . He argued that if we planted grapevines,

Virginia could solve its balance of payment problems [with Britain]."

The *Sketch* explains that Bolling had planted a vineyard at Chellowe, his Buckingham County estate, on Mount Willis, where kyanite is now mined; it is an excellent site for a vineyard, on a well-drained southeast-facing slope. Despite the paucity of documented survival of vineyards in the commonwealth in the colonial era, Bowles maintains that Bolling wrote *A Sketch of Vine Culture*—an impressive two hundred pages long—"to encourage the Virginia gentry to plant wine-grape vines, since there was a political backlash against tobacco in England at the time." Bowles says the Virginia Assembly awarded Bolling fifty pounds sterling to plant a vinifera vineyard at Chellowe.

In 2009, Bowles taught a course titled "The Curious History of Wine in Virginia: A Sociotechnical Systems Approach" at UVA's School of Engineering and Applied Science. "My mission is to get [*A Sketch of Vine Culture*] published," declares Bowles, who has already approached the University Press of Virginia.

After being leased by Horton Vineyards for a time, the Montdomaine label has resurfaced. The wines are very Old World–style, with minerality and delicate, vibrant fruit. The chardonnay has a gentle touch of oak but firm acidity; the viognier is not as fruit-forward as most Virginia viogniers but has intriguing floral and mineral nuances. The merlot is very reminiscent of Saint-Emilion and its satellites, and the newly launched reserve cabernet is solid and firm in a Bordeaux style.

Meanwhile, Philip Carter Strother, who established the Philip Carter vineyards in Rappahannock County in 2008, discovered fascinating documentation in the records of the Royal Society of Arts (RSA) in London showing that an ancestor named Charles Carter successfully raised grapes and made wine on his Virginia estate a decade before the publication appearance of Bolling's *Sketch* in 1774. This overturns the belief that no evidence existed of successful grape and wine production in Virginia prior to the discovery of the norton grape in the 1820s.

Like Michael Bowles, Strother—who is an attorney—made his discovery as a consequence of reading Pinney's *History of Wine in America*. He relates the story of how he became aware of Charles Carter successfully making Virginia wine in the mid-eighteenth century, nine years before Jefferson first planted his vines at Monticello. "It was the 2007 Thanksgiving weekend, and I was reading in my home study. Pinney's book contains a chapter on the early developments in wine that covers Virginia. The chapter has a half a page about [Charles] Carter and his efforts and success. When I came across the name, I thought that it must be the same Carter family. I then traveled to the Virginia State Library and began to research the reference." Strother discovered that in 1762, Carter—who by then had 1,800 vines growing at Cleve (his plantation on the James River east of Richmond)—sent to the London-based Royal Society for the Encouragement of Arts, Manufactures and Commerce a dozen bottles of his wine, made from the American winter grape ("a grape so nauseous till frost that the fowls of the air will not touch it"—probably the native *Vitis cordifolia* is meant) and from a vineyard of "white Portugal summer grapes."

Strother explains that the library of today's Royal Society of Arts contains multiple documents relating to Carter's involvement with the vine and wine production and the recognition of this success in the form of an award from the society. "I then contacted Royal Society of Arts and they searched their archives and located additional correspondence. One document in particular is very important. It is a certificate signed in 1763 by Royal Governor Francis Fauquier that certifies that Carter was successfully growing a vineyard of European grapes both red and white."

An act had been passed by the Virginia Assembly in 1760 lamenting the high tariffs paid on imported wines and establishing a prize of five hundred pounds for the first Virginian who could successfully grow grapes and make at least ten hogsheads (55-gallon wine barrels) of wine. The money was to be raised by "public-spirited gentlemen," and those who volunteered to put up the money demonstrate how strong sentiment was among leading Virginians; signatures included Carters, Randolphs, Nelsons, and Lees (including Richard Henry Lee), George Wythe and James Blair of the College of William and Mary, and none other than George Washington. Charles Carter himself volunteered some of the prize money he later won back.

Strother is currently working to get complete copies of this and other documents archived in England.

While researching the award Charles Carter received from the society, Sophie Cawthorne, archive and records management trainee at the RSA, found that Carter was actually mentioned in *A History of the Royal Society of Arts* by Sir Henry Trueman Wood, which was published in 1913. In the chapter "The North American Colonies," Wood writes:

> The first offer of a prize for wine appears in the 1758 list, in which the amount of £100 is promised for five tuns of good wine made at a plantation in any colony, provided that one tun was imported to London. In 1763 Mr. Charles Carter sent a dozen bottles of two kinds of wine from grapes which grew in vineyards of his own planting in Virginia. One of these samples was the product of vines brought from Europe, and the other of American wild vines. The gold medal was awarded to Mr. Carter "as the first who had made a spirited attempted towards accomplishment of their views respecting wine in America."

Strother is also working with Camille Wells, a noted historian on colonial houses in Virginia. "She and I visited Cleve last year," he said, "and discovered what we believe to be the ruins of Charles Carter's wine cellar, where those first internationally recognized fine wines would have been stored." The Philip Carter Winery, its historian collaborators, and the RSA "have collectively started the planning for the 250th anniversary, in 2012, of the RSA Carter award, which will hopefully include a multiple-day event starting at Christ Church and ending at Philip Carter Winery."

Some people in the industry are annoyed with the Philip Carter Winery's slogan: "Before Jefferson, there was Carter." However, these recently discovered documents seem to prove that the marketing is based in fact. Both Carter and Bolling seemed to be practicing Virginia viticulture as if it were a natural thing to do, and we owe the discovery of these missing chapters on Virginia wine to the great American wine historian Thomas Pinney and his sharp-eyed readers Michael Bowles and Philip Carter Strother.

It remains a tantalizing mystery whether Thomas Jefferson was aware of Carter's and Bolling's efforts, or of Bolling's publication, and how it was that Carter was able to succeed in a way that was confirmed at the time, where Jefferson's decades of patient efforts seem to have failed. Was Carter aware of the threat of birds and deer to the ripening grapes? And what methods did he employ to ensure his crop ripened to maturity? How many years did his vineyard continue to produce a crop? What were the varieties he planted in today's nomenclature? And were they hardier than other vinifera varieties, or was he just a superior vineyard manager? We'll probably never know the answers to all these questions, but the new information unearthed by Bowles and Strother has given us a more complicated and tantalizing view of this period in Virginia's viticulture and winemaking history.

The Nineteenth Century:
Dr. Norton's Virginia Seedling

Dr. Daniel Norton was a hobbyist gardener and grape hybridizer. Todd Kliman tells of Norton's work and the spread of the grape that bears his name in his book *The Wild Vine*. It is unclear whether Dr. Norton manually "created" the variety by physically hybridizing it, or whether hybridization was accidental, due to cross-pollination in his garden, but we know he propagated the variety and, after harvesting a crop, found it made quality table wine, quite unlike the foxy concord and scuppernong varieties. Leading British wine writer Jancis Robinson says norton "produces some of the finest red wine made anywhere from non-vinifera vines."

Fifty years after Norton's grape was introduced, the Monticello Wine Company was founded in Charlottesville in 1873, and its "Virginia claret" based on the norton grape went on to win many awards nationally and internationally. Whether Dr. Norton created a new grape or simply introduced a wild grape or accidental hybrid into commercial cultivation, his contribution to American wine is gigantic. The hardiness and disease resistance of the norton, combined with flavors that were much better than those found in concord and the other members of the *Vitis labrusca* family, meant a viable native American wine industry was possible from the shores of the Chesapeake Bay to the Missouri River (it won't ripen much farther north than the Mason-Dixon Line).

Unfortunately, just as the promise of quality commercial Virginia viticulture was being realized, Prohibition took hold there in 1914. The vineyards were abandoned or grubbed up, and only a few documents, photographs, and the occasional bottle remained of the era.

Fortunately, settlers carried the norton vine west, where it found a grateful home in Missouri and Arkansas, and cuttings from old vines revived the grape and the industry in those states. Eventually, norton was reintroduced to its native Virginia by Dennis Horton of Horton Vineyards in the early 1990s; now, many Virginia wineries produce a norton. Evidence of norton's revival in Virginia is how quickly some wineries sell out of it, and how the price has climbed above $20 in several wineries.

THE RENAISSANCE OF A FINE AMERICAN WINE REGION

Except for Sciutto Winery, which briefly operated and closed in the 1950s, the renaissance of the Virginia wine industry began in the late 1960s around the town of Middleburg, in the northern Piedmont east of the Blue Ridge Mountains on US Rt. 50. First to open was Farfelu Vineyards, established in 1967, followed a few months later by Meredyth Vineyards (both are now defunct). The post-Prohibition pioneers grew the hardy French hybrid varieties championed in the East by Philip Wagner in Maryland, to avoid the vineyard woes experienced by Jefferson and the Jamestown settlers, setting the pattern for small Virginia wineries for the next twenty years.

The best French hybrids for Virginia are seyval blanc and vidal blanc for whites, with chambourcin for red. In the beginning, a plethora of second-rate hybrids were also grown, including villard noir, rayon d'or, and others with equally forgettable names. Also in Middleburg, Piedmont Vineyards was the site of the first planting of commercial vinifera vines (chardonnay) in post-Prohibition Virginia, in 1973, led by the Vinifera Wine Growers Association.

Important steps forward were realized in 1980 and 1985 with the passage and reauthorization of the Virginia Farm Winery Act, establishing favorable tax and regulatory status for wineries with their own vineyards and small commercial production using Virginia grapes. In 1984, the Virginia Winegrowers Productivity Fund provided that the excise tax of forty cents per liter assessed on Virginia wine would go to fund enology and viticulture research and staff positions at Virginia Tech, as well as for marketing. As is frequently the case, the long arm of state revenue collectors appropriated some of the funding, but current governor Bob McDonnell, a strong supporter of the Virginia wine industry, sponsored a bill rededicating the funding to the wine industry in 2011, a rare case of a regional wine industry receiving a funding boost in the Great Recession.

Thanks to the investment in research positions at Virginia Tech, enologist Dr. Bruce Zoecklein and viticulturist Dr. Tony Wolf have been able to contribute immeasurably to the evolution of quality grape and wine production in the commonwealth.

Also in the mid-1980s, there was a varietal shift from plantings of French hybrid grapes to vinifera (European) varieties. At first, chardonnay, riesling, and cabernet sauvignon were dominant. With time, riesling was largely abandoned due to its rot problems in the humid climate, while cabernet sauvignon was recently surpassed by cabernet franc, since the latter produces better wine most years with its earlier ripening, smoother tannins, and better tolerance of clay soils.

By the mid-1990s, vinifera grapes led Virginia production. The decade saw a further evolution in Virginia viticulture, with great experimentation in vinifera grapes—most notably viognier—pioneered at Horton Vineyards. Virginia has since earned a national reputation for the consistent quality and finesse of its viognier (a white grape from the northern Rhône). In addition, petit verdot (a red Bordeaux grape), touriga naçional, tannat, albariño, tempranillo, pinotage (from South Africa), a range of Italian varieties, and the rather obscure petit manseng (an aromatic white grape from the Jurançon region of France) have all made an appearance, often with impressive results. This period also saw the introduction of a new hybrid, traminette, which was developed by Cornell University at their Geneva, New York, research station. Traminette is a cross of a white French hybrid (Seyve 23.146) and gewürztraminer, and gives a wine with intensely perfumed gewürztraminer aromas and flavors but with better acidity and much better winter- and disease-hardiness in the vineyard. Both traminette and petit manseng are frequently blended with other white grape varieties for balance.

In addition to these shifts in grape varieties, the 1990s saw several other major developments in the Virginia wine industry. The extension work and research carried out by Drs. Wolf and Zoecklein at Virginia Tech greatly improved the average wine quality in Virginia, and winery tourism was becoming big business for the state, with the multiplier effect of money spent in wine tourism generating financial benefits both in tax revenue and in money spent in the general hospitality industry and local economy near wineries. Politicians and officials in state government couldn't help but notice the benefits to the rural economy of attracting well-heeled wine tourists to the tasting rooms and vineyards of one of the most breathtakingly beautiful states in the country.

Part of the improved perception of Virginia wine quality came from the branding of the state as having ideal terroir for viognier. (Terroir is the combination of climate and soil characteristics that gives expression to any particular grape variety in a specific place, and to the final wine. "Good terroir" is when these characteristics favor the best varietal expression of a particular grape.) Dennis Horton, of Horton Vineyards (awarded a lifetime achievement award by the industry in 2011), has become the leading grape iconoclast in Virginia. In the late 1980s, he was the first to commercially plant viognier and other Rhône varieties, while at the same time reintroducing the native norton grape commercially (he grew up a block away from the iconic Stone Hill vineyard in

Hermann, Missouri, a leading producer of norton there). In 1993, his 1992 vintage won more awards than any other viognier in the country, and caused a stir with the national wine press and the Rhone Rangers association in California.

Viognier had declined to a mere eighty acres planted world-wide by 1986, according to wine authority Jancis Robinson, because it is a low-yielding variety and therefore commercially unrewarding. Condrieu, the appellation in the northern Rhône Valley, where viognier reaches its apogee, makes some of the most expensive white table wine in France, but outside this limited zone it doesn't pay well for growers. Dennis Horton solved the problem of low yields for viognier in Virginia by training the vines on a quadrilateral open-lyre trellis. The usual two-sided vertical shoot positioning (VSP) training system is modified; above the horizontal cordons (where the trunk divides into two horizontal canes running in opposite directions) there is a trapezoidal frame (with the shorter end on the bottom) with notches to hold trellis wires. The shoots growing up from the horizontal cordons are trained to grow out along the lyre-shaped frame in opposite directions, with shoots and leaves pulled from the middle lyre zone to allow light and air penetration. Combined with the moderately high vigor typical in most Virginia Piedmont vineyards, this allows a larger yield per vine, while avoiding the crowding of shoots and leaves in a conventional two-sided VSP canopy. (Note: while yields per vine are improved, materials and labor cost for managing this system also increase.)

Horton proved that viognier grown in Virginia this way would not only produce commercially rewarding yields, but wine of fine quality. Virginia's climate allows viognier to ripen most years to the ideal benchmark of at least 23.5 degrees Brix (a measure of sugar level in the juice of the grapes), where the delicate floral and tropical-fruit aromatics and flavors are realized. At the same time, the climate is usually not hot enough to burn off the delicate fruit aromatics, and Virginia vintners usually can harvest classic viognier between 13 and

14 percent potential alcohol. In warmer regions in the New World, it can be difficult to keep viognier from overripening, losing delicate fruit aromatics, and getting a coarse alcoholic burn. Since Horton's success with his 1992 vintage, Virginia's reputation for a classic style of viognier has only grown. Viognier has a broad appeal as a varietal in America; the tropical fruit and floral characters satisfy the "fruity" wine crowd, while the dry style and complexities that time on the lees (yeast cells) adds to the wine please many chardonnay drinkers. Since wineries can make a good profit selling viognier between $18 and $30 a bottle, everyone wins.

Virginia also saw a string of strong vintages in the 1990s, especially for red wines. Dr. Bruce Zoecklein recalls 1993 as the first vintage where the industry finally proved they had listened to what he had been telling them about fermentation and post-fermentation management for red wines. The 1995 vintage was a solid success, and although 1996 was a washout because of Hurricane Fran, 1997 and 1998 were back-to-back classics, especially the reds. The 1998 wine was like the 1989 in Bordeaux—ripe and fruity but with structure to last—and some 1998 Virginia reds are still fruity and youthful.

The Twenty-First Century and the Fifth Phase

The new century began with a benchmark vintage in 2001. It was a long, hot growing season, but without the drought stress seen in some 2002 wines. Reds were ripe and tannic, and wines from the more tannic varieties such as nebbiolo and cabernet sauvignon may still be too young.

Red wines from the 2001 vintage have won accolades at international wine competitions and from leading wine authorities such as Michael Broadbent, who praised Barboursville Vineyards' 2001 Octagon (merlot-based Bordeaux blend) in *Decanter* magazine.

In the first decade of the twenty-first century, it was clear that the attitude of industry participants had changed. Through the 1980s and 1990s, many of the newcomers to the scene still fancied themselves "gentlemen farmers," with a passion for wine turned into a hobby that happened to be a business (if they paid attention). Since 2000, however, most recent arrivals have been well funded, well educated, and focused on succeeding in a commercially competitive market; this new level of professionalism in the industry has helped everyone. Aside from grape and wine quality, the new professionalism is seen in everything from winery and tasting-room design to attendance by winery owners at major conferences and trade shows, the adoption of wine clubs, and the proliferation of high-end events such as weddings at the wineries. "We're not just in the wine business, we're in the wedding business," remarks Andrew Hodson of Veritas Vineyard, near Afton, whose stunning views, fine wines, and well-appointed facilities make it one of the state's leading event destinations.

The year 2007 marked the four hundredth anniversary of the Jamestown Settlement and the fortieth anniversary of the renaissance of the Virginia wine industry. To mark the occasion, several wineries organized a tasting of Virginia wines for members of the media and trade in London, where it all began for Virginia in 1607. London is the center of the world wine trade, and home to the most respected wine journalists. Sixty-four Virginia wines qualified after a blind judging presided over by Dr. Bruce Zoecklein, and were poured at two events in London in May 2007.

Leading wine writers Hugh Johnson (author of an annual encyclopedia of wine and coauthor of *The World Atlas of Wine*), Steven Spurrier (who engineered the famous "Judgment of Paris" tasting in 1976), and Andrew Jefford (twice winner of the Glenfiddich Wine Writer of the Year award) all tasted Virginia wines alongside other writers and members of the trade, and seemed both surprised and impressed. Spurrier noted that the wines were up to international quality standards, but alcohol levels were "refreshingly not." Jefford devoted a column in the London *Financial Times* to the event, the wines, and Virginia wine history, titled "Vineyards to Make a Founding Father Proud." By 2011, the number of Virginia wineries had exploded from just over fifty at the start of the century to nearly two hundred, and some Virginia wines are now being exported to the United Kingdom.

With the maturing of the industry has come a more sophisticated understanding of wine and grape production that showcases what can work best in Virginia. Jim Law of Linden Vineyards acknowledges that fifteen years ago he was using too much new oak in his wines, and says he now strives for more integration and finesse, a trend echoed by other experienced winemakers.

Stylistically, Virginia wines have evolved in the past twenty-five years from simple, bold, and rustic, often with heavy-handed oak and obvious technical flaws, to having finesse, integration, balance, rare flaws, and increasing regional distinctiveness across the various species (norton, French and New York hybrids, and vinifera varieties).

White Wines

Chardonnay and viognier are the leading white varieties today, and they're increasingly made with little or no oak (or older, neutral oak) and partial or no malolactic fermentation, to retain natural acidity and freshness. Optimal harvesting timing retains delicate varietal expression and keeps alcohol levels moderate. Viognier is noted for its floral fragrance, with aromas of white flowers, peach, apricot, and tropical fruit flavors. Acidity can be low, so barrel-fermented viognier is often blended with tank-fermented chardonnay to tone down the flowery character of viognier and give it more acidity. Viognier needs to ripen to 23.5 degrees Brix to reach its optimal aromatic and flavor potential, and Virginia's climate provides this reliably, but viognier is harvested as soon after it is practical, to avoid high alcohol and low acid, and to preserve freshness.

Especially in the northern Piedmont and Shenandoah Valley, chardonnay makes wines both more flavorful and fresher than most of its West Coast incarnations. Some producers are making a very impressive New World interpretation of Burgundy, ranging from high lemon citrus acidity to those barrel-fermented in French oak that give a meursault-like style, lower in alcohol and viscosity than the dominant West Coast style. Among hybrid varieties, vidal blanc and seyval blanc are still strong, but seyval, which used to be coarse and harsh, is now stylistically very much like Loire Valley whites, with Rappahannock Cellars, Lovingston Winery, and Linden being leading examples. Vidal blanc, which used to be the "poor man's riesling," has a dual identity, as a table wine (which can show some elegance when partially barrel-aged) and as a backbone for artificially frozen dessert wines. Officially known as cryoextraction, this process makes intensely sweet but balanced (high acid) dessert wines at a fraction of the cost of vine-frozen and harvested grapes.

The rare petit manseng resembles traminette in its strong, fruity aromatics and mid-palate viscosity, but retains acidity like riesling while yielding fruit character ranging from passion fruit to mango.

Red Wines

A decade ago, the shift in top Virginia reds was from straight varietal wines to red Bordeaux blends (even blending other varieties into wines labeled with the dominant varietal). This category is still the signature style for Virginia reds, but it has gone from being dominated by cabernet sauvignon to leading with merlot and cabernet franc, with a significant amount of petit verdot, the grape that may well be Virginia's future signature style in this category. Since the wines of Bordeaux's Right Bank (Saint-Emilion and its satellites) are always popular and easy to drink, this stylistic shift means Virginia will be producing supple, subtle, nuanced red Bordeaux blends that avoid the juicy fruit-bomb style.

Cabernet franc and merlot are still made as varietals, with cabernet franc the most produced red Bordeaux varietal in the state. While there is a range of styles, there is an increasing focus on neutral oak and clean, vibrant fruit, mirroring the stylistic evolution of Virginia white wines. Those who prefer a happy medium between the rich, higher-alcohol, and intense style of West Coast red Bordeaux blends, and the more austere, acidic style of Bordeaux, will enjoy today's Virginia red Bordeaux blends and varietals.

While syrah, mourvedre, tannat, and touriga nacional have long been grown by Horton Vineyards and increasingly by others, recommendations by Drs. Zoecklein and Wolf have favored increasing acreage of tannat, which is showing up in more Virginia wines, usually as part of a blend, as a nonaromatic variety that delivers the tannin levels people look for in cabernet sauvignon, which is less reliable in the vineyard. Another esoteric grape that is now being championed by Lovingston Winery's South African winemaker, Riaan Rossouw, is the specialty of his homeland: pinotage.

The only red French hybrid which has performed consistently well in both the vineyard and the winery in Virginia is chambourcin, which also grows well throughout the Mid-Atlantic. With its bright cherry aromas and flavors, crisp acidity, and low tannin level, chambourcin resembles the gamay grape of Beaujolais. Part of the Fifth Phase of the industry in the new century is how winemakers are returning to this grape and treating it seriously, avoiding over-oaking while making wines of concentration and depth of fruit. Keswick Vineyards and Lovingston Winery excel, while Shenandoah Vineyards has set the benchmark for chambourcin for many years, fermenting it with some cabernet sauvignon skins for added tannin. Pippin Hill makes an excellent blend of chambourcin and cabernet franc.

Sparkling and Dessert Wines in Virginia

Another part of the Fifth Phase of developments is how both the sparkling and dessert wine categories have evolved in Virginia since the century began. While respectable sparkling wines have been made in Virginia in the past, the category has been taken to a new level by the work of Claude Thibaut, a native of Champagne. Having first worked for Kluge Estate Vineyards with their debut sparkling wines, Thibaut now consults for other Virginia wineries, including Veritas Vineyard, where he introduced a pale pink, dry *méthode champenoise* wine of cabernet franc called Scintilla, delightfully dry and delicate. His Blanc de Chardonnay, under the Thibaut-Janisson label, was served at the first Obama White House state dinner, and his Virginia Fizz (also a chardonnay blanc de blancs) was rated the top Virginia sparkling wine by a group of Virginia wine writers and bloggers in 2010.

Charles Gendrot also worked at Kluge Estate, not only maintaining standards set by Thibaut but introducing two new products: a blanc de blancs reserve and a blanc de noirs. The reserve is rich, with new-oak hints, and needs more time to fully integrate, but the blanc de noirs is amazingly elegant, with subtle pear aromas and flavors, rich, creamy mid-palate, and clean, lingering aftertaste. Indeed, the reserve was poured blind at an industry dinner I attended, and none of the trade professionals present guessed it was not real champagne.

Some people disdain dessert wines as being only for novices, but sauternes, tokaji, German and Austrian ausleses, Loire botrytis chenin blanc, and the entire port category are testaments to the great potential of fine dessert wines. In Virginia, the category of cryoextraction sweet wines (artificial ice wine) has been fine-tuned to the point where it can produce some of the best dessert wines in the country. Shepherd "Shep" Rouse, of Rockbridge Vineyard, is an acknowledged leader, blending four grape varieties (vidal blanc, riesling, traminette, and vignoles) in his V d'Or, a cryo-process wine that balances sweetness with refreshing acidity. White Hall Vineyards' Soliterre contains vidal blanc, petit manseng, and white muscat, and is made in the same way. Veritas's Kenmar, made of traminette, is luscious and fragrant and won the first National Women's Wine Competition (for wines made by women in the United States).

Port-style wines are an entire subcategory of dessert wines, and while they have been made in Virginia for a while, they have lacked distinction until now. Veritas's Othello is a bold and creative ruby-style blend of tannat, touriga, and petit verdot. It has the characteristic spiciness and rich, dark fruit flavors of traditional port varieties, as well as the structure (from tannat), but avoids the prune-like overripeness that plagues a lot of New World port-style wines. Cooper Vineyards and Glass House Winery are making delicious and tastefully balanced chocolate norton ports.

Rosé and Blush Wines

Finally, we can't forget rosé and blush wines, a big category that is experiencing a surge in popularity, especially dry rosé. Barboursville Vineyards has made a cabernet blush for years, but recently introduced a dry rosé made from sangiovese, nebbiolo, and cabernet franc—delicate but bone dry and excellent with food. Other leading rosé producers are Sharp Rock, Prince Michel, White Hall (using touriga), and Veritas with their sparkling version. And Chrysalis and New Kent Vineyards produce blush wines from norton. Some wineries like King Family Vineyards report such a demand for their rosé that it sells out within weeks of release.

So, if you like drinking wine, you are sure to find something you like in Virginia today. And thanks to the hard work of Drs. Bruce Zoecklein and Tony Wolf, and the winemakers, grape growers, and winery owners of Virginia, we have some of the most distinctive high-quality wines on the regional US wine scene.

There are several major political issues facing the Virginia wine industry today. One is regulatory restrictions; thanks to a well-funded, well-connected wholesale lobby, in 2006 Virginia wineries lost the right to self-distribute (sell directly) to trade customers. This was a backlash from wholesalers both angered and worried about the implications of the 2005 *Granholm v. Heald* Supreme Court decision, which said that states had to be consistent in how they allowed wineries to direct-ship to consumers. Formerly, out-of-state wineries were prohibited in some states from shipping in wine, but native wineries could ship intrastate. As a result of wineries losing the right to self-distribute, the state had to step in and set up the Virginia Winery Distribution Company, adding a layer of regulation and paperwork that hadn't existed before.

A regulatory issue that may become even more important concerns the tension between Virginia wineries and their residential neighbors. Certain antidevelopment counties (particularly Fauquier and Albemarle) have begun to look unfavorably on winery events as disruptive to the local community. Marterella Winery, unfortunately located within a Fauquier County development that includes a residential community with a homeowners' association, found itself sued by that association, which claimed selling wine was not approved by its bylaws. The suit continued for three and a half years, and in January 2011, the winery had an injunction issued against it. In June, circuit court judge Jeff Parker ordered winery proprietors Jerry and Kate Marterella to post a bond totaling nearly $105,000 in order to appeal the case to the state supreme court, and awarded nearly $100,000 to cover the homeowners' association's legal fees (these fees were added to the bond). In the face of the mounting costs, the Marterellas decided they could not afford to continue the litigation and would close the winery instead.

Related to this issue is the question of whether large events at Virginia wineries are detrimental to the local community and should be restricted, or are permissible under the Right to Farm Act and other legislation.

Another issue of concern to many Virginia wine producers is the inclusion of out-of-state fruit in wines made by Virginia wineries, whether these wines are being labeled correctly, and whether such labeling is explicit enough for customers to know the difference.

Now let's move from the "big picture" into more detailed and close-up views of the Virginia wine scene, focusing on the people who live and work in it.

THE PRIMACY OF
VITICULTURE AND BLESSINGS
AND CHALLENGES OF NATURE

Jefferson's predictions for Virginia and American wine have been criticized as overenthusiastic boosterism, but he was basing his assessments on empirical observations of the world around him, comparing America to the great wine regions he had visited in Europe while ambassador to France. The upper Piedmont countryside around his Monticello home must have seemed particularly promising, with a topography closely resembling the Piedmont of Italy. In an 1881 letter, Jefferson described the Colle site as having "an abundance of lean and meager spots of stony and red soil, without sand, resembling extremely the Cote of Burgundy from Chambertin to Montrachet where the famous wines of Burgundy are made."

Indeed, on the surface Virginia seems a promising place for viticulture. It has been observed that "if you have a good view, you probably have a good vineyard site," and a moderate climate and ample rolling hills seem to provide endless opportunities for well-appointed vineyards in many parts of the state.

Due to its temperate climate, Virginia grows a wide range of native, hybrid, and classic vinifera grape varieties. In fact, there are more commercial varieties of vinifera grown in Virginia than anywhere else east of the Mississippi. This is important for marketing and branding purposes; vinifera varieties have more cachet on the market than the lesser-known hybrids, and are therefore usually easier to sell.

Virginia offers some of the best views in the country, diverse soils, and plenty of hillside locations and a favorable climate, so who could blame Jefferson for his optimistic outlook? Now for the bad news: Virginia also provides particular challenges to viticulture (especially of the European vinifera varieties) that largely explain why a native wine industry took until the late nineteenth century to become established, and until the late twentieth century to reemerge after Prohibition.

The most enduring threats, year in and out, are fungal diseases caused by high relative humidity in the growing season, including frequent rainfall, especially in the hurricane months of late summer as the grapes are getting riper and their skins thinner. This is true across the viticultural East in North America (east of the hundredth meridian or about the western edge of Minnesota). Wine regions such as the West Coast, Chile, Argentina, Australia, and South Africa have minimal threat of rains during harvest, making viticulture there both easier and cheaper.

Farming according to strict organic protocols, which is possible in dry climates such as California's, will not work in Virginia. However, there are some environmentally friendly synthetic fungal sprays that are very effective, including those against black rot, for which there is no effective organic treatment.

One of the reasons Virginia wine is seldom found priced below $10 is the high cost of production; Virginia lacks the economies of scale found in the wine behemoth of California, and the cost (in both labor and materials) for vineyard spraying in Virginia is high. Chris Breiner, owner of Stone Mountain Vineyards in the Monticello AVA (American

Viticultural Area), farms twenty acres of vines and estimates his fungal and weed management spray in 2010 took nine hours of labor per week over sixteen weeks in the growing season. He also pays $18,000 for spray materials, and the 2010 vintage was remarkably dry! A vintage such as 2009, which was much rainier, might bring a much higher spray bill, while simultaneously giving a reduced volume of grapes after a quality selection sorted out those damaged by rot or other problems.

Some varieties, such as the native norton, are far more disease resistant than the vulnerable European vinifera, but most grape growers (whether they simply sell the fruit or make wine commercially) are looking for a good return on the considerable investment in vineyard establishment, and so look to the tender, disease-prone European varieties that bring the highest market prices. One salient example is chardonnay. Winemakers and marketers love chardonnay for its versatility, name recognition, and salability. Virginia chardonnay has excellent regional style, combining ripe apple and pear fruit with balanced acidity. However, the variety is one of the most problematic in the vineyard in Virginia. It is as prone to disease as any vinifera variety in the state, and accordingly is expensive to grow when losses are factored in.

Chardonel, a hybrid of chardonnay and the French hybrid seyval blanc, on the other hand, is a much better economic bet in the vineyard, but unfortunately not in the marketplace. Chardonel produces a wine very much like its chardonnay parent, with delicate apple-pear notes and good balancing acidity. The grape yields well and is much cheaper to grow, but also brings less money into the winery because it lacks the brand recognition of chardonnay.

What is the ideal vineyard site in Virginia? If you have a good view, you probably have high elevation (compared to the surrounding land), which helps with air and water drainage.

In 2000, Virginia viticulturist Dr. Tony Wolf coauthored a paper with Virginia Tech colleague John Boyer on GIS (geographic information system) mapping for Virginia vineyards. A range of six factors were given relative weight, and each area mapped had a potential score from less than fifty-five (for poor) up to a hundred (for ideal). The top two quality factors alone were given fifty-five potential points—these were site elevation and soil characteristics. Major factors in vineyard soil quality outlined by Dr. Wolf include soil fertility, soil depth, water drainage, and soil pH. Every Virginia county has now been mapped, with a color-coded scale showing composite scores.

Virginia Tech's Center for Geospatial Information Technology (CGIT), under the direction of Peter Sforza, received a USDA grant in 2011 to expand and further refine a new Web-based, interactive GIS platform that allows users to evaluate their property for vineyard suitability and match the property's location to appropriate grape varieties. "Not only will users be able to review the climatic and physical attributes or liabilities of their site," says Dr. Wolf, "but we'll be able to offer recommendations on which grape varieties could be grown at the property, based on length of growing season, summer heat, and winter low-temperature considerations."

He points out that grapevines need enough days in the growing season to ripen their crop, and planting above 1,800 feet makes it doubtful that the vines will get enough heat in the season to do so reliably. At the same time, an ideal minimum elevation of 820 feet is also recommended (except for vineyards close to the moderating influence of the Chesapeake Bay). Planting between extremes of elevation also helps the grower take advantage of thermal belts in hilly terrain.

Air drainage is critical in Virginia vineyards for a couple of reasons. The movement of air through the vineyard dries the foliage and keeps fungal spores from settling easily, reducing the threat of fungal disease. In addition, good air drainage reduces the threat of freezes, as cold air ponds at the bottom of slopes. Sites with enough—but not too much—elevation can benefit from the settling of cold air in the winter and spring and the draining of humid air in the growing season.

Grapevines evolved in the semi-arid Caucasus, and they naturally prefer well-drained soils for optimal vine metabolism. Recent research has also shown that vineyards planted on poorly drained, heavy clay soils do not yield as much fruit and are much more prone to winter kill; the same vineyards retrofitted with underground tile drainage see improved winter survival rates and crop yields.

Overly fertile soils put too much plant vigor into producing shoots and leaves, compromising fruit ripeness and optimal chemistry (too much potassium and high pH) and making the grower spend resources fighting nature and fending off fungal diseases. Grapevines can put down roots as far as thirty feet, but shallow-soil vineyards mean the roots hit hardpan close to the surface and are prone to drought stress; young vines die easily, and even mature vines are stressed.

Dr. Tony Wolf is a tall, trim, handsome man who is almost Germanic in his straightforward professionalism and clear, focused manner. He has been the state viticulturist since he was hired by Virginia Tech in 1985. In addition to his research and extension work for Virginia Tech, Dr. Wolf frequently presents at professional meetings and conferences, and his work is relevant to issues elsewhere in the Mid-Atlantic. In 1995, he published *The Mid-Atlantic Winegrape Grower's Guide*, which in 2009 was revised and expanded with the work of colleagues, and published under the title *Wine Grape Production Guide for Eastern North America*.

I asked him what conclusions he had drawn about the most important parameters for predicting commercial vineyard sustainability and potential wine quality in Virginia. He reaffirmed that elevation (both absolute and relative) and soil are still of paramount importance. "More specifically, I'd say that relative elevation is even more important than absolute elevation." This is because a valley can still be at high absolute elevation but low relative elevation, and airflow can be blocked by adjacent slopes.

To put the modern history of site selection in perspective, explains Dr. Wolf, the emphasis throughout the eighties and nineties was on seeking sites that promoted consistent cropping and vine survival—winter low temperatures and spring and early fall frosts had to be considered first and foremost, and frost hazard is still a prime consideration. "From the turn of this century on, we have increasingly added a more stringent soils evaluation as our attention has evolved from simply crop survival to crop quality." Dr. Wolf says this means looking for soils with excellent internal and surface drainage, features often found on convex landforms. Fortuitously, convex landforms are often good vineyard sites from a climatic standpoint.

Dr. Wolf summarizes a good vineyard site in Virginia as one that has excellent relative elevation for cold-air drainage, excellent internal and surface soil drainage, moderate fertility, and good sunlight exposure, a site that experiences sufficient frost-free days most years to ripen the crop, with enough surplus carbohydrates for the vines' permanent wood to last through the winter, and that can be brought into production with minimal inputs other than for the vines, trellis, and labor. "A *great* site is more exacting. A great site has soil with modest water-holding capacity but availability of either ground water or surface water for irrigation as needed, has a modest (roughly 1 to 2 percent) organic-matter content, is at low risk of certain biological risks such as Pierce's Disease and grapevine yellows, and is removed from restrictive local ordinances or sensitive environmental or civil features." For practical and commercial reasons, Dr. Wolf feels that a winery should be included in the discussion and, therefore, "a great site would also include ease of access and aesthetic viewsheds that attract customers."

When I asked Dr. Wolf what he believes is necessary for a grape-grower to be a commercial success in Virginia, he pointed out that this depends on one's definition of success. "Business success might mean staying in business for one person, or producing grapes that result in a ninety-plus *Wine Spectator* rating for another, or maybe just trying to meet a three-out-of-five-year IRS profit rule for others."

Dr. Wolf explained that the profit margin for grape growing alone in Virginia is quite small, due to the small size of operations in the state, the high capitalization requirement of vineyards, the high cost of labor (including that of the owner), and the occasional losses to environmental and biological threats. He says, "it's little wonder that so many grape growers eventually build wineries. That said, I do know some grape growers sans wineries who are making money growing grapes. They are on good or great sites. They are growing high-value varieties that are in demand in the state. They don't make management mistakes that will cost them crop quality or crop loss. They are generally careful about avoiding unnecessary but expensive vineyard inputs that don't have a proven benefit. And, perhaps most controversial, they are cropping the vines at levels that generate a fair return on their effort while meeting the buyers' specifications for the intended quality or wine price point. This does not mean overcropping the vines, and it certainly does not mean undercropping the vines' capacity." On this last point, Dr. Wolf alludes to the widespread assumption that the lower the crop yields per acre, the higher the resulting wine quality, but it's not possible to make a blanket assumption that applies in all situations. Balanced viticulture means cropping the vines in a way that gives both the grapes and the permanent vine adequate but not excessive nutrients.

Jim Law is always cited by those who know the industry well as one of Virginia's leading winegrowers (a term he prefers over *winemaker*, as he believes "the more time I spend in the vineyard, the less I have to spend in the winery").

Originally from Ohio, Law is a traditionalist when it comes to winemaking style. He believes strongly in the primacy of site in the character and quality of wine, and although he has been farming Hardscrabble—his home vineyard at Linden Vineyards—since 1985, he says he's still learning about his site and how it interacts with different grape varieties; recently he had planted the *ur*-Bordeaux variety carmenere, but then decided to pull it out after it performed poorly.

When asked about site requirements in Virginia, Law says, "It's all about soil water evacuation. Virginia is a wet place to grow grapes, as is Atlantic-influenced Europe. We can learn a lot from them." The steeper the slope the better, as rain runs off and drains quickly. "This is true for all varieties." However, he believes it's important for growers to match soil texture, depth, and water-holding capacity to a specific variety's preferences. "As long as a vineyard is planted on a steep slope, I have found that whites, along with merlot, do best in clay, and the cabernets prefer more meager, droughty, and less fertile soils."

As to what is required for commercial success, he says, "A frost-free, steep slope managed by a full-time professional with many years of experience on that site." He adds that there is a cost to such management, and he believes the grape and/or wine-bottle price needs to reflect the site and farming effort. Law's red wines are notably pricier than the Virginia average, but he does not lack for discriminating trade and tasting-room customers or critical acclaim.

Chris Pearmund is a tall, confident, and highly energetic man. As if owning and managing two vineyards weren't enough (Pearmund Cellars and the Winery at La Grange), Pearmund opened a third winery, Vint Hill, specializing in custom crush. Pearmund's original chardonnay site, Meriwether Vineyard, was much sought after when he was selling the fruit to other wineries.

Chris says that many people agree on what makes a good vineyard site in Virginia, adding that less than four-foot in-row vine spacing is often recommended for reducing yields. "A great site has the shadow of the owner with passion and drive. It's attitude over latitude," he concludes.

As to how a grape grower can be a commercial success in Virginia, Pearmund says, "this can go to many levels, by basically 'understanding wine.' So many [in the industry] do not understand farming; so many think it's glamorous. Understand the winemaker's and winery's needs and desires. Grape flavor should trump Brix, or sugar level, alone. Don't be afraid to drop fruit [in the vineyard] several times. Understand the timing of vineyard tasks and spray schedules, with vine nutrition playing an important role. Prune for next year's crop, drop fruit for this year's crop."

Barboursville Vineyards, north of Charlottesville, is owned by the Zonin family, the largest private wine producers in Italy. The winery and the hamlet it's in take their name from Virginia governor James Barbour, a friend of Thomas Jefferson's, for whom Jefferson designed a now-ruined mansion on the property.

The Zonins started their Virginia vineyard and winery in 1976. With the deep pockets and professional experience the family brought to Barboursville, they were able to take the long view about adapting their Italian techniques in the vineyard and winery to Virginia's quite different climatic conditions.

Luca Paschina, the current general manager and chief winemaker, has been on the job since 1989. Barboursville boasts one of the largest vineyard plantings in the state, currently 162 acres (twenty-four of which were just planted in the largest expansion since 1976). A major element in the success of Barboursville's wines has been the way that Paschina has paid careful attention to the vineyard and adapted cultural practices as necessary. He also credits the fine work of his long-time vineyard manager, Fernando Franco.

Franco believes that site selection and vineyard management should be a function of the winery's intentions for the final product and its price. "Different sites for different varietals is my recommendation for optimal use of a site," he says. As to what's required for commercial success, he says simply, "Get well informed of the challenges that Virginia viticulture presents and be quality-minded in your management."

Paschina adds that he prefers soil with medium vigor over meager or poor soils, and he rejects high-fertility soils. "I have come to disagree that vines have to struggle in order to produce a great wine. Instead I believe that they have to grow in a balanced way, like people should. Somebody asked me one day, 'How come your wines are so balanced?' I replied, 'I have a balanced life.'"

Chris Breiner is the owner and winemaker at Stone Mountain Vineyards, located high up in the Blue Ridge Mountains in Greene County off a very long and winding road, with a stunning view east from the ample deck of the winery's tasting room over three acres of vines just below (he has more than twenty acres total, most of them out of view). It's an idyllic vista, like something out of a Renaissance-era painting of the Tuscan countryside.

Breiner is about six feet tall, with dark hair, a nearly constant smile, and an enthusiastic but soft-spoken manner. He began clearing land on the mountainside for his vineyard in 1995 and has been producing wine since 1998.

Breiner's vineyard site is on steep hillsides, with excellent air and water drainage. "We talked to Gabriele [Rausse] and Tony Wolf, so we knew the site would work before planting it," he says. While the material cost of installing a good commercial vineyard is not cheap (between $11,000 and $15,000 per acre, not including the land), Breiner explains, "Your labor of building the vineyard is more than the actual posts, wire, etcetera. So site and varietal selection have huge implications [for long-term cost and viability]. It's important to do it right the first time." Breiner agrees with Jim Law that "the more time you spend in the vineyard, the easier life is in the winery."

Breiner says the biggest thing he's learned is that "there's no such thing as an average growing season. If you don't stay awake to meet the challenge of every specific season, you'll find yourself behind the eight ball." Also, he's still learning to match site to cultivars "in ways that weren't obvious" when he started.

It should be said that some regions of the state without steep hillsides—such as the Eastern Shore or the Tidewater region—can have well-draining soils, as is the case in Bordeaux. A steep slope is not necessary for quality viticulture in Virginia, but those with vineyards on flat sites need to be extra careful to ensure success.

Reflecting on the fast growth in the number of wineries in Virginia, Breiner says, "I think the growers understand the issues more than maybe some new winery owners. They don't really realize what goes into growing an acre of grapes to make a good bottle of wine. I don't think they quite understand you can't make good wine from bad grapes; a lot of them are still in the romantic-vision phase."

He's also seen supply and demand dynamics change for grape varieties. He notes that Rock Stephens, a commercial grower and former president of the Virginia Vineyards Association, says there are still some vineyards that are dropping fruit and not selling it. In 2000, he couldn't find cabernet franc to buy at harvest, but "now you can't give it away." He feels there should be better industry coordination in what gets planted.

Asked if he had any words of advice for people considering planting a vineyard in Virginia, he laughed. "Don't do it. But if you do, do your homework on site selection and grape variety. If you're going to be a grower only, get a contract with a local winery and sell them what they want to buy."

Oliver Asberger is a gregarious German, the proprietor of Wine & Vine Care, a consultancy for winery and vineyard management. He smiles easily and is a familiar figure at Charlottesville's "Fridays after Five" event, where he is known for his interpretive dancing. Despite this artistic bent, he is precise and methodical in his work. He has been a vineyard manager in Virginia, Michigan, and Georgia, but he is also a winemaker, which is in the European tradition.

Asberger insists on the importance of an optimal soil pH range near 6.5 (in the 6.2 to 6.8 range); avoiding a north-facing aspect; a slope that's not too steep (dangerous for machinery and physically demanding for workers); rows spaced appropriately to safely use machinery such as harvesters, hedgers, and mechanized weed control; and not planting near trees, bushes, or forest, to minimize animal pressure and shading. Other practical factors he recommends are good access roads for easy transport of material and grapes and a location close to the winery for faster processing of grapes, to avoid spoilage. A great vineyard site, he declares, is "where all the ranges [of the above factors] are optimal."

Asberger gives some very helpful economic advice on the question of what is necessary for a grape grower to be a commercial success in Virginia. Of foremost importance is, "*To know your costs!* Write down all the costs and time you and others spend! Value your own time. You are worth something, too." He also recommends management strategies by vineyard blocks and variety. "The more specific you are, the better you are!" Reflecting on his vineyard management and establishment costs per acre per year (not counting the cost of the land), Asberger concludes simply: "If you have a four-ton yield per acre at two thousand dollars per ton, you break even. If you sell less you are . . . [screwed]." (Asberger's specific cost estimates per acre are detailed in "Additional Information" at the end of this book.)

As with vintages anywhere, what makes a good vintage in Virginia varies with the subregion and grape variety. And part of the difficulty is agreeing on what makes a good vintage—the definition depends on who is asked and their economic stake in the answer.

Often, what makes a good vintage for whites is not quite the same as for reds. White wines are best where grapes are disease-free and ripe but not overripe, so that fresh-fruit flavors and acidity are highlighted.

Good vintages for red wines require a growing season that is fairly dry, especially in the late phase (after Labor Day), so the phenolic compounds such as tannins and anthocyanins (color compounds) in the skins of the grapes can polymerize (forming three-dimensional polymer chains with each other) and develop deep color, ripe-fruit aromas and flavors, and smooth textures. Some vintages, such as 2009, are excellent for most white wines, with high acid and bright citrus fruit, but not as good for many reds (2009 was a cool growing season, with rainy spells during harvest of earlier-ripening reds), without the hot and dry conditions quality red wine demands. The 2010 vintage was California-like, with weeks of sunshine and no rain, resulting in high sugar levels, with well-developed flavors, but some wines that are unbalanced and high in alcohol without a corresponding ripe-fruit flavor. As with many things, in viticulture you can have too much of a good thing.

THE TIDEWATER REGION

Virginia's Eastern Shore

The wine world is changing rapidly. There used to be an Old World style and a New World style, clearly delineated by geography and philosophy, but the industry today is much like someone's description of world music: everyone's "ripping each other off" stylistically. This is understandable; lots of consumer dollars are at stake in a competitive market, and even the French have learned that if you can't sell your traditional-style wine anymore because consumers have changed their preferences, you'll have to swallow your pride and change, or get out of the business.

We now set off on a guided wine tour across Virginia, journeying from east to west, but covering the north and south as well (driving directions are based on the annual *Virginia Winery Guide*, available from the Virginia Wine Board Marketing Office). We'll meet growers, winemakers, winery owners, marketing mavens, wine writers, and politicians. We'll see the vast diversity of Virginia wine, from large wineries to brands without wineries that hire custom-crush facilities to make the wine for them. We'll travel across the state, from the Eastern Shore to the Blue Ridge Mountains and beyond, and from two-hundred-year-old plantation estates to brand-new wineries, and experience the rich diversity these wineries offer, from classic European vinifera varietals like cabernet franc, chardonnay, and merlot, to uniquely Virginia blends with petit verdot, and from obscure vinifera like petit manseng to old and new hybrids like traminette.

Some important words of advice for wine tourists: First, don't taste and drive. Have a designated driver. Second, even if you're not driving, you'll find that your specific impressions (of the wines, the wineries, the people, the places) will fade into a blur if you don't take the simple step of tasting professionally; that is, taking notes and spitting the wine out instead of swallowing it. Just bring a small, opaque plastic cup with you, and don't worry about being "gross" or getting scolded. This is how professionals taste wine all day, by spitting diligently, writing and focusing, drinking lots of water, and not tasting on an empty stomach. If you're taking the time and trouble to visit wineries in a vehicle, you may as well be awake and alert enough to remember the experience and distinguish what's good and what you really like from what you don't. This requires staying fairly sober, and I need to add that even spitting wine out, you won't avoid swallowing some, and this will creep up on you after a while; be alert and pace yourself.

Personally, I like to visit three to four wineries a day at the most. You'll be amazed how much time it takes to travel, taste, talk to the staff, buy what you want, get back on the road or wait in line for the bathroom, eat lunch, etc., etc. Also, the fatigue factor (even with spitting) sets in after the fourth winery for me, and then you still have to get back to your home base.

We start our journey in the Tidewater region, where the English settlement in North America began. Virginia's Eastern Shore, which has its own AVA, is defined by two major features: the moderating maritime climate between the bay and the ocean, and well-drained sandy loam soils.

Let's assume you are driving south down the Delmarva Peninsula; the Virginia section is the narrow southern end. Soon after crossing into Virginia on Rt. 13, Rt. 175 heads to the east, past the Mid-Atlantic Regional Spaceport and NASA, to the islands of Chincoteague and Assateague, where the famous Chincoteague ponies roam wild, and home to an antique lighthouse and National Seashore beach (the Eastern Shore has longest stretch of wild coastline left on the East Coast). Chincoteague also houses the Oyster and Maritime Museum.

Virginia's Eastern Shore is, for the most part, like Maryland's Eastern Shore, only without Ocean City or the giant poultry-processing plant in Salisbury. After the novelty of the space center and Chincoteague, the countryside settles down to placid farmland. Virginia's Eastern Shore is only ten miles across at its widest, and there's a sense of having left the twenty-first century behind, with the wide Chesapeake Bay to the west and the Atlantic Ocean to the east, as the miles of farmland and small towns slip by, mixing traditional English place-names such as Northampton and Oak Hall with Native American ones such as Wachapreague and Machipongo.

Heading south on Rt. 13, you'll find **Bloxom Winery**, the oldest extant winery on Virginia's Eastern Shore, near the town of that name. Take Rt. 681 west (left for one mile, left at the vineyard, and follow signs to the winery). Wines include chardonnay, merlot, cabernet franc, Red Kiss, and Some Like It Blush.

In Onacock, you can take a ferry to Tangier Island, in the middle of the Chesapeake Bay. This was at one point an important oyster fishing community (stocks have dropped drastically, but the fishing tradition carries on). The island is carless, and besides tourists attracts linguists *posing* as tourists, surreptitiously trying to record the dialect of the locals, which is said to be the closest to seventeenth-century English in the country.

Rock Stephens is a large, tall man with a muscular jaw and the presence of a football coach or a Marine sergeant, although he is friendly and not intimidating. He is one of the few commercial vineyard owners who does not also make significant amounts of wine from his own grapes, and has been a leader in the industry, having recently stepped down as president of the Virginia Vineyards Association. His property is called the **Vineyard at Point Breeze**, located in Belle Haven, west of Rt. 13 between Painter and Exmore. The vineyard isn't open to the public currently, but Stephens is a leading Virginia commercial grape grower, and it's worth hearing his recommendations for successful viticulture in the state.

Like others, he emphasizes the need to grow varietals that will succeed in Virginia (and on the individual site), but he adds the importance of avoiding close proximity to residential neighbors. "There are times that you need to drag the sprayer out at 1:00 a.m. or get the old shotgun out to take care of some pesky critters, and you do not want to be hampered by having a subdivision right next to the vineyard."

South of Exmore is **Holly Grove Vineyards**. In Nassawadox, turn east on Rodgers Dr. and follow the grape cluster signs to the winery. Major wines are chardonnay, merlot, and a High Tide traminette.

The last winery on the Eastern Shore before you cross the Chesapeake Bay Bridge-Tunnel is **Chatham Vineyards**, owned and operated by Jon and Mills Wehner. Jon claims to be the first Virginia client of viticultural consultant Lucie Morton to move to the now-dominant paradigm for vineyard spacing in Virginia: close in-row spacing (about a meter), with cane pruning instead of spur pruning. "At the time [the late 1990s], everyone else in Virginia (except Barboursville Vineyards) was moving to wide spacing for vigor management," he says. "We went with Lucie in the opposite direction."

There are several advantages to this cane-pruned, close-planted system. Vigor management is a priority for most Virginia growers, and the more you can establish a vineyard that self-regulates its vigor, the more labor and time you'll save as a grower. The theory behind tight vine spacing (within the row) is that it encourages competition between plant roots for nutrients, thereby limiting vine vigor. Another advantage is that with higher vine density, you can limit per-vine yield but still get more per-acre yield from the vineyard.

With spur pruning, permanent cordons are laid out horizontally from the vine, and shoots grow vertically from them, bearing fruit. The problem in Virginia, with its fairly vigorous soils, is that shoots will compete for space on the trellis as the cordons grow toward one another, creating a tangle that is labor-intensive to manage. Also, permanent cordons will diminish fruit productivity as the vine ages.

With cane pruning, all the previous year's canes are cut from the trunks, leaving just a few buds for the next year's growth. The horizontal space competition is now gone. The new shoots are trained vertically, and even though the vines are only a meter apart (six-foot in-row spacing had been common), the shoots are easy to manage, and the grape clusters hang in neat, orderly lines at the base of the foliage.

Jon Wehner is a second-generation Virginia winegrower; his parents had a vineyard in Great Falls in the 1970s, and Lucie Morton was also their consultant. "We produce site-expressive wines that reflect the unique climate of Virginia's Eastern Shore," says Wehner. He farms twenty acres of French vinifera grapes, including first-generation Dijon clones, and produces about 3,200 cases annually, harvesting approximately seventy-five tons.

Aside from pioneering close in-row spacing in Virginia, Wehner claims theirs was the first commercial winery to plant the then-new Dijon clones (so-named for their Burgundian origin) of chardonnay that had just been released in 1999 (clones 76, 95, and 96) as well as the UC Davis clone 4. Aside from five acres of chardonnay, his grapes are all red Bordeaux varieties: the two cabernets, merlot, and petit verdot (his largest planting is ten acres of merlot).

Wehner has had over a decade of experience working with his new spacing and the new clones, so he's confident about what works for him, although he won't speak for other people's sites. What difference does a Dijon clone of chardonnay make, compared to the UC Davis clone 4? "Clone four is a production [volume] clone; these clusters can weigh a half pound and look like a football. Growers like them for that reason. Dijon clones have small berries, and the clusters are the size of your fist." There's more concentration in the smaller berries, and also high acid.

Chatham Farm has been a working farm for four centuries (the land was patented in 1640), and Wehner describes himself as a stylistic traditionalist. "It's a reflection of our climate and soils," he says. The Federal-period brick house, Chatham, was built in 1818 by Major Scarborough Pitts and named for William Pitt, the earl of Chatham and friend of the American Revolution. Although tastings are now held in the winery, future plans include the relocation and restoration of an 1890s farmhouse adjoining the winery to serve as a tasting room and special-events facility.

"We made a decision to leave northern Virginia for a better quality of life," says Wehner of himself and his wife, Mills. "We got married, moved to the shore, and planted a vineyard in the same year. We felt it was important to raise our children in the country." He says he grew up working in the vineyard and making wine in the cellar of his parents' dairy barn in Fairfax County. "I have very fond childhood memories."

Wehner notes that vineyards are located in beautiful places, attracting winery tourism that generates tax revenue and is a high-dollar, low-impact business that preserves farmland. "The State of Virginia has been very supportive, particularly the governor [McDonnell] and his cabinet. The big issues [in the future] will be small farm wineries' rights and county ordinances, direct shipping to out-of-state consumers, and wholesale relations."

The Virginia Peninsula (Hampton Roads Region)

There are many miles of high-density development in Hampton and Newport News. To their north is Yorktown, in Virginia's historic triangle (the other two points being Jamestown and Williamsburg). At Yorktown in 1781, American forces under George Washington and their French allies defeated General Cornwallis's British army, effectively ending the Revolutionary War.

It isn't until you leave Newport News well behind that the trees return in number as you approach Williamsburg and Jamestown. Turning off I-64 at Exit 242A, you take Rt. 199 west and watch for signs and turns for the **Williamsburg Winery**.

The Williamsburg Winery is the Virginia winery with the longest-standing association with our colonial heritage. It has a style harking back to the Jamestown era and, in fact, the winery and its vineyard stand on "the Wessex Hundred," land that was first cultivated by English settlers in the Jamestown era. Several of its wines have names evoking the early Jamestown Settlement, such as the Acte 12 of 1619 Chardonnay, the John Adlum Chardonnay, the Gabriel Archer Reserve, and the Governor's White. The winery also has a museum with a large collection of eighteenth-century bottles salvaged from the wreck of a Dutch trading ship of that era. "We are a part of the history of the wine world," says winery president Patrick Duffeler Sr., who owns and operates the winery with his son Patrick Jr. The winemaker is Matthew Meyer, who was formerly winemaker at Hanzell in Napa Valley.

Patrick Duffeler Sr. is trim and bald, with a wide and quick smile. He was born in Belgium and educated in the United States, earning a degree in economics and finance from the University of Rochester. His previous career was in marketing, first for Eastman Kodak then as director of marketing for Philip Morris in Lausanne, Switzerland. He also worked in the wine industry in Burgundy. Duffeler Sr. has taken a leadership role in the industry, promoting not just his own wines but the positioning and reputation of Virginia wine as a whole; he was named Virginia Wine Industry Person of the Year in 1998 at the Governor's Cup ceremony. With his marketing background and European experience, it was natural for him to form the idea of the Virginia Wine Experience, which in 2007 brought sixty-four prescreened wines to London for leading trade and media members to taste (full disclosure: the author was executive director of the event).

"For twenty-five years I've been here in Williamsburg," he says. "What made me settle here was the history. I think of Williamsburg as the 'soul of America'; it was logical to me to have a winery that was consistent with the history of the state." The 300-acre farm was purchased in 1983, and he and his wife, Peggy, founded the Williamsburg Winery in 1985. The main winery facility was built in 1988, and after expansions now includes a large hall for dinners and receptions, enlarged barrel rooms and retail shops, and the adjacent facilities of the Gabriel Archer Tavern and Wedmore Place, a luxury hotel.

The Williamsburg Winery is one of the largest wineries in Virginia. From its 1988 level of 2,000 cases produced annually, it has grown to a current 55,000–60,000 cases, twenty-three wines, and over 65,000 visitors a year. "Our long-term goal is not to grow total case production, but to focus on increasing premium varietals and reserve wines; they've increased 25 percent over the last three years," explains Duffeler Sr. Sales volume and dollar volume per label vary widely: The two top production labels are the Governor's White and Two Shilling Red, both attractively priced proprietary blends, at 10,000 and

8,000 cases produced per year, respectively. Both are made from non-Virginia fruit. These are also top sellers in the tasting room, while the higher-tier Gabriel Archer Reserve (a red Bordeaux-style blend) and Virginia Trianon (cabernet franc) are the top two dollar-grossing labels and are Virginia products.

One example of Duffeler Sr.'s focus on the higher end of wine quality and its corresponding market is the introduction of the new Adagio label with the 2007 vintage. A proprietary red Bordeaux blend, it is notable for its high percentage of petit verdot, which works well in Virginia. The inaugural vintage drinks like red velvet—very smooth and rich, but fruit driven, in a style that is distinctly Virginian. Production was only 120 cases the first year; that has risen to 250 cases with the 2008 vintage. The wine is pretty pricey at $60 retail but, says Duffeler Sr., "We've sold out every year since we launched it." The 2007 and 2008 vintages both won silver medals at the *Decanter* World Wine Awards in 2010 and 2011 (only forty-three total silver medals were awarded for the entire United States in 2011).

"Our selling proposition is to meet or exceed consumer expectations in each tier of our wines," he says, "and reflect the character of Virginia. But what is the character of Virginia's wines? That's why we don't try to compete with very rich cabernets from California, or Tuscan wines; we'll never have those kind of flavors here." Duffeler Sr. believes Virginia should focus on grapes "that have a future for Virginia, like cabernet franc, petit verdot, merlot, and Bordeaux-style blends using those components. Those varietals are done very well here; we grow more cabernet franc in Virginia than any other place [in the United States]."

Like Jon Wehner at Chatham Vineyards, Duffeler Sr. describes himself as a stylistic traditionalist. "I see us as working on establishing a flavor profile for Virginia wines. Virginia is neither Europe nor California, but should be making Virginia wine. Rob Bickford [a former employee] jokes that, 'Europeans are trying to make California wines and Californians are trying to make European wines, so they're all trying to make Virginia wines,'" quotes Duffeler Sr. with a laugh.

Duffeler Sr.'s goal for Virginia wine style is "elegance: a lot of flavors that don't have uncharacteristic intensity but have a delicacy of multiple flavors joining together, with a long finish. Our pursuit is literally to make a fabulous cabernet franc, merlot, or blend that reflects the terroir of Virginia, elicit a positive response from wine people that, regardless of its origin, they'll say it's the best merlot or cabernet franc they've ever had."

If Duffeler Sr. is so bullish on making wine that reflects what's special about Virginia, why does he make three labels of chardonnay? "This is responding to the market," he explains. "There was a time that people were saying 'ABC' [anything but chardonnay] because there was a lot of poor chardonnay on the market. I had a terrible California chardonnay last night; it was sweet, lacking in flavor. But there are a lot of people who appreciate great chardonnay. Oz Clarke commented [at the London International Wine Fair in 2010] that he was impressed by our Acte 12 of 1619 chardonnay; he said that it was going in the direction of fine white Burgundy instead of the direction of California. It's also a lot less expensive than a Puligny-Montrachet or meursault."

The Williamsburg Winery has replanted its vineyards (now thirty-seven acres total), and Duffeler Sr. explains they have added a fair amount of calcium and lime to the soil to raise pH for optimal vine metabolism. But despite their new vineyards, they still purchase 80 percent of their grapes from outside growers. And despite his enthusiasm for branding Virginia wine, Duffeler Sr. concedes that, "We have purchased grapes from other states for wines in popular consumer price points. We think that people want well-made wines that don't have to be Virginia wines, but all our reserve and premium varietal wines have the Virginia appellation."

Duffeler Sr. touches on a paradox in the Virginia wine industry: the lack of affordable, everyday Virginia table wine, due to growers' focus on top-dollar grape varieties and the expense of farming grapes in Virginia's humid climate. "I would like to see us in a few years making a hundred percent Virginia appellation wines. I'm concerned about the lack of vineyards of economical size. The cost of grapes will have an important impact on the Virginia wine industry. The average grape price per ton in Virginia is unrealistically high to be able to produce popular-priced wines. We have to think about the right equilibrium for the industry." The winery's own vineyards are an example; they are planted mainly to top-market red Bordeaux varieties and viognier, with just twelve acres devoted to white hybrids vidal blanc and traminette (the winery produces a dessert vidal blanc retailing at $24 for a half bottle).

Duffeler Sr.'s public relations background plays a part in the decision to focus both on the high end and on red wines. "When I came to Virginia in the late 1970s, red wines were only 15 percent of the market; today they are almost half of the dollar volume of the wine market. Ultimately, wine lovers will appreciate wines that have the capacity to age. We did a vertical tasting of the Gabriel Archer Reserve recently; people were thrilled about tasting older wines with depth of flavor they don't ordinarily see, but the market would not expect producers to put on a vertical tasting of chardonnays." Accordingly, he's positioning the winery to appeal to the kind of wine drinkers who appreciate high-end reds.

Duffeler Sr. buys and blends grapes from across Virginia. "We like to blend grapes from different areas of the state for flavor complexity; grapes from the Eastern Shore with grapes from the mountains, for example." He adds that Shep Rouse, of Rockbridge, does the same. "You cannot just say 'my grapes or my location' will make the very best grapes in the world year in and year out. Even in Burgundy it's not possible to have that level of consistency. I saw a hailstorm in the vineyards of Nuits-Saint-Georges that was just terrible. So nobody can generalize that they'll always be best every year. We all know nature is unpredictable." (The Williamsburg Winery's 2007 crop was wiped out by hail.)

Duffeler Sr. has watched the Virginia wine industry for the last ten years. "I think Virginia has been on the cusp of becoming known as a fine wine region. The growth of the US wine industry has been very impressive, but has also taken place in many other states. The growth in the percentage of the market is totally dominated by California, but Oregon branded itself with pinot noir very well; Washington and New York have also branded themselves. Regional wine is a good thing. I go back to Europe twice a year and am always struck by the favor given to regional wines there. Then again, the issue of pricing comes in. You have to be able to support a regional wine industry with wines most people can afford. I want to affirm that the best is yet to come; we're always asking ourselves how to improve the food or the visitor experience or the winemaking."

He sees winery tourism as a natural strong suit for Virginia. "It's not just wine tourism; there's a general trend as the country becomes more urbanized for people to escape to the countryside for relief. This is an extraordinarily scenic state; the diversity from the beaches to the mountains, and the beauty of our forests . . . Farmland is very attractive for agritourism—ecotourism." He points out that this isn't unique to Virginia. "Lifestyles over the last fifty years have changed. When I started the winery, the [US Travel Association] had found that by the mid-1980s, among the top factors deciding vacation destinations was people's desire to explore local wine and food. Twenty-five years later, there's no question that people will make a detour to visit the Inn at Little Washington [Virginia] for its great food and wines and scenic setting, for example."

Duffeler Sr. is an optimist and believes strongly that the Virginia wine industry offers its customers not just a product, but an experience. "When I go into a fine-wine shop, I feel like it's an adult version of a candy store. We're offering people joy through our wines and how they experience them. Most people work in stressful situations. We offer them a respite from all that. We who are passionate and enjoy what we do in this industry should communicate our joy to our customers."

❧   ❧   ❧

Sustainability and ecotourism go hand in hand. West of Williamsburg, in New Kent County (take Exit 211 from I-64, north on Rt. 106), is a remarkable example of winery planning that incorporates heirloom, reclaimed materials; a heritage design; strongly environmentally friendly features; a business plan that welcomes and encourages tour buses as well as the adjacent affluent retirement community; and of course fine Virginia wine made by an experienced and respected winemaker: winemaking consultant Tom Payette.

Pete Johns is the principal of **New Kent Winery**. An amiable man in his sixties, with the calm, genial comportment of a Virginian, he's actually beyond Yankee north: His family is originally from the Niagara region of Ontario, Canada, home today to a thriving vinifera-based wine industry. "I used to play in my grandfather's garden and small vineyard as a child. I had no idea that growing grapes was as much work as it is," he says with a laugh.

Johns is a real estate developer and a former NFL player. The New Kent vineyards and winery are actually the centerpiece of a much larger planned community that carries the name of the vineyards. Johns explains that the project encompasses more than 2,500 acres and will mature to 2,500 homes and 860,000 square feet of commercial space. Amenities for the community include a signature Rees Jones golf course—the Club at Viniterra—a neo-traditional village, and of course the distinctive winery and vineyards. "In working with my partners, Boddie-Noell Enterprises, I suggested we create a unique lifestyle for this upscale community. In addition to the traditional golf course and village, I suggested vineyards and a winery. We have created a remarkable project and one that will endure," he says.

The winery was constructed using recycled antique building materials that included massive heart-pine beams and columns taken from an 1852 warehouse in Connecticut, handmade pre–Civil War bricks out of nearby Richmond, cypress siding and shingles formed from sinker logs that were underwater in the northern rivers of Florida for more than 150 years, and 1902 trusses that came from the Southern Railway depot in Richmond.

Johns plans for the big picture, which is why he located the winery—the centerpiece of the planned residential community for affluent baby boomers who enjoy wine as part of their lifestyle—with convenient access to I-64. He notes that the winery is located in the middle of a major growth corridor of the future—the I-64 corridor that will link Hampton Roads harbor and Richmond, with Williamsburg in the middle. The corridor is also the major tourist corridor for the commonwealth, with millions of people passing near the winery each year on their way to the Outer Banks of North Carolina, Williamsburg, and other tourist destinations in this historic region.

Johns has even planned a separate tasting facility just for tour buses, with exactly the number of seats at a table for a full bus, so that visitors in the upstairs tasting room wouldn't be inconvenienced by the crowds.

New Kent has just over twenty acres of vines planted, some of which are thirteen years old. Their vineyards include the following grape varietals: chardonnay, merlot, cabernet franc, vidal blanc, and norton. They produce about half of the grapes necessary for production, and the rest they secure through contracts. Until now, all wine sales were at the winery or at the dozen or so wine festivals they attend each year, but New Kent has just begun distributing wines throughout Virginia.

The wine that is probably the standout, for its novelty, is New Kent's white norton. "Rather than making a more traditional red norton," Johns explains, "we developed a new version—white norton. This wine won great praise and awards when we introduced it to the general public. Each year we have sold out of this wine, and that prompted us to find a replacement wine until our own vines mature enough to produce the quantities we needed for additional production.

The replacement wine has also been a great success—white merlot, a true white wine made from the merlot grape. These wines are very different from the norm and have won great acclaim for our winery."

While some may scoff at "blush" wines, Johns points out that it's hard to argue with success. Although they began by selecting traditional wines that would grow in their region, "we have expanded on this theme with unique variations and styles. While our goal is to constantly strive to improve the quality of our wines, we also must be practical and make wines that will sell. Many of our wines are designed for the largest segment of the wine-drinking public. Our terroir limits the varietals of wines we can successfully grow, but we strive to make each of our basic wines the best they can be," he says.

"We believe Virginia is on the verge of becoming a very important element within the US wine industry. California and European wineries see Virginia as an ideal market to enter and expand their interest to the East Coast. Our population is well educated, wine savvy, and they are willing to try new wines. It would not surprise us to see one or more major wineries from California or Europe purchase an interest in an existing winery in Virginia."

The Northern Neck AVA and Nearby

After leaving New Kent Winery, you'll most likely return to I-64 on Rt. 106. If, however, you take Rt. 249 heading east instead, you can turn left on Rt. 623 and stop at nearby **Saudé Creek Vineyards**. When you arrive at West Point, where the York River meets the Chesapeake Bay estuary, what if you continue your Tidewater exploration on a sailboat? Sailing down the estuary, you'll pass Yorktown on your right before reaching the bay, where you can head northeast, then north, perhaps stopping at Tangier Island, before heading west, below Point Lookout, Maryland, and up into the Potomac River estuary. After landing at Westmoreland State Park and visiting George Washington's birthplace, you'll re-embark for a short sail west, up the river, following the southern shore into an estuary bay. Disembarking, you'll follow signs into the town of Oak Grove, location of **Ingleside Plantation Vineyards**. You're retracing the route (at least up the Potomac) taken by the Belgian Jacques Recht, who had decided in 1980 to retire from winemaking and sail around the world on a catamaran with his wife, Liliane, when by chance they came across Oak Grove and Ingleside Vineyards.

The story of Jacques and Liliane's fortunate arrival at Ingleside has been called "The Winemaker from the Sea," says Chris Flemer, brother of owner Doug Flemer. On arriving in the region, "They happened to meet some family friends of ours who, upon learning that Jacques was a winemaker, suggested that he meet my father, Carl, who was starting a winery. So Jacques and Liliane came to meet my parents and tried some wines my father made. I believe Jacques saw some potential in the wines and my father was impressed with Jacques's vast knowledge and experience with wine. We were able to convince Jacques to stay and help us with our first harvest. This was our first commercial harvest. Jacques ended up staying on and becoming our full-time winemaker for about fifteen years. He also consulted with other wineries in Virginia and the East Coast. I think Jacques found the potential of a new wine industry in Virginia an intriguing challenge, and we were very fortunate to have him as our winemaker."

Recht's expertise helped Ingleside—and many other Virginia wineries—establish themselves with sound winemaking practices at a critical time in the industry's revival. Sadly, Recht passed away several years ago, but his contributions are well remembered by the Virginia wine pioneers of the 1980s.

Oak Grove is located in the middle of a peninsula known as the Northern Neck. Like Virginia's Eastern Shore, it also has an AVA, with a formal name possible only in Virginia: Northern Neck George Washington Birthplace. Like the Eastern Shore, the Northern Neck's climate is moderated mostly by the Chesapeake Bay to the east, but it also benefits from air and water drainage of the Potomac and Rappahannock rivers to the north and south.

For many in the Washington exurbs of Virginia, the Northern Neck is much like the Eastern Shore—a welcome time warp where they can leave behind traffic congestion and high-tech, high-stress environments, but it's much closer than the Eastern Shore. Today there are ten wineries on the Northern Neck, and they have their own wine trail.

Ingleside Vineyards is located on a historic antebellum plantation. Built in 1834, it was used during the Civil War as a garrison and later a courthouse. Since 1890, the Flemer family has owned and operated the estate, which encompasses more than three thousand acres. For its first fifty years it functioned as a dairy farm.

The winery began its current business as a grapevine nursery after Carl Flemer realized that the plantation's location (at the crest of the peninsula, with good air and water drainage) offered prime conditions for growing high-quality wine grapes.

Ingleside Vineyards is one of Virginia's oldest and largest wineries, producing about twenty varieties of wine from estate-grown grapes, and the first winery on the Northern Neck. In the 1980s, Ingleside's cabernet sauvignon was consistently among the best red wines in the state, and its wines have won top honors in state, national, and international wine competitions, such as the Virginia Governor's Cup competition, the San Diego International Wine Competition, and the London International Wine and Spirit Competition. The current winemaker is Bill Swain.

Ingleside currently produces 10,000 cases per year with fifty acres of vines. Top varieties include merlot, petit verdot, pinot grigio, and sangiovese. The latter three, introduced relatively recently in the thirty-year history of the winery, have gained particular notice, as has their premium red Bordeaux blend, Virginia Gold.

Ingleside produced Virginia's first *méthode champenoise* sparkling wine in 1980. "We were also the first winery in Virginia to bottle a varietal petit verdot, which has proven to be a popular wine in Virginia," Chris says.

If you didn't want to drive west into the modern world and the multihighway intersection and traffic that you'll meet in Fredericksburg (and who would?), you'd again embark in your sailboat up the Potomac estuary, navigating northwest off the Potomac River into Aquia Creek (first researching details on where you can dock and berth the boat). A ten- to fifteen-minute cab ride and you'll arrive at **Potomac Point Vineyard & Winery**.

Skip and Cindi Causey are the proprietors of this elegant, Mediterranean-style winery that offers a respite from the crowded roads to the west. In contrast to Ingleside—one of the oldest Virginia wineries—Potomac Point is fairly new, but thanks to the talented Simone Bergese, their Italian winemaker, has established itself on the Virginia scene for its quality wine. The winery is located between Fredericksburg and the nearby Quantico Marine Corps base.

Cindi Causey thinks the synergy of a favorable climate, the agri-tourism trend, and the support of state government is "great for the entire well-being of the commonwealth. To me it's a win-win for all."

Considering the future of Virginia wine, she says that "what stands out most in my mind is that as an industry, we are taking winemaking seriously; hiring educated winemakers and raising quality grapes to make quality wine, and putting a quality alliance program in place. These are all positive signs."

Simone Bergese brings a blend of traditional and New World approaches to his winemaking, having worked in the ultratraditional Piemonte of Italy, then in Australia for two years to get a different perspective. He describes his winemaking style as keeping from tradition what he thinks works well (probably 70 percent of his techniques) and adding "all the new techniques I know to make wines that can somehow inspire our customers. So, I'm product-oriented, but with ears open to the world."

In 2008, Bergese made a norton that won a double gold medal in the International Eastern Wine Competition in 2009. Norton is problematic for winemakers; it combines high acid with high pH, which can compromise both balance and microbial stability. It also has a ratio of malic acid to tartaric acid that is four times higher than that of vinifera red varieties, and low tannin at the same time. This produces a wine that can seem both tart and flat to people used to traditional red vinifera varieties.

Bergese's approach was creative. The main thing, he explains, was sorting for high fruit quality in 2008, which was a fine vintage for norton. His second key was blending the norton with red vinifera grapes, in this case touriga nacional and petit verdot, to balance the texture of the wine. "I believe that you must use at least 10 percent of vinifera grapes to find the balance with norton," he explains. Finally, he fermented the wine in a large oak tank, avoiding small new oak, which can give norton a chewy vanilla edge that clashes with its tartness. The resulting wine still tasted like norton, but was balanced and elegant, phrases not often used to describe wines made from that grape.

NORTHERN VIRGINIA

Rappahannock and Fauquier Counties

If you've driven to Potomac Point, get directions to I-95 south, then take Exit 133 and head west on Rt. 17; you're on your way to the northern Piedmont. On the way you can stop at **Hartwood Winery** on the right, **Rogers Ford Farm Winery** on the left (some distance from the road), and **Molon Lave Vineyards**, also on the left. Continuing on Rt. 17, at Opal you'll meet Rt. 29, which you'll take north, then follow signs for Business Rt. 17 into Warrenton, turning left on Rt. 211 to head west. You'll first encounter **Unicorn Winery** on the right (technically in Culpeper County), then, reaching Amissville, you'll have a pair of wineries close together: **Gray Ghost** on the left and **Narmada** on the right (now in Rappahannock County).

Following this route, you're on what had been the front lines during the Civil War, 150 years ago, along the Rappahannock River. If you continued into Fredericksburg, you could visit the battlefield where General Ambrose Burnside's Union attack on the city in the winter of 1862 ended in a disastrous slaughter. To the west along Rt. 3 is the Fredericksburg & Spotsylvania County National Military Park, commemorating the battles of Chancellorsville, in 1863, and Wilderness, in 1864.

Gray Ghost Vineyards (named after the nickname of Confederate colonel John Mosby, whose raiders operated in the area) is a small but high-quality winery owned and run by the Kellert family: Al and Cheryl (co-winemakers), their son Al (vineyard manager), and daughter Amy (marketing manager). Although production and product line are modest, Gray Ghost has established a reputation disproportionate to its size. Amy says they receive at least one hundred awards annually, many from out-of-state competitions. Although they make fine dry wines from both vinifera and hybrids, they are best known for their consistently excellent Adieu, a proprietary late-harvest vidal blanc that, unlike most in Virginia, is not made from frozen grapes but from grapes left on the vine to be picked late, developing complex, rich apricot flavors from botrytis, as is the case with top French and German late-harvest wines. Adieu has won "Best of Class" for the last three years in the Los Angeles International Wine & Spirits Competition and "Best of Show" in 2009 in the Mid-Atlantic Southeastern Wine Competition. The Adieu, Reserve Chardonnay, Reserve Cabernet Sauvignon, vidal blanc (off-dry), and their Bordeaux-blend Ranger Reserve also perform consistently well in competitions, including those in California.

Al and Cheryl Kellert got the wine bug while Al was still working as a marketing manager at the US Postal Service and planted grapevines in their suburban backyard (they actually transplanted them to the Amissville location). Several things drew them into the wine world. First, while studying for a degree in chemistry, Al was introduced to winemaking during a summer job in a research lab in 1969. After he and Cheryl were married, they continued making wine as a hobby until 1981, when he was sent to the West Coast to head up the regional marketing office for the Postal Service in San Francisco. "We had the opportunity to meet and work with some very renowned winemakers while in the area. One was Justin Meyer of Silver Oak. It was that experience that tipped the scales for us to move from hobby to the real thing."

After spending three years searching for property (in both Virginia and California), they selected their current location because the topography and climate are ideal for grape growing. "It was then a matter of meticulously developing the vineyards, the future winery, and Gray Ghost was the result. For us, this is truly a dream come true."

"We focus on the Civil War history," he says, "with primary emphasis on Colonel Mosby, since we are located at the southern edge of Mosby's Confederacy. Coupled with the emphasis on highly acclaimed wines and a beautiful setting, this makes the winery an attractive stop for wine enthusiasts as well as history buffs." He notes that tourists tend to look at winery groupings as destination areas for spending a day in wine country.

Stylistically, Kellert explains, "we place ourselves in both the traditional and New World categories, depending on the wine being produced. Our barrel-fermented and aged wines utilize Old World methods, including aging chardonnays on the lees for texture and flavor complexity and producing dry reds as unfiltered [to retain flavor]." Meanwhile, the stainless-steel-fermented wines use contemporary technology, giving them the ability to cold-ferment and stop fermentation with residual sugar. "This blend of tradition and technology gives us both elegant, velvety, finished reds and chardonnays as well as beautiful fruity-style wines from stainless steel."

Kellert reflects that many factors work together for the growth and benefit of the Virginia wine industry. "As Virginia becomes more recognized as a winegrowing region, the rapid growth in the industry is a natural follow-up. Virginia's wine industry is in the enviable position of being located in a state that supports the industry with research in both viticulture and enology. The state is also very business-friendly, which helps encourage entrepreneurs. Finally, vineyards represent alternative agriculture, which fits very nicely into the state's objectives of keeping land open, beautiful, and in viable agricultural programs."

One difference Kellert sees in the industry today compared to twenty years ago is that "Wineries appear to be starting less because of a passion for wine, and more driven by individuals with accumulated wealth wishing to be a part of what is perceived to be a 'romantic' lifestyle. This has resulted in a number of disenchanted individuals who may have gotten in a little over their heads. We feel that over time the cream will rise to the top."

Before leaving Amissville, look out for the refreshingly original **Narmada Winery**, a few miles north of Rt. 211. The winery is owned by Pandit Patil, and his wife—Dr. Sudha Patil—is the winemaker (she also owns and runs a periodontal practice). The couple is Indian, and at the winery you can enjoy Indian tapas thoughtfully matched with their wines, which are mostly proprietary blends.

Continue north on Rt. 211 and watch for signs for Rt. 522 north. Turn right on it, heading toward Front Royal, where the north and south forks of the Shenandoah River meet and the famous Skyline Parkway Drive along the crest of the Blue Ridge Mountains begins. If you want to enjoy lunch at this point, the town of Flint Hill is a nice place to stop. North of Flint Hill, look for Rt. 630 (Hittles Mill Rd.) on the left to visit **Berry Hill Vineyard**. (Turn left; after the bridge stay left to Rt. 466 on the left.) For ten years, Berry Hill grew cabernet franc and sold it to others, but now they are making wine themselves; at the current writing, the 2009 vintage is their only wine.

Returning to Rt. 522, turn left to continue north. Watch for the familiar state winery road sign on the right just past the hamlet of Huntley. Turn right on CR 635 (you can't miss the vineyard at the crossroads) and turn left into **Rappahannock Cellars**.

John Delmare is the proprietor of Rappahannock Cellars, and Jason Burrus is the winemaker. Aside from their own product line, they also provide some custom-crush services to other Virginia wineries.

Delmare is a large, affable man with wavy hair, and is one of several Virginia winery owners who first owned a winery in California (in his case, Savannah-Chanelle, in the San Francisco Bay area). Explaining why he decided to relocate to a lesser-known, more challenging wine region, Delmare says, "I really came because it was the confluence between a great place to raise my growing family and a region that was capable of making world-class wines. I can't think of another region in the country that offered the best of both worlds."

Rappahannock Cellars' product line spans the major vinifera varieties produced in Virginia, but also includes norton (a stunning example, in a port style) and the French hybrid seyval blanc, interpreted brilliantly in a Loire Valley style. While the winery has garnered a deserved reputation for viognier and cabernet franc, a very stylish Meritage is also noteworthy, and for fans of singular chardonnay, their "native yeast ferment" is astonishing for its layers of deftly interwoven flavors and textures. Stylistically, you could say they represent a skillful synergy of the best of Old and New World styles. Delmare considers Rappahannock Cellars "mostly traditionalists, but that somewhat depends on the varietal and the vintage. Meritage, cabernet franc, and chardonnay are done in traditional styles, but the viognier is New World at its best—but really, it's Virginia. Seyval blanc is definitely New World; norton is norton!" He points out that vintage character plays a role in wine style. "Our 2007 cab. franc was very New World (California in style), where 2008 screamed Loire Valley—Old World."

For a marketing message, Delmare says, "we focus on the wine, and also play up our California roots. We are known for high quality across all our wines. Our philosophy is that we will never allow a substandard wine to be poured in our winery." Notably, they focus a lot on their wine club, which accounts for over 60 percent of their business. "We market mostly by word of mouth and by providing a superior environment, service, and wine quality."

Commenting on the larger industry, Delmare notes that "Virginia wines are growing in quality, and the world is waking up to that fact. For many years, we have produced great wines, but now a larger percentage of the industry here in Virginia is making quality wine. The word is getting out, and the robust economy in relation to the rest of the country has allowed us to move forward during this national recession."

Looking to the future, he sees a continued (and accelerated) refinement toward quality "both in wine and the winery experience," and a continued growth in the average size of wineries, which will help to open doors to sales channels that are viable only for larger wineries.

Before proceeding on Rt. 635, go back to Rt. 522 and drive north again, up the mountain, being prepared to turn quickly just at the crest of the hill as you see a barrel and a flag reading "Open." This is the aptly named **Chester Gap Cellars**, sitting on the east side of the crest of the Blue Ridge Mountains at Chester Gap.

Owner and winemaker Bernd Jung is a tall and fit German (he was an accomplished member of the German waterskiing team for fourteen years). Although he is focused and passionate, he's laid-back enough to have an ironic sense of humor about the business. Instead of seeking out publicity, he doesn't cultivate bloggers, no buses or limousines are allowed at the winery, and large groups are not encouraged. Chester Gap is very Old World in its singular focus on growing and making fine wines (all wines except one viognier are from estate-grown fruit). The tasting room is spartan (it's about the wine), but there is a deck with a breathtaking east-facing view of the valley below.

Jung explains that he never really planned on opening a winery, but the fruit and vegetable business was his family's trade in Munich, where he grew up. As his family made some wine sales to corporate clients, he got to meet vintners, and his interest was sparked. When he moved to the States in the 1980s (his wife, Kristi, and his children are American), he settled in Florida, where he had a lot of friends from his waterskiing days. "It all started with some advice from an extension agent in Florida," Jung recalls. "He was growing a wide variety of field crops, and the agent asked if I'd ever thought of growing grapes—said it was the next big thing. So I got suckered into that, and next thing you knew I was a grape grower. I don't think I ever planned to be in this." He began growing and selling native muscadine grapes and some of their hybrids, such as blanc du bois.

How, then, did he learn winemaking? "I've read every Geisenheim [the German winemaking academy] textbook there is. There's hardly an enology book I haven't read." He also took a lot of courses and attended trade shows and local winemaker meetings. "It's important to listen to what people have to say." For some years he also worked at Euro Machines, a company supplying the wine industry with processing equipment such as presses, and that experience "really helped me see viticulture and enology from Canada to Texas; I got to learn more technically about the interface between grapes and wine."

Chester Gap is a very small, artisanal producer, farming nine acres of vines. The first vintage was 2004, and they started selling in 2005. "A long time ago I realized that a small vineyard [I can afford] only is not going to pay the bills," but Jung notes that he's never taken out a loan to plant a vineyard.

The vineyard site lies at 1,300 feet and is, he says, on "extremely rocky soil, and being in the Gap, it has a constant breeze, with night temperatures lower than surrounding areas [aiding wine balance with good malic acid retention]. I only buy viognier from one other vineyard, at half the elevation, and there's quite a bit more acidity in my grapes."

Jung describes himself as a "fairly traditional" winemaker. "I haven't had to do any additives [to correct wine chemistry] like tannins or acid; the only thing that goes into the wine are grapes, sulfites, and yeast. I will always try to keep it that way. I also don't add concentrate [concentrated grape must]; I'm not interested in predictability, but in expressing my site. I would rather learn from what the ground gives me every year, learn from that rather than mess with it in the winery. To me vintage character is very important."

Chester Gap wines do have a traditional European subtlety and nuance, but are marked by firm acidity and fruit concentration (alcohols can be high, but the wine doesn't taste that way). While the petit manseng wines are a party in a glass, with lots of pineapple and hints of Jimmy Buffett music, all the viogniers are more similar to the northern Rhône style—with delicate, floral minerality—than many other in-your-face Virginia viogniers, with their lush fruitiness. In fact, while most viogniers don't hold up in the bottle for more than a couple of years, Chester Gap viogniers need a few years before they fully evolve. The 2007 reserve I tasted in June 2011 was richly layered with fruit and floral nuances, despite being over 14 percent alcohol, and with good acidity.

Jung says he doesn't "really market a whole lot." His wines are distributed by Margaux & Company, and 20 percent of the production goes into distribution. "Margaux gets the brand into nice restaurants; sometimes those people will come out to the winery and buy a case. The point of distribution is great marketing, if you have someone who does a good job for you." Jung has planned for the vineyard and winery to grow together, so there wasn't a need for a big marketing campaign, and he's been "hoping for a word-of-mouth thing."

He explains that his major marketing angle is "that I don't over-price my wines." They're all below $20, except for the cabernet franc, which goes for around $22. "This retains people, especially the good customers I already have. I don't go to festivals. I don't have a parking lot that's very large. Hopefully, with decent wines and good prices, I'll have the customers I need. Sometimes, overpricing wines tells people that it must be good due to the price, but how many people will buy it?" He says with a laugh that colleagues in the business give him a hard time about charging too little for his wines.

Considering trends for the future, Jung says, "events will continue to be a huge driving force for the industry. Will that put us on the path of quality winemaking? Probably not. Hopefully we can all make good wines, where the industry can thrive on a reputation for good wine. The amount of [nonlocal] grapes that have infiltrated Virginia wine is ridiculous. I hope that the influx of non-premium fruit from other states doesn't drag down our quality reputation. We're kind of at a crossroads. I think we'll either have the industry focus on quality or mediocrity and events. There are people who make a whole lot of cash quickly by making fruit wines, but also make a few high-end wines to support their reputation." On the other hand, he adds, "I can't fault people for making money by making wine of any kind."

Regarding a proposed Virginia quality-control alliance, he's willing to consider it, but cautiously. "In general, it's a great idea, but how that really works is questionable. I'm open-minded on that, but don't know exactly what their parameters will be. It could become a very silly exclusive club to which only a few people belong. I think every grape should be included. If only vinifera is included, we'll never get to more restrained chemical use in the vineyard. All the vinifera require a huge amount of sprays. It would be wrong to punish people farming more sustainably by growing less-high-maintenance varieties. Grape prejudice has nothing to do with wine quality."

Returning to Rt. 522, turn right and continue north into Front Royal, Canoe Capital of Virginia. At the first major intersection, with the shopping center on the right, turn right onto Rt. 55 (South St.), passing through the town of Linden, turning right on Rt. 638 (Fiery Run Rd.) for two miles, and watch for **Linden Vineyards** on the right.

Hardscrabble is the name of the mountain on which Linden Vineyards is located. This small vineyard has been in the forefront of Virginia wine's reputation with critics, the trade, and the discriminating public over the last twenty-five years, having an impact disproportionate to its production of only 4,000–5,000 cases annually.

Jancis Robinson, one of the world's leading wine writers, says owner-winemaker Jim Law's wines "have been exceptional almost from when he started in the 1980s."

Law sources fruit from thirty acres, focusing on red Bordeaux varieties: cabernet sauvignon (4.5 acres), petit verdot (2.5 acres), cabernet franc (1 acre), merlot (2.5 acres), vidal blanc (3.5 acres), chardonnay (2 acres), seyval blanc (2.5 acres), riesling (1 acre), and petit manseng (1.2 acres). The first six acres were planted in 1985, and the estate now has twenty-one dedicated acres (he also buys sauvignon blanc and red Bordeaux varieties from the neighboring Avenius and Boisseau vineyards, accounting for the other nine acres).

Law says that he continues to learn from his site even after twenty-five years and adapts growing practices such as training systems and row spacing as needed. He has given seminars to other members of the industry at his winery and has mentored apprentices who have started their own wineries.

Law is a highly intelligent, soft-spoken, and contemplative man. He is hard to read at first, with an ambiguous appearance. He is trim, with a beard and a ponytail. This might suggest a Californian, but put a beret on his head and look at him straight on so you don't see the ponytail, and he looks like a Frenchman from the Languedoc. Law admits that his real inspiration and love in the wine world is fine Bordeaux, which explains those grapes' dominance in his vineyard.

Since Bordeaux is in a tidal estuary, does it make sense to seek Bordeaux terroir in the mountains? Law explains that the name Hardscrabble is the local name for the steep, poor, rocky slopes that were difficult to farm but are in fact wonderful for quality viticulture. Elevation is near the top of Dr. Tony Wolf's recommendations, at 1,100–1,400 feet. In Bordeaux, the best-drained sites with low vigor correlate with high wine quality.

There's also a New World model for top cabernet sauvignon in mountaintop locations: A cabernet from Ridge's Monte Bello vineyard, in the Santa Cruz Mountains, was one of the wines in the landmark "Judgment of Paris" tasting in 1976, where the California cabernets and chardonnays trumped the top French wines of the day. Cabernets from the Mount Veeder and Howell Mountain AVAs in Napa Valley are also noted for their fruit, tannin, and flavor concentration.

Despite his European inspiration, Law has grown white hybrids from early on: The seyval blanc is crisp and Loire-like, and the vidal blanc–riesling blend is fruity but elegant. Three labels of chardonnay reflect their respective vineyard sites. A long-standing late-harvest vidal blanc has been complemented by a late-harvest petit manseng, barrel-fermented and aged with lees contact for added complexity; it seems far more vibrant and interesting than the more commonly seen late-harvest vidal blancs. Law says his Bordeaux reds, chardonnay, and recently added sauvignon blanc are the most well known.

Law's traditionalist winemaking shows particularly in the reds. Wine drinkers who like a big, heady, fruit-forward, and new-oak-slapping kind of red wine won't be likely to warm to his style. His reds need several years in the bottle before they are ready to drink and enjoy. Red wines are like racehorses: The ones that are flashy right out of the gate tend to drop off in the home stretch, while those that hold back at the start have length, breadth, and style to last to the finish. Law makes his wines in the latter mold.

Linden Vineyard's "discovery" by young professionals driving out from the Washington, D.C., suburbs to overwhelm his small tasting room, "playing backgammon for hours" as a colleague says, led him to allow access to a limited seating area only to wine club members. "My regular customers told me they weren't coming to the winery anymore because it had become overrun. I said, 'Wait, I can't afford to have them alienated.'" He decided to make the porch area for wine club members only, and although he took a whole year to inform everyone about it, he says there was hell to pay when the policy finally went into effect. "It was ugly for a while," he says, shaking his head.

Nevertheless, the plan worked. "Our winery traffic decreased, but total sales dollars did not." When I ask him what his marketing message is, he replies simply, "Focused on growing grapes and making wine for over twenty-five years." Instead of social media networking, he prefers to rely on word of mouth. Linden is now a magnet for Metro D.C. foodies and B and B/inn gastro-tourists.

We go into the winery and he opens a 2001 cabernet franc. It was a great year in Virginia, but we tasted the wine in 2009, when most cabernet francs (which are not nearly as tannic as cabernet sauvignon) from that year have faded. This one is bright, fresh, and young, with loads of ripe cherry, black pepper, and smooth tannins, tasting more like a 2005. Law cultivates trade and customers who appreciate and understand his wines enough to lay them down for a few years so they can reach their prime. A 1997 Fiery Run red Bordeaux blend I drank at ten years of age was round, rich, supple, and smooth; mature but by no means fading.

During the zoning debate in Fauquier County about winery events, Law told me he was against wineries holding large events, because he feels they disrupt the life of the rural community. He wants to be a good neighbor and steward of the land, he explains, and if large events alienate others in the community, it could turn many against farm wineries.

Law notes that major cultural trends like the combination of "staycation" tourism and eat/buy-local movements are increasing winery visits and visibility. He's also impressed with a few of the winemaking newcomers in the last few years. "Finally, a few individuals are thoughtfully selecting good growing sites and focusing on quality from the ground up."

Return down Fiery Run Rd. If you have a companion in the car, have your copilot watch for where the Appalachian Trail crosses the road; incongruously, Rt. 638 crosses over the crest of the Blue Ridge Mountains into the Shenandoah Valley. Stay north on Rt. 638

(Freezeland Rd.) as it crosses Rt. 55 and then I-66, and continue for three miles to the entrance to **Fox Meadow Winery** on the right at 3310 Freezeland Rd.; you have now crossed over the crest of the Blue Ridge, back into its upper eastern slope in the Piedmont.

Like many Virginia winery owners, Dan and Cheryl Mortland had long nurtured a dream to open their own winery. They both worked in the corporate world in suburban Philadelphia, and in the late 1990s, they took steps to put the dream into action. They decided on northern Virginia only after spending three years considering various sites and states along the Mid-Atlantic Seaboard.

Dan believes in hiring the best local experts—people who knew the dynamics in Virginia—based on referrals from those in the industry. He brought in veteran consultant winemaker Tom Payette and Jeanette Smith of VineSmith Vineyard Services to help find the right balance of elevation, a southern exposure, and the right soil conditions. "After meeting Tom," Dan says, "we realized that he understood and shared our vision of wanting to make world-class wines in Virginia."

The Mortlands took their time, focusing on northern Virginia, then finally on their current site, after looking at more than a hundred other locations. One of the deciding factors was that several other wineries were making some great wines in this area. The winery opened in 2008.

Fox Meadow Winery and vineyard is just below the crest of the Blue Ridge Mountains, at 1,750 feet above sea level (their motto is "Visit us and look down on the tops of mountains"), with a southern exposure that allows the grapes to ripen well, but very slowly, and retain good acidity. Currently they grow eight acres, including cabernet franc, merlot, cabernet sauvignon, petit verdot, chardonnay, pinot grigio, and riesling. Since they are a small, artisanal winery, Dan feels they grow too many different varieties and intends to phase some out while adding up to seven and a half new acres in the next two years, mostly of their popular pinot grigio.

Although Fox Meadow is a fairly new winery, winemaker Payette's skill earned the wines critical acclaim early on. The 2006 estate cabernet franc, 2008 pinot grigio, 2009 barrel-fermented chardonnay, and 2008 Le Renard Rouge Meritage have taken consistent, impressive medals, including the Virginia Governor's Cup award for red wine in 2011.

Dan explains that for the reds they use both extended aging techniques and relatively young oak barrels, primarily French oak. "Our chardonnay is a classic oak-barrel fermented and aged chardonnay. Now it is being made in French oak and the fruit flavors are exceptional. . . . Our pinot grigio has a minerality not seen in other wines of its type." The wines are made in a deft balance of Old and New World techniques and should please most fine-wine lovers.

Return on Freezeland Rd. to Rt. 55, then turn left (east) and continue to the I-66 exit and the town of Markham. You can use this as a jumping-off point to visit a significant cluster of Fauquier County wineries to the north, south, and east. Two miles to the north, off CR 688 on the right, is **Naked Mountain Winery & Vineyards**, a small veteran winery with a reputation for consistently fine barrel-fermented chardonnay, and one of the best slogans in the business: Drink Naked!

Continuing north on Rt. 688, then south on Rt. 17, on the left is **Delaplane Cellars**, fairly new but with impressive New World–style reds. Founded by Jim and Betsy Dolphin, Delaplane Cellars makes only vinifera-based wines and specializes in vineyard-designated wines. A specialty is a syrah with 13 percent tannat. A commitment to the environment extends from winery to vineyard and includes in the tasting room recyclable water cups made from corn that will compost in three months. The tasting room is elegant, with a fine view of the nearby mountains to the southwest. Farther south on Rt. 17 on the right is **Three Fox Vineyards**.

Three Fox Vineyards calls itself "the original northern Virginia home of sangiovese." Proprietors Holli and John Todhunter founded the winery in 2002, with a focus on Italian varieties (sangiovese, nebbiolo, pinot grigio) as well as chardonnay, viognier, and the usual red Bordeaux varieties. The couple declares themselves "passionate about life, love, wine, and Italy," and the winery's slogan is "We make La Dolce Vita a part of your life!" The winery takes its name from an omen: As Holli and John were viewing the property with a real estate agent, Holli spotted three foxes on the slope, "and that sealed the bargain for 'Three Fox Vineyards.'"

A couple of miles after Rt. 17 merges with I-66 east, take Exit 27, go left on Free State Rd., left again on CR T185 (Grove Ln.)/F.-185 to the stop sign in Delaplane, and you realize you've gone to the dogs—at **Barrel Oak Winery** (on the left).

It won't take you long to realize that "BOW," the acronym for Barrel Oak Winery, is no accident. Brian Roeder, a large, genial, confident, and straight-talking man who is the winery's owner and general manager, explains that "we wanted to be a place of community, where relationships would be created and families, kids, and dogs would be welcomed. Most of our customers like that welcoming and friendly attitude." In fact, dogs are also part of the branding of Barrel Oak's wines: The most popular wines in the tasting room are BowHaus White, BowHaus Red, Chocolate Lab (a dessert wine), and a norton—and the wine club is the "BOW Club."

Brian jokingly holds his "lovely wife, Sharon" responsible for their arrival in Delaplane. "It was her dream to grow grapes in the countryside that led us here." As he explored how to achieve her dream, Brian realized that they had to make and sell wine to afford the land they'd have to buy for the vineyard. "Fortunately, I'm on about my eighth career," having managed several small businesses, owned restaurants, built military housing communities, managed nonprofits and boards, provided executive training, been a hands-on builder, and also worked in sales. "The reality is that I am using every single one of those skills. What really amazes me, though, is Sharon who, with no background in making wine, has so quickly come to understand its needs and its challenges."

Sharon actually is co-winemaker with Rick Tagg. "Rick gets wine in ways that many do not. They are a great team, and they cover for each other's weaknesses. I believe having two rather than one wine-maker has been key to our success," Brian says.

Barrel Oak currently has twenty acres of vines, growing nine varieties. While they've won a number of medals for their classic dry Virginia varietals (cabernet franc, petit verdot, norton, reserve char-donnay, and viognier), "forty percent of our customers prefer off-dry wines; forty percent of our sales are of off-dry or sweet wines. So, the general public does not necessarily want our best wines."

Barrel Oak opened in 2007, but used a very different marketing and business model from other small wineries, such as that of Fox Meadow. "The role of electronic social networking media cannot be overempha-sized" in launching a winery and keeping a buzz going, says Brian, who claims they had the most successful winery opening in Virginia history because of the buzz that the bloggers created for them. He emphasizes, though, that "if the wine is bad and service is great, people are not coming back. If the wine is great and the service is lousy or rude, people are not coming back." Weekly e-mails to winery customers "reminded them about what they loved about BOW and kept them coming back."

Barrel Oak gained a reputation for having lots of events in their first few years, and Brian realizes that he earned some enmity. Now that the winery is firmly established, he's scaling back events. "After three years of operations, we are moving back from what has been a very aggressive events schedule and the effort to market those events online. The truth is that we were the most aggressive [courting winery visitors] because almost all of our investment is debt. We had to do those things to pay the bills. Thank God it worked."

Brian continues, "Our experience shows that events are a crucial tool for start-up wineries. They are the primary way that a winery has to initially attract the public and to generate a critical mass of supporting customers. However, events are a high-load effort on staff and plant and carry the disadvantage of the perception that a winery is not about the wine. The reality is that if a winery makes very good wine and is knowledgeable and welcoming in its service of that wine, its customers will return and will promote the winery." Brian says that while many wineries focus on weddings, "we have made it a point to host charitable benefits at the winery. These come to us from community members, and we always donate a portion of our proceeds to the organizer. The rewards include customers who care about us because we care about their issue, community recognition for our role as a supporter of local causes, organizations that effectively drive customers to us, and earlier closing hours closer to 9:00 p.m. for benefits than the typical 11:00 p.m. for weddings." He adds that about 35 percent of Barrel Oak's winery clientele are locals—an unusually high number.

Brian explains that in their scaling back of events, Barrel Oak now has good relations with the county. "We actually have not had any problems with neighbors regarding traffic or noise from our events. In fact, our neighbors are very supportive of our events. Where we have had complaints, ironically, is from other winery owners, who have suggested to the county that we are behaving irresponsibly." He says county officials "recognize that there are no grounds for these complaints, because we are situated on a large piece of property, far from neighboring homes, on a high-traffic-volume frontage road, and adjacent to an interstate that masks much of our noise under the white noise of traffic.

"Success in the Virginia wine business is doable," Brian affirms, noting that "we are thirty-seven months into this and about two hundred thousand dollars in the black." How have they done it? "Have the owners there and thank people for arriving, for leaving, for buying your wine, for staying, for bringing their dogs . . . kids . . . parents . . . friends . . . picnics . . . motorcycles . . . wacky T-shirts . . . smiles . . . fun shoes . . . everything! In everything that you do, show gratitude to your staff and your customers. Keep the bathrooms clean. Stay humble and work your hearts out every . . . single . . . day. Take a little time for yourselves. Have fun. Remember how this is so much better than the alternative. Get a good night's sleep and then start all over again. Rinse . . . repeat. We need to sell the dream along with the wine," Brian concludes. Then he adds that he has to get back to his customers "not because I have to, but because I want to." Attitude, as they say, is everything.

Leaving Barrel Oak, complete your circuit of the western Fauquier County wineries by following signs to I-66 east, then take Exit 27 in Marshall onto CR 721 south and west and turn immediately right onto CR 647. Turn right again on CR 635, continuing to Hume. Watch for the crossroads and turn left on CR 688 (Leeds Manor Rd.), then right on CR 734, to **Hume Vineyards**. They opened only in early 2011, describing themselves as "a little Virginia winery with big ambition . . . respectful of tradition, unbound by convention." Their four wines, at this writing, are one white—a vidal blanc—and three reds: chambourcin; cabernet sauvignon; and Detour, a red Bordeaux blend.

Going back to CR 688 in Hume, continue north on that road and you'll reach **Philip Carter Winery** on the right, where the forgotten chapter of eighteenth-century Virginia wine history was unearthed by owner Philip Carter Strother, as we read on page 23. As fascinating as its history is, the Philip Carter Winery is also worth a visit for its wines and its tranquil Rappahannock County location. The chardonnay reserve and cabernet franc are the strong suits, both showing the freshness and firm acidity of the cool location, but all the wines are solid, and the Governor Fauquier is a very fun, versatile, off-dry vidal blanc. You can taste the cool climate manifested in the wines: The cabernet franc is fresh and bright (with minimal oak), and the Reserve

Chardonnay—which reminds me of a Puligny-Montrachet—has won major accolades.

Turning left then quickly right out of the winery driveway back onto CR 688 north, you'll intersect Rt. 55 again. Turn right and you'll find a cluster of nearby wineries: **Chateau O'Brien** and **Aspen Dale**, just off Rt. 55, and **Capitol Vineyards**, to the south of the road (please consult your GPS, the Virginia Wine in My Pocket app, or the state winery guide for more specific directions).

Chateau O'Brien has a range of wines from apple wine and bistro red to reserve wines. They aim high and the prices show it. A specialty is their Limited Reserve Tannat; subtle on the nose, the wine is initially smooth then packs a powerful tannic punch typical of the variety. The price also packs a powerful punch at $79 (not so typical for the variety). Also impressive are the petit verdot and petit manseng.

Aspen Dale Winery is owned and operated by a seventh-generation farm family. "A Breath of Fresh Air" is their motto, and the atmosphere and aesthetic are very comfy down-home country, but that doesn't mean the wines are not to be taken seriously. In 2011, their cabernet sauvignon and sauvignon blanc both took "Best in Class" awards in the Atlantic Seaboard Wine Competition. Sarah's Chapeau, an original blend of 60 percent vidal blanc and 40 percent sauvignon blanc, took "Best of Show" in the Mid-Atlantic Southeastern Wine Competition. Their Hildersham Sauvignon Blanc is one of the most elegant in the state, in a Loire style with bright lemon/citrus aromas and flavors. The Rockawalkin' Cabernet Sauvignon is beefy and robust, but not coarse.

Nearby Capitol Vineyards, so-called because it is owned and operated by young professionals of the Capitol region, offers "accessible wines for affordable prices," currently traminette, cabernet franc, cabernet sauvignon, merlot, and a Meritage, all from Virginia-only grapes. The tasting room—a newly renovated general store from the early 1900s—was once home to the first African-American postmaster general in Virginia.

From Capitol Vineyards, return to I-66 east, exiting at The Plains and heading north on Rt. 245. At the intersection with Rt. 55, in the town of The Plains, turn right, then take the next left, following the sign "To Middleburg" on CR 626, a designated "Virginia Byway." The road is certainly scenic, but the driver should keep his or her eyes on the road (and speed limit), as it is narrow and winding.

The first winery you'll encounter, on the left, is **Piedmont Vineyards,** with its landmark plantation house, Waverly, a Virginia historic landmark. The site has another historical feature: It is where the first commercial vinifera (chardonnay) vines were planted in Virginia in 1973. The winery is owned by Gerhard von Finck, a German. Contrasting with the plantation house, the winery tasting room is designed in a very hip Arts and Crafts style. The signature wine for some years has been a native-yeast-fermented chardonnay.

Continuing north on Rt. 626, you'll soon come to **Boxwood Estate Winery** on the left before you reach Middleburg, but it's open only by appointment to groups of fifteen or fewer. Tours last forty-five minutes and are followed by a tasting for a fee of $20. Their tasting room in nearby Middleburg is easier to visit.

Boxwood could be called the "jewel box" winery of Virginia. The focus is on a few wines of the highest quality, and all aspects of the operation, from sixteen acres of close-spaced vines to processing equipment to architecture and design, reflect this commitment. The winery was completed in 2005 and is owned by John Kent Cooke, son of the late Washington Redskins football team owner Jack Kent Cooke. The professional winery crew includes Stephane Derenoncourt, a noted Bordeaux consultant enologist; Adam McTaggart, a winemaker from Ontario; and Rachel Martin, executive vice president, who trained at Napa Valley College and the University of Bordeaux and is Rita and John Kent Cooke's daughter.

The winery takes its name from the estate, a national historic landmark, which was one of the earliest horse farms in the Middleburg area. Boxwood's production is small: 2,000 cases, with expansion capacity to 5,000 cases. The vineyard is expanding to twenty-one acres, all planted to the five major red Bordeaux varieties, and the winery produces only four wines, all variations on the red Bordeaux theme. The 2007 vintage, the debut for these wines, was a very good year, and the wines were stylistically correct. The other wines include rosés made from each of the two blends and named accordingly, and a blend of the press wine from each of the reds, named Trellis. Despite the high level of investment and ultra-premium positioning, the wines are reasonably priced: The reds are $25 and the rosés are $14.

Critical acclaim has come through favorable mentions in a wide variety of media, from *Washingtonian* magazine and the *Washington Post* to *Wine Enthusiast*, *Wine Spectator*, *Decanter*, and the blog of wine media superstar Jancis Robinson. One of four silver medals won by Virginia wineries in the 2011 *Decanter* World Wine Awards competition was earned by the Boxwood Winery 2007 Topiary.

Boxwood takes an original approach to sales and marketing. While the winery is not open to the public except by appointment, they own and operate four satellite tasting rooms: in nearby Middleburg; in Reston, northern Virginia; in Chevy Chase, suburban Maryland; and at National Harbour in Oxon Hill, Maryland. These locations also host private parties. The winery has a strong program for retail and restaurant sales (clients include top restaurants in London), and sales are also available through their online store.

In June 2011, Boxwood made headlines in the American sustainability movement when it was announced by MADE: In America (an organization protecting sustainable and green American businesses as historic treasures) that the winery will be the recipient of the 2011 American Treasure Award.

Rachel Martin is also active in the effort to establish a new Middleburg AVA. Does Virginia really need another AVA? I asked her.

"The more AVAs that are established in Virginia, the more recognized Virginia will be as a winegrowing region," she answered. "It will help bring the consumer's attention to different regions in Virginia, thereby enhancing their experience with Virginia wine and educating them about the differences in those wines." Also, Boxwood Winery would then be able to label their wines "estate bottled" she explains (inexplicably, current Alcohol and Tobacco Tax and Trade Bureau [TTB] regulations do not allow wineries to use the term, even if they otherwise qualify, unless the winery is located within an approved federal AVA).

Running in a narrow northeast band to the Potomac River, the AVA would be bounded on the east by the Catoctin and Bull Run mountains just east of Middleburg, a line from Big Cobbler Mountain to Rattle Snake Mountain (paralleling I-66) to the south, and to the west, by the Blue Ridge and Short Hill mountains, and the Potomac River to the north, taking the northern half of Fauquier and the western two-thirds of Loudoun County. The salient feature of the proposed AVA, says Martin, is the alluvial soils: well-drained rocky clay and gravelly silt loams. First filed in 2009, the Middleburg AVA should have been approved by the time you're reading this.

Loudoun County

Continue north on Rt. 626 and you'll soon come to Middleburg. Middleburg has been a tiny country retreat for the Washington elite since at least the Kennedy administration, and is also the center of the northern Piedmont hunt and horse country. Turn right on Rt. 50 and continue slowly through town. You're now in Loudoun County and the town around which the nascent post-Prohibition Virginia wineries began to emerge, in the late 1960s.

The next stop will be **Swedenburg Estate Vineyards** and **Valley View Farm**, on the right after you leave town. Founders Wayne and Juanita Swedenburg wanted to establish a working farm when they retired, and the farm raises Angus cattle as well as wine grapes (the first crush was in 1987). Marc Swedenburg now runs the operation. Swedenburg makes three whites (a riesling, a seyval blanc called Chantilly, and a barrel-fermented chardonnay), a rosé, a pinot noir, and a cabernet sauvignon.

Continuing east on Rt. 50, watch for the grape cluster sign and the road sign for Rt. 629 (Champe Ford Rd.) on the right; drive one mile south on Rt. 629 and look for **Chrysalis Vineyards** on the left. The name is a metaphor for the wine emerging from the barrel as a caterpillar emerges from its cocoon.

Winery founder Jennifer McCloud came to Middleburg in 1996 to found the vineyard and winery and realize her winemaking dream. She enlisted the talent of winemaker Alan Kinne, and in 1997 they produced their first two wines: a chardonnay and a viognier. (Since then, Kinne has spent a nine-year hiatus on the West Coast but has returned to Chrysalis.)

The Locksley Estate vineyard at Chrysalis has grown and now farms over twenty varieties, including vinifera unusual for Virginia such as albariño, fer servadou, tannat, tempranillo, and graciano, although McCloud's passion (and the mission of the winery) is to proudly restore Virginia wines to world renown, and promote norton, which McCloud calls "America's real grape." Accordingly, she claims to have the largest planting of norton in the world at her estate. Chrysalis makes five wines using norton, including two rosés.

Returning on Rt. 629 to Rt. 50, you'll turn right and continue east through Aldie, then go around the roundabout to head left (north) on Rt. 15; **Quattro Goomba's Winery** will be on the right—"The spirit and taste of Italy in Virginia."

For many years there were just a handful of wineries in Loudoun, as land prices soared due to suburbanization pressures with the postindustrial development of ever-expanding northern Virginia. In the last decade, the number has exploded to twenty-five, rivaling Fauquier and Albemarle counties for the largest number of wineries.

Loudoun County is aggressive in branding and promoting its wineries as "Washington D.C.'s Wine Country." To help group the wineries in logical touring segments, the county has organized them into clusters: the Mosby Cluster (which we've just finished); the Loudoun Heights Cluster in the northwest of the county; the Waterford Cluster running north-south between Hillsboro and Waterford; the Potomac Cluster north of Leesburg and east of Rt. 15; and the Harmony Cluster southwest of Leesburg. For the sake of space, we will focus on a few of the wineries, but for more details you can visit visitloudoun.org, or the Virginia wine website: virginiawine.org.

As you approach Leesburg on scenic Rt. 15 from the south, the next cluster you'll encounter is the Harmony Cluster, and Loudoun County's oldest winery, **Willowcroft Farm Vineyards**. Turn left on Rt. 704, immediately left again on Rt. 797 (Mount Gilead Rd.), then right on Rt. 662; the winery is on the left.

Willowcroft's proprietor, Lew Parker, is a thin, white-haired gentleman, who would look completely natural in a pith helmet and khakis somewhere in Africa. "My philosophy has been to stay small, make high-quality wines and sell out locally," he explains. The first commercial wines were made here in 1984, and Parker thinks he might be the sixth- or seventh-oldest winery currently operating in Virginia.

His daughters were in 4-H, he recalls, but "that wasn't popular in Fairfax subdivisions," so he bought the farm, then looked at how to improve profitability. He called Dr. Konstantin Frank (the vinifera pioneer of the East) in New York and asked him to send him some vines. "He refused, because he said I didn't know what I was doing, and of course he was right," Parker says, laughing. "He felt his reputation was on the line with every vinifera grapevine in the East." In the early 1980s, the Virginia Extension Service was still not recommending vinifera to growers, but French hybrids instead. Still, a dozen wineries were growing them. Parker first planted two acres of chardonnay, cabernet sauvignon, seyval blanc, and riesling. "I couldn't find anyone who knew anything about rootstock. So I planted each row on a different rootstock; some of the rows did noticeably better than others, which helped me and others in the industry."

He expanded plantings of the same varieties in 1987, and when his neighbors became interested he planted and managed vineyards for some of them. "People have these mini-farms with lots of land empty around their large houses and they had to mow it; they wanted to plant some vines there instead. I have three twenty-five-year leases with people to supply me with wine grapes, all within a mile of the winery."

Willowcroft is located on Mount Gilead, the southernmost part of the Catoctin Mountains, with a beautiful view of the Blue Ridge. "People come, hopefully, for the wine quality, but also for the view and picnic area, which is probably the best around," says Parker.

Parker is worried about the sustainability of his and his neighbors' vineyards planted to white vinifera varieties, which are susceptible to American grapevine yellows, a disease transmitted by leafhopper insects native to the northern Blue Ridge Mountains and environs (chardonnay is particularly susceptible). He is hoping albariño and the hybrid traminette will prove resistant.

Discussing the bigger picture of the growth of the Virginia wine industry, Parker is less effusive than most of his colleagues. "We still have less than five percent of wine sales [as a proportion of total wine sales] within the state. I think we have more and more wineries sharing the same piece of the public pie. Even though the pie is growing slowly, are we really growing market share of Virginia wines? It's still a very small share. We haven't reached a tipping point with overall large market share acceptability."

On the plus side, he declares, "If you're accessible to customers, you can have a successful farm winery in Virginia by making high-quality wine and selling locally, but trying to go into national or international markets is a reach too far for Virginia."

However, he sees more newcomers with more ideas today, and the level of professionalism is far above what it used to be. Like nearly everyone else, he gives credit for this progress to Drs. Bruce Zoecklein and Tony Wolf, but also to internationally acclaimed consultants who have been brought to the state by new wineries with money to spend on expertise. "Within a two-hour drive, I can seek advice from wine-makers trained in Bordeaux, Geisenheim, or UC Davis; I couldn't do that in the early days."

He thinks Virginia is singularly able to produce some wines that may be among the best in the world, but that's not the same as selling them. "Every year I taste Virginia wines that I think are just block-busters [for quality]. Quality will continue to improve; I think we still are learning about varieties that will be the best varieties for us. That will be a lifetime quest."

Returning to Rt. 15, you can first stop at **Zephaniah Farm Vineyard** (left on Rt. 770). Back on Rt. 15, turn left and head into Leesburg, which provides a good base of operations for making a circuit of win-eries to the north and west. For the Potomac Cluster, take either the Rt. 15 Leesburg Bypass or the business route through Leesburg; they join north of town. Three and a half miles north of the junction of the two roads, turn right on Limestone School Rd.; **Fabbioli Cellars** is 1.3 miles on the left.

Proprietor Doug Fabbioli is an affable, bearded man who worked for a winery in the Finger Lakes of New York while attending Syracuse University and got the wine bug. He then acquired more industry expe-rience in California before returning to Virginia, and has consulted for other Loudoun wineries.

The winery makes 3,500 cases, with ten acres under vine. Fabbioli regards his top wines as cabernet franc and raspberry merlot. "Our soils have a pretty heavy limestone content, and that helps greatly in defining our crisp and balanced wines," he says. The most popular wines are raspberry merlot and pear wines. "Both wines redefine what a fruit-based wine is. These wines go well with desserts as well as cheeses."

The winery slogan is "Real People. Earth Friendly. Fabulous Wines." "We work hard through our website and written material as well as all of our actions to emphasize this message," says Fabbioli, noting that "sustainability is more than the earth, it is the business and the people as well."

Although tourism is "huge," Fabbioli insists that "we need to make sure we make wines for the world market, not just wines to drink at the winery." He also feels tasting rooms, event facilities, and other on-site consumption need to be balanced with the neighbors, farms, and other activities in the rural landscape.

He's bullish about the reputation of Loudoun Valley wineries today. "I see Loudoun wineries being [known as] high-caliber boutique wineries," adding that the wine quality in this region needs to be quite high because of the close proximity to Metro D.C. and neighboring wineries. "We continue to bring up the quality bar for each other. It is a great area to make the wine as well as consume it."

Continuing north on Rt. 661, take Rt. 657 when Rt. 661 bears left, to visit **Lost Creek** and **Hidden Brook** wineries, then turn left on Rt. 658, where you'll find **Tarara Winery** on the right.

Tarara is one of the largest wineries in Loudoun, and its 475 acres just above the Potomac River helps with air and water drainage for the vineyards and provides scenic views. The winery was founded in 1985 by Whitie Hubert, a real estate developer. His wife and son, Margaret Hubert and Steve Hubert, continue as the current owners and managers. Jordan Harris, trained in Ontario, is the winemaker. Production averages around 8,000 cases a year. There are forty-two acres of vine-yards, and the product line is tiered into varietals and blends, vineyard designates, and the top-tier "Commonwealth Collection." Harris says the limestone soils, river drainage, and winds contribute to the fresh fruit and acidity of the Tarara wines.

He explains that he came to Virginia because he was working for a massive winery ("producing about four times the volume of Virginia annually") and wanted to get back into more hands-on winemaking instead of wearing a shirt and tie to make wine. "I knew the winemaker of Tarara at the time, and he wanted to move on to something bigger, so I discussed it with him and came to check it out. I learned that vio-gnier was a flagship of Virginia, and I am an absolute Rhône geek, so I wanted to come here and make viognier."

Harris is putting a major branding emphasis on viognier as the trademark variety for Tarara, but almost all their wines are proprietary blends, perhaps the best known being Charval, originally a blend of chardonnay and seyval but now made up of chardonnay, viognier, sau-vignon blanc, roussanne, and petit manseng.

The definition of quality under Harris's tenure has become vine-yard- and terroir-based. "Without a doubt our single-vineyard wines and the Commonwealth Collection are what we believe are our best wines." The Commonwealth Collection is simply a selection of their best barrels from the three single-vineyard reds, plus a syrah from their vineyard, which are sold based on an allocation; there is a waiting list. "We only produce up to one hundred cases of each of the four wines. The single-vineyard wines have developed a great following, and the only downside is the vineyard size is finite, so we cannot expand our production of the current wines."

Due to their close proximity to the northern Virginia and Maryland suburbs of Washington (and the towns of Frederick and Leesburg), Tarara has been a major destination winery for many years. Harris sees a great mix of fifty-five-plus baby boomers and Gen Xers and

Millennials as the main customers. "I see Gen Xers and Millennials being our future, as they are very interested in where their wine came from, and that is what we are more specialized in. They are less concerned with varietal makeup and more interested in the story of the vineyard and a wine that is great." Asked if he considers himself more of a traditionalist or a New World winemaker, Harris says, "I would say we simply do what we feel is best for the wines and showcasing their sites. I don't think I am New World or Old World; really, I don't see much of a difference anymore between the two."

While Tarara had a reputation for lots of winery events in the past, that is changing now. "We are no longer doing weddings or big special events," Harris says. The winery still has its "Fine Vine . . . Just Say 'Viognier'" event (now held in October), which is a celebration of local fine food with local-oriented chefs and a handful of selected local wineries with viognier-based wines. Harris notes that today's Virginia wineries operate with the support of state government and with "far more serious wine then we ever had, and more knowledgeable winemakers. We will continue to grow, but I think we need to learn what we do best, and do it." He explains this can be different for separate regions around the state, as the terroir is wildly varied so it can be tricky. "I also think we should not be setting our sights on the California wine industry as a benchmark. I believe we need to focus on high quality and therefore more premium-priced wines for a niche market, much like Oregon has done so well."

In conclusion, Harris declares, "Our mission at Tarara is to establish our brand as a household name for ultra-premium wines, creating Virginia's most exciting brand with international acclaim while adding to the local economy and community."

Leaving Tarara on Rt. 658 and continuing northwest, you'll intersect Rt. 15 again. Turn right onto Rt. 15 and make sure to put on your left turn signal and turn left on Rt. 672 before you find yourself suddenly going over the Potomac River into Maryland. At the intersection of Rt. 287, continue straight, now on Rt. 673, which soon becomes Rt. 690. Watch for signs for **Hiddencroft Vineyards** on the left, as we briefly dip into the Waterford Cluster of Loudoun wineries.

Hiddencroft has been growing wine grapes since 2001, and their far-northern location in the state, along with proximity to the Potomac River, gives all their wines a freshness not often found in wines from warmer sites. Hiddencroft grows fruits and produces fruit wines, but the quality of their table wines shows that just because you make fruit wines doesn't mean you're not to be taken seriously.

Red wines include a vintage and vintage blend of cabernet franc, chambourcin, and petit verdot, and a distinctive proprietary blend called Dutchman's Creek Blend, described as "Old World" and "Left Bank" (cabernet sauvignon–dominated but also including cabernet franc, petit verdot, and tannat). The varietal petit verdot from the very good 2007 vintage had layers of flavor, spice, and nuances of texture I don't think I've experienced in any other such wine. Whites include a dry, fruity vidal blanc, floral but dry traminette, and a partially oaked chardonnay.

Continue south on Rt. 690 and you'll come to **Doukénie Winery** on the right (we're now in the Loudoun Heights Cluster). Some readers may remember Doukénie as **Shadwell-Windham Winery**, before lawyers for the Australian brand Wyndham objected to the winery name on grounds of trademark infringement. The name was changed to Doukénie, the first name of current co-owner Nicki Bazaco's grandmother, who immigrated to the United States from Greece around 1919. Doukénie came from a farming family who grew grapes, so family links with viticulture are continued with the winery's new name. Nicki's husband and co-owner is George, and her mother, Hope (Doukénie's daughter), is part of the family and has a page on the winery's website.

Doukénie currently produces 4,000 cases per year, from twelve acres on the property (five additional acres have been planted), and also leases twenty-nine acres of other vineyards. For a small winery, they produce an impressive sixteen different wines, ranging from pinot grigio to raspberry, and from standard red Bordeaux varietals and blends to sangiovese, syrah, and original blends such as Zeus (made of merlot, tannat, cabernet franc, and petit verdot).

By 2007, Doukénie's wines were showing an impressive change under new winemaker Sébastien Marquet, a Frenchman trained in Burgundy but with other New World winemaking experience. His 2007 Bordeaux reds were very impressive, and his cabernet franc has won medals in West Coast competitions.

Marquet is enthusiastic about working in Virginia. "After thirty years of viticulture and winemaking, winery owners and winemakers have a much better idea of what rootstocks and grape varietals work here."

Continuing south on Rt. 690, you'll intersect Rt. 9 in Hillsboro; take it west and in a few miles you'll see the **Hillsborough Vineyards** on the right. The winery offers two whites, one rosé, four reds, and a dessert wine, all named after gemstones. Watch for Rt. 671 on your right, take a right turn on it, and head north. Soon you'll see a wide expanse of vineyards on the right; turn in and you're at **Breaux Vineyards**.

Located in the Little Scotland valley, which Jefferson described as so scenic it was worth a trip across the Atlantic, this is one of the best sites for a vineyard in the state. The slope behind the winery (planted to nebbiolo at the highest point) faces southwest, and near-constant breezes blow through the valley, refreshing both visitors and vines and reducing the pressure of fungal diseases. The hundred-plus acres of vineyards grow eighteen varieties of grapes, many of which are sold to other wineries. Taking advantage of its scenic location, Breaux hosts events, including weddings—their specialty.

Breaux Vineyards was founded in 1997 by Paul Breaux (also

founder of Sun Realty in North Carolina); he remains CEO, but day-to-day management is shared by the husband-and-wife team of Chris Blosser and Jennifer Breaux Blosser. Recently, David Pagan Castaño joined Breaux as winemaker. You are now in the Loudoun Heights Cluster of county wineries.

Breaux offers a wide range of dry, semidry, and sweet wines, many as proprietary blends that are distinctive and original. There is also a line of wines of limited production available just to cellar club members. One example is Six Degrees (representing the degrees of latitude separating Breaux from Piemonte, in Italy), an original blend of barbera and nebbiolo. Breaux's viognier, seyval, and chardonnay have had a solid reputation for delicate fruit and fine acidity, while Jennifer's Jambalaya is a spicy, fruity, and semidry white blend evoking the Breaux family's Cajun roots, and was blended to accompany that cuisine.

On the serious red side, Breaux's 2007 Cabernet Franc was both a blockbuster and a velvet hammer. The Lafayette Cabernet Franc has been of consistently high quality and a brand banner, with black cherry and dark chocolate hints.

Breaux is one of the few Virginia wineries devoted to making nebbiolo, which has its best vineyard site. The wine is varietally correct, but not as intensely tannic as a barbaresco or barolo. The 2007 Meritage was another Virginia wine that won a silver medal in the 2011 *Decanter World Wine Awards*. Breaux is unusual in offering library vintages of reserve wines as well. In the dessert-wine category, Breaux makes a truly unique wine from frozen nebbiolo grapes—a rare treat.

After visiting other wineries in the Loudoun area, you could take Rt. 7, just under the West Virginia panhandle, and head across the northern Blue Ridge Mountains into the Shenandoah Valley, but we'll take that route later in the book. For now, take Rt. 7 east to Leesburg, then Rt. 15 south, back the way you came, continuing around the roundabouts and heading south past Rt. 50.

Rt. 15 marks a sort of development boundary between outer-suburban northern Virginia to the east and rural Virginia to the west. Soon you'll cross into Prince William County; if you turned east on I-66, in a few minutes you'd arrive at Manassas and its legendary Civil War battlefield park, site of two important Confederate victories in 1861 and 1862; the "third battle of Manassas" occurred in the late 1980s over plans to build a shopping mall adjacent to the park.

Prince William County, Fauquier County, and Fairfax County

Before reaching I-66, you'll come to three neighboring wineries owned by one energetic winemaker with thirty years of industry experience—Chris Pearmund. The three wineries are different from one another, and regular exit surveys confirm they attract differing clienteles. Aside from juggling three wineries, Pearmund has helped open and acted as a partner on wineries in Virginia, North Carolina, and Washington State, and is a respected consulting winemaker in the region. We heard his comments on viticulture earlier, on page 49.

To reach Pearmund's **Winery at La Grange**, turn right (west) from Rt. 15 onto Rt. 601, then left on Antioch Rd. to the winery. The winery bills itself as "Prince William County's premier winery," and makes an appropriate impression with the tasting room, which is located in a restored manor house built in 1790 from imported British brick. The business model is a premier winery funded by investors, close to a large, affluent suburban population yet with a country set-ting. Production is 8,000 cases, with a vineyard of five acres of cabernet sauvignon and two acres of petit manseng. La Grange encourages you to linger—they even have Wi-Fi throughout the property.

Returning to Rt. 15, continue south (right) through Haymarket, over I-66 to the intersection with Rt. 29; turn right and you'll soon cross into Fauquier County. Shortly after crossing the county line, turn left on Rt. 215 (Vint Hill Rd.); you'll find **Vint Hill Craft Winery** on the right.

Vint Hill specializes as a custom-crush winery but features a small cabernet sauvignon and petit verdot vineyard. The winery identity, explains Pearmund, is "one hundred barrels, made one barrel at a time." Clients are both private individuals and groups and trade customers. The fruit he uses come from "several of the best vineyards in Virginia, California, and Washington [State]." Vint Hill pledges full access to the winery facilities for custom-crush clients. "We guarantee that we'll make a good wine, together."

Returning to Rt. 29, turn left (south) for about a mile, watching for the grape cluster sign on the right; turn right on Rt. 674 and watch for the entrance to **Pearmund Cellars** on the left.

For many years, Chris Pearmund grew chardonnay grapes at his **Meriwether Vineyard**, established in 1976 and now legitimately labeled as "old vine," but eventually he built a winery on the premises. About his wine style, Pearmund says "Virginia is geographically and stylistically between California and France. We are Virginia, or 'New World' for me. I push our ability to ripen fruit, which means strict (and expensive) canopy management."

Pearmund likes the growth of the industry but sees some challenges. "We are young, growing, and only have 5 percent [wine sales] of our market share in-state. Our winery visiting experience is good, but most wines are too expensive for the quality in the bottle. We need to improve that more to grow."

Asked for details on how his custom-crush-focused model at Vint Hill differs as a business model from a regular farm winery, Pearmund explains he has issues detailing his nearly thirty years of professional wine knowledge "in an industry where people copy my nearly every move."

❖   ❖   ❖

Before leaving greater northern Virginia, be aware that Fairfax County now has a winery, almost at the Prince William county line in Clifton. Called **Paradise Springs**, it was founded in 2007. It's not a convenient stop on this route, but since it's much closer to many suburban northern Virginians and residents of Washington, D.C., it's worth noting.

The winery is owned by a mother-son team, Jane and Kirk Wiles. A unique feature is the location of the tasting room in a remodeled log cabin dating to the early 1800s, redesigned and expanded in 1955 by Howard Richter, a protégé of Frank Lloyd Wright. Despite the fact that the farm had been in the family for generations and that most Virginia counties welcome green businesses and family farms, the zoning department of Fairfax County decided to fight the permit for the winery, even though state law allowed it. This is especially ironic considering Fairfax County is notorious as an example of suburban development run amok, and you'd think profitable, green family agriculture would be something the county would want to cultivate.

Fortunately, supported by national and state-level laws and some influential industry friends in state government and the wine industry (Philip Carter Strother represented Paradise Springs in legal action), the permit was granted, and the winery opened in 2010 with a bang, winning that year's Governor's Cup Competition with an impressive 2009 chardonnay (Chris Pearmund was the winemaker).

CENTRAL VIRGINIA AND THE MONTICELLO AVA

Orange County

Returning from Pearmund Cellars to Rt. 29, turn right and continue south, following the signs for Rt. 29 south and the Rt. 17 bypass around Warrenton. Once you pass Rt. 17 at Opal, you leave the congestion of greater northern Virginia behind as you slip into the tranquil countryside. Soon after you cross the Rappahannock River into Culpeper County you pass the historic marker for the Civil War battle of Brandy Station in 1863, the largest cavalry battle ever fought in the Western Hemisphere.

The battle was fought at the start of General Lee's Gettysburg campaign and was inconclusive on the field. However, historians note that from this point in the war, the dominance of the Confederate cavalry under J. E. B. Stuart ended, and cavalry units on both sides became more evenly matched.

Once you reach Culpeper, you could simply continue south on

Rt. 29. If you did, you'd reach **Prince Michel Vineyards and Winery**, in Leon. The best wines are the Vineyard Designate series, some of which have won impressive awards. The winery has two labels that help support preservation causes: Journey Through Hallowed Ground, and Patrons for Bellaire Parks.

To take a more scenic route, however, follow signs for Rt. 15 south when Rt. 29 passes Culpeper, onto the James Madison Highway toward Orange. Almost immediately, you'll feel enveloped in the bosom of a timeless Virginia farmland, and when you reach the charming town of Orange you'll feel you've reached a slower, kinder, gentler Virginia than the one you left behind with the traffic, farther north. Taking this route, you'll miss wineries to the east, which you can learn more about by looking up the Heart of Virginia Wine Trail on the virginiawine.org website.

In Orange, turn right on Rt. 20. You are now on the Constitution Route, named for three important framers of the Constitution who lived near it: James Madison in Montpelier, Thomas Jefferson at Monticello, and James Monroe at Ash Lawn–Highland. You'll see signs for Montpelier, most of whose original construction and furnishings were recently restored. To visit, turn left across the railroad tracks.

Rt. 20 will T-intersect Rt. 33; turn left where they join for a short distance, then turn right on Rt. 20 again, and take the next left—Rt. 678 (Governor Barbour St.)—and continue straight. You'll see the **Barboursville Vineyards** on the right. Continue to the next intersection, where you turn right on Rt. 777 (Vineyard Rd.), then take the next right on Mansion Rd. onto the property. Turn left at the end of the first block of vines on the left and drive up to the winery.

You are now in the Central Piedmont and within the Monticello AVA. Bounded on the east by Southwestern Mountain and on the west by the crest of the Blue Ridge Mountains, it is at this point the most well-known Virginia AVA. The terrain is very hilly, giving good air and water drainage, and the region is cooler than the lower Piedmont to the east.

Barboursville Vineyards is one of the oldest wineries in the state and the oldest still operating in central Virginia and the Monticello AVA. It is also an iconic winery, with Tuscan-style arches along two right-angle wings, a distinctive cupola, and sweeping views of its vineyards and the Blue Ridge Mountains in the distance and Southwestern Mountain just behind the winery.

The vineyard and winery are owned by Gianni and Silvana Zonin, whose family business is Italy's largest private wine producer. Original general manager and viticulturist Gabriele Rausse recalls that he and Gianni liked the challenge of attempting vinifera viticulture in a region where everybody said it couldn't be done. The wine being produced in Virginia at the time was, says Rausse, "interesting, but I would not call it wine." Virginia Tech was not recommending planting vinifera, but rather the French hybrids. State Department of Agriculture officials offered them cigars and told them, "This is the future of Virginia viticulture."

Thanks to their pioneering spirit, and the financial clout the Zonins brought to the investment in vinifera vineyards and modern winemaking equipment, the Virginia wine industry was given a shot in the arm. Barboursville showed that commercial vinifera viticulture was possible in Virginia, and others learned much from their example.

Some thirty-five years later, now under general manager and winemaker Luca Paschina (also a native of Italy), Barboursville is still in the forefront of defining and refining Virginia wine quality and style. Barboursville was one of the first wineries to introduce close (one-meter in-row) vine spacing, which has become the reigning paradigm in Virginia. In keeping with Italian custom, it has established a premier restaurant at the winery—Palladio—which showcases the food-friendly style of the wines to great advantage. There is also an inn on the property for those who want to enjoy themselves and not worry about driving elsewhere.

Barboursville Vineyards is best known for its flagship proprietary red Bordeaux blend, Octagon (named for the trademark design Jefferson used at both the adjacent Barbour mansion and at Monticello). Octagon is a Right Bank–style blend with around 60 percent merlot, plus varying amounts of cabernet franc and just a token amount of cabernet sauvignon.

While Octagon receives international acclaim, Italians are also known for pinot grigio, and Barboursville's has been a consistent benchmark. Paschina harvests in August to retain the bright, fresh acidity that falls rapidly in that grape as it ripens; this pinot grigio is not just crisp and refreshing, but elegant. Another example of Barboursville's continuing innovation is their use of several clones of sauvignon blanc that combine the best of Loire and Marlborough styles; the clones they used before would rot too easily and had nothing like the classic aroma and flavor of the replacements. Another innovation is a few acres of newly planted petite sirah. A consultant for the Zonin Wine House in France suggested trying it.

They cultivate the Piemontese grapes barbera and nebbiolo, with impressive results, and Paschina introduced a vin santo–style dessert wine. Select white grapes (muscat ottonel in this case) are carefully picked and dried on straw mats in special humidity-controlled rooms to avoid the risk of rot. The result, called Malvaxia, is a delicious, aromatic, but balanced and concentrated sweet white wine, with far less sharp pungency than is often found in Italian vin santo. Since it's not too sweet, it can be matched with dark chocolate or rich cheese as well as desserts. The shed where the grapes for Malvaxia are dried is adjacent to the parking lot and is prominently labeled, so it can also function as consumer education and promotion.

Paschina has a calm and gracious manner, with striking features that suggest he could have stepped off the canvas of a Renaissance painting (though in modern clothes).

The majority (60 percent) of production is sold in distribution, the rest at the winery. "To me, both channels are very important," says Paschina. "I've met so many customers over the years who told me they tasted one of our wines in a restaurant" (like the Inn at Little Washington, where Barboursville is the house wine, or the Boar's Head Inn near Charlottesville). "In building a new market," he continues, "the first step is always building the restaurant trade through tastings. To buy your wine, people have to taste it. Find a friendly restaurant and then build the retail sector. As a small producer, just being in grocery stores doesn't really help if people don't know the brand."

Paschina explains that the main focus of their marketing effort is personal brand-ambassador work. "What we're now doing a lot is going many places to pour our wines; also wine and food events, and special tastings at the vineyards." He mentions high-visibility initiatives, such as being a sponsor of the 2011 national Wine Bloggers' Conference in Charlottesville. "It's very important to network with the public and the trade. We are ambassadors of our wines and Virginia wines. 'Quality Virginia Wines' is the important message, and we can only get that word out if we meet these people."

Most of the praise goes to Octagon, but Paschina says the style of their viognier is also well liked by restaurant people and critics. It isn't as popular in wine competitions, he says, because it's "not as high in alcohol and sweetness as some others here or in California." This speaks to his Old World winemaking style. "The white wines of many other producers are too sweet and soft. I focus on picking before you have sugars too high and too high alcohol, with low acid."

Paschina sees Virginia's wine industry moving in one of two directions. Some, he feels, will "aim at producing fine wines from Virginia grapes with a majority focused on successful varieties. Another trend is people producing 'gimmick' [non-grape] wines and cultivating a clientele for that. It will be interesting to see which will prevail in the long run."

Still, he is pleased with the evolution of the industry. "Virginia doesn't have as many restrictions as Italy, with its DOC regulations;

there are very few limiting factors on blending grapes here. When I arrived, the wine was so bad. I realized most producers were amateurs, just doing it for fun, I guess. Now, we have a lot of professionals in the industry; people are much more prepared when they start up new vineyards and wineries."

Returning the way you came, instead of turning left on Governor Barbour St., turn right. When Rt. 678 merges with Rt. 33 east, watch for the grape cluster sign on the right—**Horton Vineyards** will be ahead on your left shortly.

Horton Vineyards was the first to prove viognier's suitability for Virginia's terroir. At the same time, Dennis Horton reintroduced the norton grape to its native home, but he points out (as if these achievements weren't enough to cement his reputation) that he was also the first to make a varietal cabernet franc, which is now the most widely planted red-wine grape in the state.

Although cabernet sauvignon was more widely planted than cabernet franc until after 2000, Horton ripped his cabernet sauvignon vines out because they didn't hold up during the rains. He found cabernet franc performed much more consistently in late-season rains. He says that even though cabernet sauvignon has thicker skin, cabernet franc's pH doesn't "get out of whack." If an inch of rain gets dumped on cabernet sauvignon during harvest, he says, "the sugars drop and pH rises, but cab. franc consistently keeps its chemistry. Cab. sauv. can drop as much as two or three degrees Brix and lose acid, too." Living up to his well-deserved reputation for straightforwardness, he adds, "I don't think Jesus Christ could grow pinot noir in Virginia; you can do it, but it doesn't taste like pinot should."

The unapologetically opinionated Horton received a lifetime achievement award from the wine industry in 2011 (his wife, Sharon, received the Vineyard Manager of the Year award some years ago), and I asked him why he thought he had been given the award.

"I think if I have any claim to fame in Virginia wine, it's because I've probably ripped up as many vines as I've planted here because they didn't work." Thus his frank assessment of Virginia pinot noir. "It's like people; we know all men are not really created equal, and it's the same with grapes. In Napa, they have three-tenths of an inch of rainfall during harvest; we call that a dew. We get consistent rains at harvest and need grapes that don't mind an inch of rain."

Horton's wife, Sharon, manages the vineyards; the winemaker is Mike Heny; and Horton runs the winery, which is where I interviewed him in his office. He has been a large figure on the Virginia wine scene, in more ways than one. However, since surviving a terrible car accident in 2010, during which he was clinically dead and then in a medically induced coma for five months, he has lost a great deal of weight and is now tall and thin. He has several artificial joints, but you'd never know it; he gets around just fine.

Since it opened twenty years ago, Horton Vineyards has been one of the larger Virginia wineries, and today farms one hundred acres of vines. Even in very competitive markets such as Washington, D.C., Horton's market share is increasing. "We're kinda getting to the limit," says Horton of their volume capacity. "We need to decide what to do if we grow."

In the 1980s, he and Sharon had been looking at potential vineyard property in California. Sharon told him she didn't want to live in California; he had no intention of commuting. That settled the issue of staying east, and he decided to focus on Virginia. "I can make a world-class viognier; if you can do that, why not?"

I asked him what research he did to give him the confidence to plant eighteen acres of viognier. He explains it was basically enlightened pragmatism. "I didn't know for sure that viognier would work, but I was impressed at the comparison between ripe chardonnay and viognier clusters. The viognier had some rotten berries but the rot would not spread; chardonnay rot would spread all over the cluster from a few rotten berries. Before harvest, the rotten viognier berries would dry up and blow away; you wouldn't even know they had been there."

Horton's practical approach to making wine in Virginia is to start with grape varieties that will ripen well, hold proper chemistry during harvest rains, and resist rot. He points out that Virginia has twice the annual rainfall of Bordeaux, and high humidity makes managing fungal disease imperative for any successful grape grower.

Another aspect of Horton's viticulture-driven approach is his use of divided canopy training systems in the vineyard. As you may recall from earlier (page 31), the lyre trellis manages vine vigor while allowing a fairly high crop load. Horton points out that the increased sunlight penetration in the center of the lyre (when rows are oriented north-south) is key in achieving maximum air and light penetration of the canopy, which also means a better shot at ripening the fruit. "The closer you get to north-south orientation, and if you clean out the middle zone of a lyre trellis, the sun will ripen the fruit on all sides."

Horton says that viognier makes "gorgeous" wine, especially on the lyre trellis. "VSP [vertical shoot positioning] training is convenient, but I and others believe that the quality of lyre fruit is much better than what comes off VSP. But VSP fruit can be machine harvested and is easier to manage." When asked what the per-acre cost of VSP training is versus his lyre system, he laughs. "I don't want to know." The increased cost comes not just from materials but also from labor (in part because of the impracticality of machine harvesting). Lyre training is clearly a more expensive way to farm, but based on Horton's track record, it pays off. "Virginia viognier," says Horton, "offers an aromatic, extremely flavorful bottle of white wine that can be made consistently well."

Another example is malbec, the tight-clustered star of the Argentine wine industry, which in Virginia is notoriously rot-prone. Horton has grown it for twenty years on lyre trellis where, he says, it gets the light and air it needs. "I've never lost a crop."

When the Horton 1992 viognier won a slew of national awards in 1993, the winery designed a shirt with the slogan "Viognier: Virginia's Great White Hope." Horton says, "When we went to the first viognier guild meeting in California, I asked Dick Arrowood what he thought about Virginia viognier. He said, 'Quite frankly, Dennis, you've cleaned everybody's clock.' The key is you can ripen it but keep the chemistry right where you need it, and the better the chemistry is, the less you have to work with it in the cellar." Horton made a point of printing the technical data for the '92 Horton viognier on that shirt: Brix 22.3^0, titratable acidity 7.35 g/l, and pH of 3.29. His pinotage is similarly successful because it ripens with balanced chemistry. Horton also pioneered varietal petit manseng in Virginia. It's very fruity with balancing acidity, and customers like it. "I've never seen rot on a berry of petit manseng," says Horton, emphasizing the importance of a grape working in the vineyard first.

Horton is proud of his distribution success. "Republic [National] is picking up six hundred cases [total of Horton wine] every other week. We're in Maryland, D.C., and New Jersey, and looking seriously at Florida now. Whether it's [Robert] Parker or customers, people like the wine. How many other wineries are doing three thousand cases of viognier per year? It goes away, too, and doesn't just sit. My distributors have good pricing; if you go into Kroger's, they sell my wine for less than I do, and I have no intention of competing with them." The reputation he has established for himself and Virginia viognier helps. "I made two hundred and thirty-six cases of viognier in 1992 and it took all year to sell it, putting it in competitions like crazy. Now, I don't even have to promote the current three thousand cases."

His other two large-volume varietals are cabernet franc and norton (2,000–3,000 cases each), but he's found a ready market for his fruit wines, especially at festivals. "Fruit wines are very desirable to the consumer, and very desirable to us financially. They are big every-where; Kroger's has seven or eight of my fruit wines. Why? Because they make money, too."

I asked Horton how the consumption of Virginia wines can be increased. "If more people were producing commercially competitive wines, I think there'd be more Virginia wine sold. How many people will go to a winery to buy a bottle of wine? And even in grocery stores, I can stretch my arms from one end of the Virginia wine section to the other. Pricing is also out of line for a lot of commercial wines. For the Virginia wine industry to develop, you have to make it accessible to the consumer."

Ten years from now, what does Horton think Virginia wine will be known for, nationally and internationally? "I would hope the wine industry would continue to grow. I'd also hope people will experiment more with grapes. Jancis Robinson's book [*Vines, Grapes and Wines*] has over three thousand wine grapes; if more people experimented, we'd have a more cosmopolitan attitude toward grapes. Tony Wolf brought petit manseng into Virginia and many other things; that research is important. Albariño is a nice grape to deal with, but it's a tough sell. I made a beautiful roussanne from vines that have been in the ground for years; it's delightful, and it took me all year to sell my two hundred and twelve cases, but it's a proven grape that works well here."

Leaving Horton Vineyards, turn left and continue east on Rt. 33 over the Southwestern Mountain. When you intersect Rt. 231, turn right and head south toward Keswick; in a few miles you'll enter Albemarle County, the heart of the Monticello AVA, and encounter **Keswick Vineyards** on the left.

Albemarle County

The countryside around Rt. 231 is some of the most handsome in the state, and the road is appropriately designated a Virginia Scenic Byway. This section of Albemarle County is also as tony and exclusive as the estates surrounding Middleburg. There is a substantial county tax break for land that is actively and commercially farmed, but some of the local landowners were shocked to learn that a commercial farm winery would bring the common public driving their common cars into Keswick to taste wine. Not only that, they might even stay for hours for on-site events. This seemed to violate an understanding that the local gentry were to live in quiet self-congratulation. There goes the neighborhood!

Keswick Vineyards had to go through hearings with the county zoning commission due to neighbors complaining about noise, though some suspected they just preferred not to see or hear the public from their property at all. Keswick agreed to limit the size and noise of its weddings and other events, and an uneasy peace now prevails, though Keswick Vineyards plans to increase the number of its events.

Proprietor Al Schornberg retired early from the high-tech business—not unheard of for a Virginia vintner—and he and his wife, Cindy, started searching the country for an ideal place to either buy or start a winery. "We searched for five years around the country: Sonoma, Napa, the Hill Country of Texas, North Carolina, Michigan, and Virginia. We had narrowed our search down to Healdsburg in Sonoma and the Charlottesville area of Virginia. When Edgewood (an old Keswick horse farm) popped up, we looked at it and made an offer the next day." He feels that Virginia had the edge in that it was just beginning an exciting growth phase, "and being an entrepreneur, that appealed to me. Cindy, meanwhile, liked the idea of having access to some of the best services and infrastructure available while still being able to live in a rural area."

You drive through a very tidy vineyard next to a pond as you turn off Rt. 231, and then you catch sight on the left of the breathtaking manor house that is featured on Keswick's wine labels; the tasting room is actually to the right, at the winery.

"Our site is generally one of low yields and amazing quality, with the normal Virginia threat of early spring frosts," says winemaker Stephen Barnard. A native of South Africa, Barnard is a talented young winemaker who helped establish the winery's reputation as a high-quality boutique winery from the start. In a romantic storybook twist, he also married Al and Cindy's daughter, Kathy (the wedding took place at the estate, of course).

Barnard believes Virginia is "starting to create a style of wine, and we are playing to our strengths in that we are focusing on varieties that are better suited to our climates, such as petit verdot, cabernet franc, and viognier." His winemaking style aptly reflects the fusion that makes Virginia unique in the wine world. "I love the history of the Old World [wines], but I would say I am more of a New World winemaker. I am a traditionalist in a few ways, in that I ferment wines without the addition of [commercial] yeast, and I try to make wines that reflect the character of the fruit. I want you to taste in a glass of wine how the fruit was grown, the soils in which they are grown, and to that end I try not to interfere too much when making wine. However, I am New World in that I favor wines that are more fruit dominated yet age-worthy, and that might be catering to the American palate at the moment."

He sees Virginia's future as "nothing but bright as long as we work together and continue to grow and make better wines. A lot of the hard work that needs to be done is fine-tuning the vineyard. I think we have winemakers who know how to make wine, but we have to produce the quality fruit that will allow us to make competitive international wines."

Although viognier has made Keswick Vineyard's reputation, Schornberg believes that cabernet sauvignon–based blends may emerge as the winery's strength in the future. "In 2010, my personal favorites were syrah and malbec. However, those cannot be produced consistently from year to year." He believes that Virginia wine's recent emergence is the result of several factors. "I think the wine world was looking for something new but did not want to sacrifice quality. In the last ten years, winemakers from all over the world have congregated here and developed a significant industry. I also believe the efforts of Dr. Bruce Zoecklein to develop quality and share information have contributed to the improved quality."

As you leave Keswick Vineyards by turning left out of the driveway and continuing south on Rt. 231, the town of Keswick is off the main road after Rt. 231 merges with Rt. 22. Watch for signs. An early scene in the classic 1956 movie *Giant*, starring Rock Hudson, Elizabeth Taylor, and James Dean, was shot at the nearby Belmont estate and included shots of the Keswick railroad station (relabeled "Ardmore" to represent Ardmore, Maryland, in the story).

Continue on Rt. 22 until you come to Rt. 250. Merge right to take it west, toward Charlottesville.

Charlottesville is the heart of central Virginia wine country. The city is home to the University of Virginia and bills itself as a world-class city with a friendly small-town feel. Thomas Jefferson's Monticello is nearby, and Charlottesville is a convenient base of operations for striking out into the surrounding countryside and Monticello.

Assuming you're continuing on your winery visits, you'll follow signs in about two miles to turn left and take I-64 west only one exit, to Exit 121. Turn left when you reach Rt. 20, at the end of the exit ramp heading south under the interstate. On the right you'll pass Piedmont Virginia Community College, which features a workforce services division that includes apprenticeship courses in viticulture, enology, and marketing for those considering a commercial wine career.

At the second traffic light, turn left on Rt. 53 (Thomas Jefferson

Parkway). You'll pass the Carter Mountain Orchard on the right, an excellent place to take a scenic diversion by driving to the summit, where a commercial apple orchard and vineyard offer spectacular views of the lower Piedmont to the south and Charlottesville and the Blue Ridge Mountains to the north.

Continuing south on Rt. 53, you'll shortly reach the Michie Tavern on the right, which features a Virginia wine museum and is a popular lunch stop for visitors to Monticello. Winding your way along a narrow road in the woods, watch for a stone bridge as you emerge into daylight; turn right and cross over the bridge to reach the parking lot and visitors' center for Monticello. The visitors' center was recently redesigned and expanded, and the gift shop has a plethora of tasteful, educational souvenirs and a selection of local Virginia wines, including Monticello's own branded wines.

Leaving Monticello, turn left on the main road (Rt. 53) and continue carefully around the twists and turns; you'll soon see a vineyard on your right. The main road makes a right-angle turn; take it and then go right again into the parking lot for **Jefferson Vineyards**. You're now also on the spot historically named Simeon, where Filippo Mazzei helped Jefferson plant a vineyard.

Since 2005, Andy Reagan has been the winemaker and vineyard manager at Jefferson Vineyards (last year he became general manager as well). Reagan has reinvigorated the Jefferson brand with elegant, classic red Bordeaux varietals and blends, and fresh, balanced whites. Viognier, reserve chardonnay, and pinot gris are the strong whites; here the gris really shows some ripeness and viscosity to distinguish it from the lighter "grigio" style.

Jefferson Vineyards is a midsize winery for Virginia, producing between 6,500 and 8,000 cases a year, currently farming twenty-six acres of vineyard with five more planned for next year. Viognier, pinot gris, Meritage, and chardonnay make up the majority of the wine produced, and the first three are also the most appreciated by the critics, while the viognier and pinot gris are the biggest sellers.

Reagan feels that the vineyard's location is very favorable for viticulture. "We have a unique mesoclimate here. We benefit much the same way Jefferson did from the location on the eastern side of Carter's Mountain, as this helps to prevent some bad weather systems from affecting our vineyard," he explains. "We enjoy a later bud break but slightly warmer temperatures that allow the fruit to ripen most years before any real threat of tropical systems in the fall."

Due to its historic connection with the Simeon farm and vineyard (under earlier owners the winery was, in fact, named Simeon), it's natural for the winery to be named Jefferson Vineyards, though there is some grumbling about the fact that they have trademarked Jefferson's signature, which they use on their reserve wines. But Reagan has a different take on the historical link to Jefferson. "It is nothing short of an amazing feeling—walking and working the same land commissioned by one of our founding fathers," he says.

Reagan is a native of Norfolk, Virginia, and has been working in vineyards and wineries since 1992, when he was a teenager working for his sister Anne, winemaker (currently business manager) at Benmarl Winery, in New York's Hudson River valley. He was hired as cellar help at Benmarl in 1997 and became head winemaker just a few years later. At age twenty-three, Reagan was in charge of a three-thousand-case winery and a twenty-five-acre vineyard. Reagan made wine at five different wineries on the East Coast before coming to Jefferson Vineyards in 2005. "Now, some nineteen years after I suckered my first vine, I still embrace the new seasons and appreciate them for what each means related to the final product."

Asked to describe his winemaking style, Reagan says, "I consider our wines 'Old World with a New World twist,' a sort of rowdy elegance maybe." The reserve chardonnay and viognier are both known for purity of fruit and elegance, as is the Meritage blend, in which oak is a restrained background component and the texture is lively and fresh.

Located as close as it is to Monticello, Jefferson Vineyards sees many tourists, yet as the closest winery to downtown Charlottesville it also attracts a lot of UVA graduate students. "Most of the visitors are here for the history, but they return for the outstanding quality of the wine."

Commenting on the wider scene Reagan says, "As an industry we are still a very long way from achieving a consistent high-quality product. We have made huge strides toward doing so, but we still need to focus on the varieties that do the best. Still, I think we are definitely on the right track." He feels Virginia will continue to be a more boutique-based wine industry that relies mainly on agritourism, "and that will only aid in promoting Virginia as a fine-wine producing region."

Tired of hearing complaints about the pricing of Virginia wine—he thought people should instead be asking themselves if the wines were fairly priced for their quality level on the world wine market—Reagan held a blind tasting for wine writers in 2010. He included three Virginia wineries and a variety of other world wines priced at least as high and sometimes higher than the Virginia wines (such as viognier from Condrieu). Virginia wines placed first in four out of six flights (all three white flights and one of the red flights—with a 2007 Meritage blend. A very impressive South African cabernet franc and an Italian merlot were the other two top reds. See Additional Information for a link to complete results.)

Returning to Rt. 53, turn right and continue straight as Rt. 53 branches off to the left; you're now on the James Monroe Parkway (CR 795). After 2.6 miles, the road becomes Carters Mountain Rd. Continue a further 2.2 miles, then turn left at Blenheim Rd./CR 727. Your first right brings you to the tasting room of the **Trump Winery**, formerly Kluge Estate

Vineyards, offering the Kluge wines for the time being until the Trump label comes on the market. Table and sparkling wines are well-made, elegant, and reasonably priced. In just 0.6 miles, make a slight left at Blenheim Farm and you've arrived at **Blenheim Vineyards**, established by Charlottesville-based rocker Dave Matthews in 2000.

For a winery owned by a popular rock musician, Blenheim is a model of understatement and good taste. The impressive reclaimed timber-frame structure of the winery was actually designed by Matthews and built by master craftsman William Johnson to have a minimal impact on the environment. It is built into the hillside for minimal movement of the grapes and wine, as well as to save energy. Other "green" features of the winery include passive solar heating, many skylights, composting, and recycling of packaging and other products where possible. The passive lighting of the wine cellar adds a striking visual feature, letting visitors look down to see the tanks and the cellar—you can even see the winemaker in action. Behind the tasting area is a deck with a breathtaking view of vineyards and the lower Piedmont to the east.

The winery was named for the historic land patent on the property dating back to James Carter, secretary of the Virginia Colony. Matthews's mother lives in the historic nineteenth-century Gothic Revival house on the property. Also on the property was the remains of an old chardonnay vineyard used by the now-defunct Blenheim Vineyards of the 1980s, so the revival of both was another way of continuing the property's history. Vineyard manager is Peter Matthews, Dave's brother.

Under the stewardship of the talented Kirsty Harmon (see pages 182–87), Blenheim's wines are characterized by fresh and vibrant fruit, minimal oak, and finesse. Harmon describes her winemaking style as "food friendly," which explains their lively and elegant style. The regular-line wine labels have a budding grape leaf represented as a fractal (a geometric figure of identical motifs multiplying themselves on an

ever-reducing scale). The two top-of-the-line wines are the Painted
Red and Painted White. For each label, Dave Matthews sketched
a rugged pair of farm boots (in different colors for each wine). The
wines are unusual proprietary blends that vary with the vintage.

If the Dave Matthews Band is performing in nearby Charlottesville the weekend you're in town, a visit to the winery is not recommended; it will be crowded. (More details on Blenheim wines follow
in "Virginia Women of the Vine.")

Returning to CR 627 (Carters Mountain Rd.), turn left and continue
until the road intersects Rt. 20; turn left on Rt. 20, cross Carters Bridge,
and continue south for another mile or so. Watch for the grape cluster
sign. Turn right at the sign for **First Colony Winery** (Harris Creek
Rd./CR 720). Continue into the woods on the dirt road past the First
Colony Winery for about 0.25 miles, to **Virginia Wineworks**.

Virginia Wineworks is a multifaceted operation, located in the old
Montdomaine winery. The principal is Philip Stafford, and his partner
and winemaker is Michael Shaps, a Burgundy-trained winemaker with
many years of experience in the Virginia wine industry as a winemaker
and consultant. The winery features two product lines: the Virginia
Wineworks label of well-made, affordable wines, and the over-$20
Michael Shaps wines. Virginia Wineworks also functions as a custom-
crush operation, servicing twenty-three clients. "The Michael Shaps
brand is based on small-lot, high-end winemaking, mostly from single
vineyards that we lease by the acre and oversee their management,"
explains Shaps. "We look for ideal sites that work best for the particular variety." The Wineworks wines are ready-to-drink blends made
for value-wine customers who want a high level of quality, he adds.

Unique for a Virginia winery is the packaging of top vinifera varietals such as chardonnay, viognier, and cabernet franc in three-liter bag-
in-the-box (BIB) format. "The Wineworks brand is all about value and

getting a wine of high quality at a reasonable price," explains Shaps. "BIB wines have really caught on in Europe, and it was a no-brainer, combining wine quality, freshness, price, and environment [package components are recyclable]. I saw the equipment in Europe and ran the numbers; it made too much sense not to do it." Though I found the bag-in-the-box chardonnay unremarkable, I was impressed with the quality-to-price ratio of the cabernet franc and, even more, the viognier—unoaked, fresh, floral, and about half the price per ounce of the average Virginia viognier.

The Michael Shaps line of wines has consistently been in the top tier of Virginia wines. The prices are as exquisite as the wines (up to $50), but those who want to see how Virginia wines can perform at these price levels should not be disappointed.

Virginia Wineworks was the first custom-crush operation in the state. It offers clients several winemaking options, from letting them be quite hands-on to creating the wine entirely for them. Services include sourcing grapes and developing a winemaking plan.

One of Shaps's custom-crush clients, who preferred to remain anonymous, pointed out the economic benefits of the arrangement. "I don't see how you could just plant grapes and be profitable; the bigger you get, the more expensive it is to run the operation. And as a winery, how can you sell enough wine to pay for it all? I don't know how anyone [with a vineyard and winery] is making any money."

Returning from Wineworks, you can stop at **First Colony Winery** on the left on your way back to the main road. They make the usual varietals, but winery specialties include varietal seyval blanc, tannat, a "claret," and a semisweet chambourcin blend.

Reaching Rt. 20, turn left and continue north past where you joined the road from CR 627; in about ten miles you'll reach Rt. 53, where you turned to visit Monticello and Jefferson Vineyards. Continue into Charlottesville or, to visit the wineries of the northern section of the Monticello Wine Trail, follow signs for I-66 west.

The first stop will be **King Family Vineyards**. Take Exit 107 for Rt. 250 and turn right, heading toward Crozet, then look for the grape cluster sign and turn left at the next road on the left (Hillsboro La./CR 797). In a short distance, the road makes a right-angle turn to the right and becomes CR 684 (Half Mile Branch Rd.). Continue about a mile and watch for the vineyard sign on the left.

King Family Vineyards is owned and operated by the King family, originally from Texas but unrelated to the King Ranch Kings. As with many Virginia wineries, King Family Vineyards began with a search for a profitable crop on relatively small acreage. When it was founded in 1998, the winery's first vintage was only five hundred cases, but today the winery produces approximately ten times that volume of wine annually. The merlot vineyard on the property produces wine with remarkable complexity. Nearly all of the wine is made with estate grown grapes, and the author has been able to identify King Family fruit in other wineries' merlots.

Situated on a plateau close to Bucks Elbow Mountain, King Family Vineyards has a stellar view of the Blue Ridge Mountains to the west. A unique winery feature is its polo pitch, where winery guests are invited to watch live polo matches on certain Sundays during the season, and are encouraged to bring picnic lunches.

Winemaker Matthieu Finot, a Frenchman, has made wine around the world in Old and New World environments, and has continued King Family's reputation for top boutique wines. His 2007 Meritage won the 2010 Virginia Governor's Cup (red); other top awards include the 2008, 2009, and 2010 Monticello Cup, and Governor's Cup Gold Medals in 2009 and 2010. Under previous winemaker Michael Shaps, the winery won the 2004 Governor's Cup.

Returning to Rt. 684, turn left now and head north; you'll soon meet CR 691 (Jarmans Gap Rd.). Turn right and continue into the town of Crozet, home of the cult favorite Crozet Pizza and the Starr Hill

Brewery. After refreshing yourself in Crozet, go north on Crozet Ave., which becomes CR 810 as you leave town. Continue for several miles until the road T-intersects with Garth Rd. in the hamlet of White Hall. Turn left, then right at the next intersection, following signs for CR 810. Continue for a mile or so and turn left on CR 674 (Break Heart Rd.). Continue straight when the road becomes Sugar Ridge Rd. **White Hall Vineyards** is 1.5 miles on the right.

White Hall Vineyards has had a well-deserved reputation for fine wine quality and reasonable pricing since the mid-1990s. Edie and Tony Champ own White Hall. They planted their first six acres of grapes in 1992 and made the first vintage in 1994. Tony has a PhD in organic chemistry, and when he joined a chemical company he did some college recruiting two weeks a year at Stanford, Berkeley, and UC Davis, so he and his wife were able to spend some time in the Napa Valley, where they became fascinated with the wine lifestyle. "Robert Mondavi had just built his new winery in the mid-1960s, and it proved very accessible," says Tony. "The dream to one day make great wine was born."

Tony eventually became president and CEO of Fiber Industries, a producer of polyester fiber. He was based in Manhattan and lived in Westchester County, New York. The Champs owned part of the company, and when it was sold in 1989, they decided to invest their proceeds in their dream. They had lived in Virginia once before and liked the state. In revisiting it, they discovered Charlottesville and then beautiful White Hall.

The vineyards and winery are located at approximately eight hundred feet of elevation, on the eastern slope of the Blue Ridge Mountains, with very good air drainage. Although they have a second story, which they rent for a limited number of functions, and host about eight weddings a year, "We do not see events or weddings growing. We want it to be all about the wine," says Champ.

Despite their moderate size, White Hall makes eighteen different wines. "Chardonnay, viognier, petit verdot, cabernet franc, and gewürztraminer are the wines for which we are most noted," says Tony. The winemaker is Mike Panczak, and he has found the fruity, spicy petit manseng a useful and appropriate blending element, in small amounts, to enhance the fruitiness of other aromatic whites like viognier and pinot gris.

An interesting feature is the finishing of their two chardonnays with different closures. Tony explains that the Reserve Chardonnay, often sold in restaurants, is finished with a traditional cork, while the basic non-oaked chardonnay is sealed with a screw cap to maximize and preserve freshness and acidity. "Our wines are clean, fruit driven, and well balanced," Tony says, adding, "We received compliments at the London International Wine Fair for our reasonable (13 percent or less) alcohol levels. White Hall wines are also very food friendly."

White Hall Vineyards belongs to a new wine trail, cleverly called the Appellation Trail, that covers wineries close to the Blue Ridge Mountains in northern Albemarle County. Another member is neighboring **Mountfair Vineyards**, located not far north on Rt. 810 (Browns Gap Tpk.) in the hamlet of Mountfair (turn right on CR 668/Fox Mountain Rd.; a quarter mile later, the winery is on the right).

Mountfair Vineyards is a small artisan winery specializing in red Bordeaux-style blends. It emphasizes small-lot viticulture, small-batch fermentation, and sustainable business practices.

Originally only producing red Bordeaux blends (Engagement, Inaugural, Belated, Indigenous, Composition, and Wooloomooloo) with different varieties dominant in the blend, Mountfair now also makes the two cabernets, merlot, and petit verdot as varietals. The blends are the winery's strength, and the most compelling for me has been the Wooloomooloo, not least for its striking lavender label and intriguing aboriginal Australian name. The 2008 vintage had a high 60 percent of petit verdot, and was dark and brooding but with distinctive aromas of violets, lavender, and sage, and incredibly smooth tannins.

Another winery on the Appellation Trail is **Glass House Winery**, on CR 601 north of Free Union. From Mountfair Vineyards, continue east on (gravel) Rt. 668, turning left where it splits and Rt. 671 continues straight. When the road intersects (paved) Rt. 601, turn left; after about 2 miles you'll see it on the left (7 miles total from Mountfair). One of Virginia's most unusual small wineries, Glass House takes its name from a large arboretum of tropical plants and trees that you pass through on your way to the tasting room. The glass motif continues in the tasting room, where the wines all feature clear film labels to highlight the bottle, and this is the only Virginia winery so far to use glass-top closures (with a small gasket of food-grade plastic), to emphasize their "Glass House" branding.

Consulting winemaker is the experienced Brad McCarthy, and the winery has gotten off to a good start. The most distinctive wines are a Reserve Barbera made in the passito style (dried, concentrated grapes) and an exquisite and sensual port-style norton called "Meglio del Sesso," or "Better than Sex." Part of the experience is the norton; the other part is the use of cocoa powder to flavor the wine. Michelle Sanders, wife of proprietor Jeff Sanders, is a chocolatier, and offers tastes of proprietary truffles with the red wines in the tasting room. The cocoa powder is filtered out after the wine is in contact with it for some months, explains Jeff.

Leaving the winery, turn right on CR 601 (Free Union Rd.), continuing through Free Union until the road T-intersects Garth Rd. at the Hunt Country Market & Deli. Turn left and follow Garth Rd. toward Charlottesville, then turn right to follow signs for the Rt. 29 south/250 bypass west. Continue under I-64 south on Rt. 29 and you'll quickly be back in the country.

First you'll come to the **Albemarle CiderWorks** on the right. A short distance down the road, in North Garden, turn right on Plank Rd. and go 0.5 miles; **Pippin Hill Farm & Vineyards** will be on the right which was detailed on pages 14–18.

Leaving Pippin Hill, turn right on the Plank Rd. and continue through Batesville (minding the speed limit) until the road ends at Rt. 250. Turn left on Rt. 250 for a short distance, watching for the grape cluster sign, and make the next right turn on CR 796, then left on Newtown Rd./CR 690. Watch for the black and yellow winery logo sign on the left for **Pollak Vineyards**.

Pollak Vineyards was founded by David and Margo Pollak in 2003, when they purchased an organic farm just west of Charlottesville. Formerly partners in Bouchaine Vineyards, in Napa Valley's Carneros district, they discovered that great wines could be produced in Virginia from well-chosen and carefully maintained vineyards. Their inaugural team of professionals included vineyard consultant Chris Hill, consultant winemaker Michael Shaps, and winemaker Jake Busching. Setting their sights on producing world-class wines, they planted twenty-five acres of French vinifera vines on their hundred-acre farm in Greenwood. Their first vintage was in 2005 and resulted in 320 cases of an exceptional Meritage blend.

The house style is defined by their fine vineyard site, which is just below I-64 as it climbs to Afton Mountain. The vineyard is on a moraine for good water drainage and faces southwest. Although it gets plenty of summer sun, the cool nights and airflow keep good acidity in the grapes, and that helps balance the wine chemistry. The reds are quite ripe but not lush, with firm balancing acidity. The whites are the same, and their bright, lively fruit and acidity are not overshadowed by high alcohol or new oak. A barrel sample of an unreleased reserve cabernet sauvignon was impressive, in an understated Bordeaux style.

Part of Pollak Vineyards' appeal, as with King Family, is their western Albemarle location and proximity to the mountains. The tasting room is reminiscent of a stylish winery in Napa or Sonoma, and features a wraparound patio overlooking a pond. An informal summer Friday-night concert series with select food vendors attracts regulars from Charlottesville.

Nelson County

Return from Pollak to Rt. 250 west, turn left a short distance down the road onto Rt. 151, which runs south down the Rockfish Valley. You soon enter Nelson County. On the left within a mile is the Blue Mountain Brewery (several area breweries have their own beer trail), which has a great view of the nearby Blue Ridge Mountains. Continuing south on Rt. 151, look for the grape cluster sign and turn right on Rt. 6. Continue about a mile until you see vineyards on the right. Turn right at the sign for **Veritas Vineyard**.

Veritas Vineyard and Winery is family owned and operated by the Hodsons. Winemaker Emily (see page 191) is the daughter of owners Andrew and Patricia, an English couple (the English motif of the rose is found on their labels). The Hodsons are unapologetically Francophile in their wine preferences and also believe Virginia wines express the Old World style of bright, fresh fruit and firm acidity to best advantage. Their reds are inspired by Bordeaux and the Loire Valley, while the chardonnay looks stylistically to Burgundy. The cabernet franc (like that of White Hall) is packaged in a sloped Loire Valley–style bottle instead of the more usual Bordeaux bottle. Veritas was one of the first Virginia wineries to make a varietal cabernet franc with a significant amount of petit verdot blended in; this made a complementary and distinctive blend. In the white wines, the Hodsons are so enamored of sauvignon blanc that they make two when the vintage allows: a classic and restrained Loire Valley style, and a more assertive and intense Marlborough-style wine.

The winery has a strong track record for both sauvignon blanc and cabernet franc (a reserve version is rare and expensive but worth seeking out) and their sauvignon blanc, cabernet franc, viognier, petit verdot, and Kenmar (a cryoextraction traminette) are consistent top performers in competitions. In excellent vintages, Veritas releases a VR red Bordeaux reserve wine, whereas their Claret is a non-reserve early-drinking blend.

Othello is Veritas's fine dessert wine, made the same way as a traditional ruby port, from grapes that have included touriga nacional and tannat. Another specialty of Veritas is sparkling wine; they rent cellar space to the top Virginia sparkling-wine maker, Claude Thibaut, who in turn assists in their bubbly production. Scintilla is a chardonnay blanc de blancs and Mousseux a merlot sparkling rosé.

Veritas is one of the most scenic Virginia wineries, with a stunning view from the tasting room and deck/veranda of nearby Humpback Mountain beyond the vineyards. With this kind of setting, it was only natural that the winery would become one of the top destinations for vineyard/winery theme weddings in the state. Andrew Hodson confesses that when they built the winery he had no intention of using the facility for weddings, but they responded to demand.

The same view also welcomes the thousands of visitors who attend the summer concert series called Starry Nights. Featuring a variety of musical genres, the concerts allow people to bring their own food and chairs, and full-bottle wine sales keep the concertgoers well lubricated.

Turn right on Rt. 6 and watch out for the grape cluster sign; turn left on Rt. 631 (Mountain Rd.), go 1.2 miles to the entrance of **Afton Mountain Vineyards** on Vineyard Lane. One of the older wineries in the area, it was acquired a few years ago by Tony and Elizabeth Smith, Albemarle County natives. Afton Mountain is very small, so large groups are not recommended. Winery specialties are gewürztraminer, pinot noir and sangiovese.

Returning to Rt. 6, turn right and continue to Rt. 151. Cross Rt. 151 onto Avon Rd. In about a mile, take a left on Rt. 636 (Batesville Rd.); 0.5 miles later you'll come to **Cardinal Point Vineyard and Winery** on the right.

Cardinal Point is an example of a longtime grape grower that decided to make wine as well. They originally sold their cabernet sauvignon grapes to Afton Mountain Vineyards, who made a vineyard-designate from them in the late 1980s and early 1990s.

Cardinal Point is owned by the Gorman family and run by a brother-sister team: Tim is the winemaker and Sarah is the business manager. Their brother, John, is an architect who designed the winery and tasting room, and Tim's wife, Susan, runs the tasting room.

Sarah explains that "cardinal point" was a training exercise her father developed when he commanded the US Army 8th Infantry Division in Bad Kreuznach, Germany, in the late 1970s. "The name of the exercise comes from the cardinal points of the compass, and the name of our farm came from the exercise." Cardinal Point wines can be easily spotted, with their distinctive logo of a postage stamp with a cardinal's head as well as the compass points illustrating the double meaning of the words.

In Germany, the Gormans learned to drink, appreciate, and love wine, and they still grow riesling in homage to their German experience. Sarah explains that many factors went into the Gormans' decision to shift from selling grapes to making wine, among them Tim's interest in and passion for winemaking, land-use considerations, and better revenue stability given the wild fluctuations in harvest conditions in Virginia.

Far from having any regrets, Sarah says, "We love that Tim can shepherd his fruit from the vineyard all the way to the bottle; that he can express his creativity in the brilliant blends he composes. We love meeting all of the people who come our way to try our wines." Of course it's not all wine and roses, as it were. "I think anyone will tell you that the least favorite part of winery ownership is the time commitment—this is not something you do in your 'retirement,' people—it's a job, for sure! But we wouldn't have it any other way."

Turn left when you leave Cardinal Point, back onto Rt. 636. Don't retrace your steps to Veritas, but turn left where the 636 meets Rt. 638, which will soon intersect Rts. 151/6. Turn left again and continue south on 151/6 for a couple of miles until you come to signs for **Flying Fox Vineyard** on the right, one of the smallest and cutest tasting rooms in the state. Owned by Lynn Davis and Rich Evans, Flying Fox, like Cardinal Point, sold grapes to other wineries for some years before deciding to open a winery. They grow merlot, petit verdot, viognier, and cabernet franc, which was a component of neighboring Veritas Vineyard's wine in the beginning and is still a strong suit. Just released is their first varietal petit verdot (2008). Rich, dark, with loads of blackberry fruit and oak, and still needing time to soften, it's like a Virginia version of petite sirah but without the high alcohol that comes with California versions of the wine.

The winery name comes from the weathervane on the roof of their main building, which has a fox on it that, after a hard day in the vineyard and a glass or two of wine, they are fond of saying, looks like it's flying. The wine labels are also cute, with a cartoon character of a Snoopy-like fox in a Sopwith Camel–like biplane.

Continue south for a mile or so, watching for signs for Rt. 6, which branches to the left off Rt. 151. Turn onto Rt. 6, watch for signs for Rt. 634 on the left after 1.5 miles, and take the turn. After about a mile, at the intersection with Rt. 616 bear left on Old Roberts Mountain Rd. and shortly you'll see **DelFosse Vineyards** on the left.

Founded in 2000 by Claude DelFosse, a Frenchman who retired from the aerospace industry, the winery is noteworthy not just for its wines but for its striking views and progressive conservation programs. Located within a steep, narrow watershed on three hundred and thirty acres, the vineyards have excellent air and water drainage, and some parts were even terraced into the hillside.

The DelFosse motto is "inspired by the French masters," and three of the labels, named for DelFosse's two sons and one daughter, are illustrated with artwork in the style of Toulouse-Lautrec.

The French inspiration also applies to DelFosse's wines. Reflecting his style preference and the cool mountain location, his wines are noted for high natural acidity and bright fruit even in warm vintages.

A few years ago, DelFosse did a carbon-footprint study of his operation and decided he could reduce his impact by using lighter-weight glass bottles, as bottles burn carbon not just in their production but also in their shipping, both empty and full.

DelFosse likes everything about having a winery except the business side. "That's very difficult," he says. He enjoys the vineyard work, the winemaking, the tasting room: "It's fun, very social, and you become a kind of star. People take their pictures with you, women come up and hug you." But there's nothing romantic about the financial challenges, he concludes.

Leaving the winery, going south on Rt. 634, turn left on Rt. 616 (Hickory Creek Rd.) and continue for less than two miles until it meets Rt. 29/6; turn right and proceed south. After passing Rt. 56 on your left, watch for signs for **Lovingston Winery** on the left.

Lovingston Winery, owned and operated by the Puckett family, is so focused on the wines that people who want a more frilly tasting room with lots of gifts and T-shirts and stuff probably will be disappointed. Hand picking, double sorting, small-lot fermentation, and gravity-flow processing are all methods they employ to minimize changes to grape and wine chemistry and maximize the flavors of the vineyard. Their winemaker, South African Riaan Rossouw, is proudly making his country's specialty—pinotage—but Lovingston is known for red Bordeaux varietals and blends, a crisp, fresh Loire-style seyval blanc, and a ripe, juicy and viscous yet lively petit manseng, these whites being finished with a Stelvin screw cap closure for maximum freshness.

Amherst County

A few miles south of Lovingston, you'll leave the Monticello AVA and cross into Amherst County. **Rebec Vineyards**, on your right alongside Rt. 29, hosts one of the oldest and most popular wine festivals in the state in October—the annual Virginia Wine and Garlic Festival. The last winery close to Rt. 29 in this part of the state is **Lazy Days Winery**, on Rt. 29 in Amherst (1351 N. Amherst Highway). Whites include a petit manseng, a viognier, and a semisweet blend named after the winery; reds include merlot and petit verdot.

While this route continues south on Rt. 29, a worthwhile side trip if you have the time is to **Ankida Ridge Vineyards**, reached by taking Rt. 60 west toward the Blue Ridge. The winery is located at the edge of the George Washington National Forest. From Rt. 60, turn right on Rt. 631, then left on Rt. 632 (Franklin Creek Rd.) to reach the winery, which makes very elegant chardonnay, as well as impressive pinot noir (see ankidaridge.com for detailed directions). Note: tastings are by advance appointment only.

SOUTHERN VIRGINIA, THE BLUE RIDGE HIGHLANDS, AND THE SHENANDOAH VALLEY

Southern Virginia

South of Lynchburg, it starts to feel like southern Virginia. Just a couple of years ago, there were fewer than a handful of wineries east of the Blue Ridge this far south and west; now ten percent of the state's total are in the region.

We're also in an area where local palate preference shifts to sweeter wines. Since the wineries here are just emerging on the scene and don't have an established track record, I will focus on those that at least include drier mainstream wines in the product line and aspire to compete on quality with their peers statewide. To plan a comprehensive tour of the region, look up the Southern Virginia Wine Trail and the Bedford County Wine Trail on the virginiawine.org website under "Regions & AVAs > Virginia Wine Trails."

While Virginia was on the front lines during the Civil War,

especially along the Rappahannock River, the southern part of the state was the stage for the war's conclusion. The Appomattox Campaign marched through Amelia, Nottoway, Prince Edward, and Appomattox counties. After a stalemate of trench warfare through the winter of 1864–65, General Ulysses S. Grant finally took the offensive in Petersburg and after the Confederate loss in the Battle of Fort Stedman turned the tide in a quick succession of battles, including the decisive Battle of Five Forks on April 1 and the Third Battle of Petersburg on April 2, which was closely followed by the collapse of defenses at Petersburg and the fall of Richmond.

General Robert E. Lee and the Army of Northern Virginia retreated southwest, seeking supplies first at Amelia Court House, then at Appomattox. Grant caught up with them, and Lee's army suffered a significant loss at the Battle of Sayler's Creek on April 6. The quick-moving Union army then seized the supplies waiting for Lee at Appomattox Station and defeated the outnumbered Confederate forces there, allowing Grant's army to outflank Lee and block his escape to the west. Lee's last hope was to break through the Union cavalry, but Lee attacked the morning of April 9 at Appomattox Courthouse not knowing that during the night the Union lines had been reinforced by two corps of Union infantry. When Lee realized the situation faced by his exhausted and outnumbered army, he decided to surrender before more lives were lost. The documents of surrender were signed in the parlor of the home of Wilmer McLean. The house is kept in period condition, and an oddly spiritually charged atmosphere prevails, with what seems like a profound sense of relief and peace.

In the southern Piedmont, you'll often see small, quaint-looking, square log cabins in the middle of farm fields, setting the region apart from the rest of the state. These are tobacco curing sheds, relics of an era when tobacco was Virginia's main cash crop.

A decade ago, major tobacco-producing states were looking for ways of phasing out tobacco and replacing it with other high-value crops that could also be profitable for small family farms. In a happy irony that would certainly make Thomas Jefferson smile, studies showed that ideal tobacco sites in the southern Piedmont correlated strongly with the best sites for viticulture. To be sure, there were strong contrasts. Tobacco is a native weed, where wine grapes (except for the norton and muscadine) are nonnative, and as we've seen, susceptible to a range of pests. Also, perennial vines have to be trained and trellised on expensive metal stakes and wires. However, the late transition of tobacco farmers into growers of wine grapes was a benefit to them in that they were able to learn from all the struggle of the previous thirty years of Virginia viticulture.

After leaving Lazy Days Winery, continue south on Rt. 29 to Rt. 60, where you turn left. In about ten miles, just as you cross into Appomattox County, turn right on Rt. 26. After ten miles or so you'll reach the town of Appomattox and you can visit the McLean House, where General Lee surrendered to General Grant.

Continuing south on Rt. 460, you'll reach the town of Pamplin City. Turn right on Rt. 47 south (Thomas Jefferson Highway), go approximately 2.5 miles and turn left onto CR 663 (Baker Mountain Rd.). The **Spring Creek Wine Cellar** entrance is 0.5 miles on the left. Spring Creek bills itself as specializing in dry wines, but it has an impressive range of red and white vinifera and French hybrid varietals.

Returning to Rt. 47, turn left and continue south through Charlotte Courthouse and Drakes Branch; watch for the grape cluster sign and turn right on CR 612. In about two miles, you'll see signs for **Annefield Vineyards** on the right.

Annefield's founders are Stephen Ballard and Michael Leary, and it's clear that they are not just passionate about wine, but about holistic viticulture as well. They grow only vinifera varieties and farm biodynamically, on the principles of the Austrian philosopher Rudolf Steiner.

Cabernet franc and viognier are excellent examples of the Virginia mainstream with these varietals. To match the stylish wines, the estate features an attractive Italianate antebellum manor house.

Leaving Annefield, turn right on Rt. 612, and right again on CR 746; in about ten miles you'll intersect Rt. 40, where you turn left to pass through Phenix. Soon after crossing the Campbell county line you'll see signs for **Sans Soucy Vineyards** on the left. Sans Soucy (French for "without a care") is a family owned and operated winery; Paul Anctil runs the cellar, while son Jackie manages the tasting room, festivals, and marketing. The winery and tasting room are in a restored barn and schoolhouse. Sans Soucy grows a variety of vinifera and hybrid vines on five acres and has an additional acre planted with heirloom apple trees. Whites include Viognier Reserve and Traminette Reserve. A unique angle for red varietal wines is a Tempranillo Reserve and a proprietary blend of tempranillo, chambourcin, and cabernet franc. The wines are priced between $25 and $30.

Leaving Sans Soucy, continue west on Rt. 40 through Brookneal. About twenty miles later you'll intersect Rt. 29 in Gretna; turn right and head north toward Altavista, taking the bypass. Take the Rt. 43 (Bedford Ave.) exit at Altavista, turn right on Bedford Ave., continue until Main St., turn left on Main St., go to the second stop light, and turn right onto CR 668 (Pittsylvania Ave.). Go approximately four miles to Level Run Rd., where you turn left. After about 200 yards, **Altavista Vineyards and Winery** is on the right.

Altavista Vineyards describes itself as "a small family-run vineyard and winery that specializes in limited production of finely crafted wines." Their vineyards currently produce syrah, chardonnay, viognier, merlot, cabernet franc, and cabernet sauvignon. The current product line includes cabernet franc, Meritage, chardonnay, viognier, and a proprietary sweet white called Vista Blanca (the other wines are dry). The 2009 Meritage won a silver medal in the 2011 Governor's Cup competition.

Returning to the town of Altavista, take Rt. 43 north/west until it meets Rt. 24; turn left and follow Rt. 24 west across the Blue Ridge Mountains into the city of Roanoke.

Before leaving this region, it's worth pointing out that **Rosemont Vineyards** by Lake Gaston, just off I-85 far to the east, has a good reputation for its wines but does not fit conveniently on this itinerary. It features a four-level, gravity-flow processing winery, and offers pinot gris/grigio, traminette, vidal blanc, a dessert wine made from lacrosse (a hybrid), and the two varietal cabernets, merlot, syrah, a rosé of chambourcin, and a sweet catawba. In 2010, their 2007 Meritage won "Best in Show" (out of over five hundred wines) at the Atlantic Seaboard Wine Competition.

Blue Ridge Highlands

Roanoke is a good base of operations for wineries on the Bedford County Wine Trail to the east, the Blue Ridge Highlands region to the south and west, and the southern wineries of the Shenandoah Valley. Leaving Roanoke on Rt. 221 (Main St. SW/Brambleton Ave.) heading south, pass through the town of Cave Spring and look for Rt. 689 (Roselawn Rd.); turn right and bear left when the road merges with Rt. 692. This road T-intersects with Mt. Chestnut Rd.; turn right, and look for signs for **Valhalla Vineyards** (6500 Mt. Chestnut Rd.).

Valhalla Vineyards (technically part of the Shenandoah Valley AVA but grouped in this section for navigational convenience) is owned by James and Debra Vascik. James is the vineyard manager (and a neurosurgeon by profession); Debra is the winemaker. The property is located on a granite cliff at two thousand feet of elevation, with a stunning view of the Roanoke Valley. The barrel cellar was blasted out of the cliff rock.

Both the Vasciks are fans of Rhône-style wines, and explain that their granite-based soils resemble those of the Rhône Valley. While the high altitude is good for acid retention in the grapes, the Valhalla style is ripe, forward fruit, and some of the reds spend up to forty months in the barrel. The twenty-one-acre vineyard is planted to viognier, chardonnay, syrah, red Bordeaux varieties, norton, and alicante bouschet, which is used in a late-harvest wine.

With their first vintage—1998—they made an impressive debut on the Virginia wine scene, winning the Governor's Cup with their syrah. Viognier and Götterdämmerung, their Château Cheval Blanc–inspired, cabernet franc–dominated blend, also won top awards, including double gold in national competitions. Wines are estate bottled and carry the North Fork of Roanoke AVA.

Returning to Rt. 221, turn right and continue south; in about five miles you'll come to **AmRhein's Wine Cellars**. Winery owner Russ AmRhein is a third-generation jeweler—AmRhein's Fine Jewelry opened in downtown Roanoke in 1921—who has always had a love for farming and a passion for wine. He was able to indulge that passion by starting the Bent Mountain vineyard in the late 1990s. His son, Chad, is now the fourth-generation jeweler managing the retail divisions of the business while Russ focuses solely on the winery. AmRhein's new winemaker is Seth McCombs.

"When we lost the right to self-distribute, we lost connections with the trade," says Rebecca Spaid, AmRhein's director of marketing. "We do use the [state-run] Virginia Winery Distribution Company [VWDC] to ship to accounts, but most of our wines are sold on-site, with quite a few mail-order clients both in and out of state. In the one year where we had no system, we lost 90 percent of our off-site accounts, and we didn't get them back. I've talked to other small farm wineries that had the same experience." In 2011, they started using the VWDC (after their private distributor retired), and Spaid thinks it's working but says the paperwork is a hassle. They still have to do all the compliance paperwork, and the state collects a larger portion of the revenue than before.

The surname AmRhein means "on the Rhine" in German, and the house style is "Eastern US/Virginia with a German influence." The vineyards were first planted in 1995, and their first crush was in 1999. AmRhein now has three vineyards (Bent Mountain, Franklin County, and Botetourt) boasting forty acres planted to twenty varieties of grapes.

Russ AmRhein is a great admirer of Dennis Horton's focus on grape varieties that work in Virginia. The winery is best known for petit verdot, petit manseng, and late-harvest vidal blanc, the last of which has won the Governor's Cup. They were even able to harvest and process a true ice wine thanks to a vineyard freeze a few years ago. AmRhein labels are colorful and sensual, and a range of proprietary sweet blended wines is packaged to appeal to female consumers and their admirers (as noted, the local palate preference is sweeter in this part of the state than in the northern and central Piedmont).

From AmRhein, return to Rt. 221 and continue south for about ten miles until you reach Rt. 8 in Floyd. Turn left and you'll climb to the Blue Ridge Parkway. When you reach it, turn right and in just about a mile (milepost 170.3) you'll come to **Villa Appalaccia** on the left.

Villa Appalaccia's motto is "Enjoy a slice of Tuscany on the Blue Ridge Parkway." The winery/tasting room is designed like a small Tuscan villa, and Villa Appalaccia specializes in Italian grapes, offering an original Virginia-Italian interpretation with what they call "innovative and traditional wines." For example, their Toscanello is a blend of cabernet franc and sangiovese, with some primitivo added for spice and acidity. The winery is owned and run by another husband-wife team, Susanne Becker and Stephen Haskill. Susanne is the winemaker—along with Jocelyn Kuzelka—and Stephen is the "winegrower."

Susanne and Stephen love Italian cuisine and Italian wine, and they also look to Italy's Old World approach for wine style. The wines are designed to complement food and especially Italian food, and run against the regional preference for sweeter wine. Whites are dry, sometimes with bracing acidity, but with fresh and delicate fruit thanks to their high-elevation vineyard site, which was planted in 1989. Its shallow soils and good air drainage are also very favorable for viticulture, and so far it's the only vineyard in the East that's been able to ripen and make a sound wine from primitivo/zinfandel, as a result of how the air drainage retards fungal disease. In 2007, they harvested their first olives from trees on the estate and have a brick oven for making traditional Italian flatbreads.

From Villa Appalaccia, turn left on Castle Rock Gorge; on re-joining the Blue Ridge Parkway, turn left and right when it reaches Black Ridge Rd.; take the first left on Winery Lane, and shortly you'll see the entrance for **Château Morrisette**. Owned by the Morrisette family, Château Morrisette is one of Virginia's largest wineries and was a major tourist destination years before winery touring became as popular in Virginia as it is today. The signature wine is the Black Dog, a cabernet franc and chambourcin blend that's not entirely dry, though it has been growing steadily drier over the years. The wine takes its name from a painting of a black dog on the label; the theme was then expanded to Our Dog Blue and The Black Dog Blanc, with a blue bottle and a blue dog in the first case and a black dog looking at itself in a mirror and seeing a white reflection in the second. There are other dog labels as well. The Black Dog is the single most popular Virginia wine label in the state.

One of the oldest wineries in the state, the vineyard was first planted in 1978, and the first wines were produced in 1982 by current owner David Morrisette. Rick Hall is now the winemaker. While there is a vineyard opposite the winery, Morrisette explains that it was sited on a plateau with no air drainage; at this elevation, the only variety to survive the cold temperatures was the native Niagara grape. The Niagara produces a Sweet Mountain Laurel that is very popular.

Château Morrisette is located in the Rocky Knob AVA (Virginia's smallest), along the upper eastern flank of the Blue Ridge, but the vast majority of the grapes used are from growers across the state. The pricing for Château Morrisette's wines is very competitive with the world market and other Virginia wines, but they do have a Reserve Tannat clocking in at $48. Between Chateau O'Brien and Château Morrisette, Virginia may have the world's most expensive tannats—a dubious achievement.

The winery has fine views to the north into the Roanoke Valley, and the winery itself is worth a view; an expansion in 1999 used over 132,000 board feet of recycled Douglas fir for the new timber-frame construction. Despite the high number of visitors, the scale of the winery and tasting room are adequate to accommodate the traffic, and the winery is one of the few with a restaurant serving lunch and dinner.

In fairness to Château Morrisette, they were the first Virginia winery to successfully brand themselves with dogs and as dog lovers. Aside from featuring a range of catchy, fun dog labels, they also have a label for service dogs (Liberty red and Independence white) and a special white-and-red wine label, For the Love of Dogs, that is custom-printed and hand-labeled per order. This special label benefits medical research on dogs with exocrine pancreatic insufficiency (EPI). For unknown reasons, the largest group of dogs afflicted with EPI are service and working dogs. Researchers are seeking to identify the genetic marker(s) of EPI to allow testing prior to breeding in an effort to eradicate this disease. Recently, EPI has begun to show up in all breeds. More information on EPI research is available at epi4dogs.com or EPI-Research-Fund.com.

Leaving Château Morrisette, turn right on the Blue Ridge Parkway and continue a couple of miles, before turning right on Rt. 58 and heading west. In about four miles, take another right, onto Rt. 638 (Dugspur Rd.). After about two more miles, look for Rt. 656 (Pineview Rd.) on the right and take the turn. In about a mile, just before the road merges with Chisholm Creek Rd., you'll come to Foggy Ridge Cider.

Hard cider is a heritage beverage dating to colonial times and the Blue Ridge Mountain counties boast a long history of apple growing and cidermaking. Foggy Ridge Cider, explains proprietor and cidermaker Diane Flynt, is at three thousand feet of elevation, a difficult climate for grapes but ideal for apples. "For over a century," she says, "this region has grown delicious and highly valued apples. Varieties such as Newtown Pippin [called Albemarle Pippin in central Virginia] were exported to England—this apple was so prized by Queen Victoria that it was the only agricultural product sent to England with no import tax."

Because of their elevation, soil, and climate, Foggy Ridge apples range from 14 degrees to 19 degrees Brix at harvest, with most in the 15 to 16 degrees Brix range. Accordingly, the ciders more closely resemble classic sparkling wine such as champagne than the sweet, fizzy national brand ciders. "While it seems popular to denigrate the public's sweet tooth, I find most customers appreciate a balanced cider that speaks of fruit, acidity, and complex flavors rather than simple apple sweetness," says Flynt. "Even our sweetest cider [Sweet Stayman, at 2.3 percent residual sugar] is about half the sweetness level of most six-pack ciders."

The packaging is heavy champagne bottles finished with crown caps, and the labels feature appetizing photos of the dominant apples. The impression from the packaging is that this is serious table wine rather than a sweet, bubbly fruit wine, and the prices match. Acid is high and refreshing, much drier than mass-market American ciders. "Other than our fortified dessert ciders, Foggy Ridge ciders are around 8 percent alcohol," says Flynt. "I look for balance in cider, and find that alcohol levels above 9 percent generally tip cider toward the harsh end of the scale for my palate. Similar to grapes, lean is better. Serious wine drinkers tend to like our driest cider, Serious Cider, and Sweet Stayman is popular with chefs."

Flynt came to cultivate heirloom apples and make cider because, after over twenty years in the corporate business world, she longed to return to a more rural way of living. "I grew up in a very small town in Georgia and have always appreciated a seasonal life. I hoped to one day be able to give up long airplane flights to cities that all look the same, hotel food, and meetings in windowless rooms," she says. "At Foggy Ridge we grow cider apples and make a handcrafted hard cider. The Foggy Ridge brochure says 'Our tasting room has no scented candles and no T-shirts.' As the owner and cidermaker, my full-time effort is on selecting and growing apples suited for high-quality hard cider, and on crafting the very best cider that can be made from this fruit."

For example, she picks apples like a winemaker picks grapes—for optimal flavor, nothing more. "This means I might pick a block of apples three or four times to allow the fruit in the center of the trees to gain flavor and complexity that comes from tree ripening. This is an expensive way to harvest fruit, but an essential practice to gain complex flavors that make an interesting cider." She explains that more than thirty American, English, and French apple varieties—ugly and hard to grow, but full of the tannin, acid, and aroma needed for fine cider— are blended to create a traditional hard cider.

Wine writers and chefs have sung the praises of Foggy Ridge ciders. "Barbara Ensrud [a food and wine writer from Durham, North Carolina] says that Sweet Stayman is the best beverage to serve with North Carolina vinegar-based barbecue. Charlie Berg, sommelier at Town House restaurant in Chilhowie, serves Foggy Ridge's First Fruit cider on their famous tasting menu. James Beard award–winning chef John Currence served all three ciders at his family's Thanksgiving last year."

Flynt says most restaurant and retail customers in the Carolinas consider Foggy Ridge a local product; the cidery is closer to Charleston, South Carolina, than it is to many markets in eastern and northern Virginia. "Cider has an interesting history and one that we've high-lighted, especially in First Fruit, which uses apple varieties grown by Thomas Jefferson. I love the stories surrounding uncommon apples, and I founded a volunteer group to preserve both stories and apples, called Apple Corps."

From Foggy Ridge Cider it's a short distance to another Virginia winery specializing in quality non-grape products: **Blacksnake Meadery**, making a range of dry to sweet meads, or honey wines. After leaving Foggy Ridge, continue north on Rt. 656 (Pineview Rd.); at the intersection with Rt. 628 (Buffalo Rd.), turn left. In about a mile, you'll come to the meadery, on the right.

Blacksnake makes a variety of traditional meads as well as a few innovations of their own: Cyser is a blend of pressed apple cider and honey, and they feature two kinds; Melomel is fruit-flavored mead, and they plan to produce one using cranberries as well as wild black raspberries and wild wineberries (a member of the raspberry genus common in the area).

Blacksnake Meadery's take on popular pumpkin ale is Squashed, featuring wildflower honey, butternut squash, and "pumpkin pie" spices.

Hydromels are lighter, lower-alcohol meads. Blacksnake's versions are carbonated, and they call them Bee Brews; one is flavored with hops, another with lime.

Connoisseurs may scoff at non-grape beverages, but in high-elevation sites, where viticulture isn't sustainable, ciders, fruit wines, and meads offer a very local product from high-quality, low-carbon-footprint ingredients that provide a welcome change from the mass-market industrial wines with cute colorful critter labels that crowd grocery-store shelves, usually imported from a great distance at considerable environmental cost.

Leaving the meadery, turn right and continue west on Buffalo Rd. to Rt. 638 (Dugspur Rd.), where you turn right and head north. When Dugspur Rd. merges into Rt. 221, merge left and head west for about ten miles, until you meet I-77; take it heading north. After crossing the

New River (one of the oldest rivers in North America), take the next exit, onto Rt. 52 (Fort Chiswell Rd.) heading northwest for approximately three miles. About a mile past New River General Store, on your right, is the entrance to **West Wind Farm Vineyard and Winery**, a fourth-generation homestead focused on making small-batch, hand-crafted Virginia wine. They make just 1,500 cases currently, with plans for slow expansion.

Though located in a cool part of the state, West Wind's vineyard site has a southern exposure, steady breezes, and well-drained soil with plenty of shale and rock throughout. The winery is located on a farm that's been in owner and winemaker David Manley's family since 1914. They had followed the wine industry in Virginia and surrounding states for a number of years, and it seemed like a business that would fit their various strengths (growing, retail, etc.). Vines were first planted in 2003, with the first harvest in 2005.

"Our interest in Virginia wine and doing a project together coincided with the farm becoming available," says Manley. "Frankly, seeing the farm sold off, chopped up, and/or developed wasn't anything we could stomach." His brother Jason came on board before they opened, and it's been a family-run enterprise since the outset. "We certainly embrace our history on this site, being the fourth generation here operating it as an agricultural pursuit. We also, however, take quality most seriously. We don't cut corners in terms of our fruit, winemaking, presentation, and the experience as a whole. It's authentic without the pretense."

Due to their location near two major interstate highways, most of West Wind's tasting-room customers are traveling through the region from Ohio, Pennsylvania, Florida, and neighboring states. "We do have loyal local followers, but their numbers are dwarfed by the visitors."

People feel comfortable at West Wind, whether they are new to wine or experienced wine aficionados, says Manley. "Our tasting-room experience invites people to savor the wine. There's nothing worse than feeling like you're imposing on the winery by being there tasting their wine. We want people to sit and savor a glass, take in the scenery and the quiet. Linger."

West Wind's tasting-room design fits the packaging design and wine style, which Manley describes as "comfortably elegant. . . We wanted our tasting room to be open, airy, and full of natural light. We are surrounded by beautiful countryside, so why not show it off?" Accordingly, they filled the walls with windows and added a clerestory on top. Passive heating is a plus during the winter, too.

Manley feels that Virginia has had difficulty persuading the public at large that their reds can compete. "We prefer to think they can make their own way on their own merits. Our reds, like cabernet sauvignon, and our blends [Heritage Reserve and Galena Creek Red] make me proud, because they are great East Coast reds. They're not—nor will they ever be—California reds, and it's part of our mission as an industry to educate the wine-drinking public accordingly."

He notes that their Alsace-style pinot gris was what really helped build their reputation locally for enjoyable, drinkable, approachable wine, although West Wind's cabernet sauvignon and the Heritage Reserve have won the most awards over the five years they've been entering competitions. The Galena Creek White is vidal blanc, partially barrel-fermented, and drinks with vinifera-like elegance. West Wind has struck a good balance between dry and sweet wines.

"Early on we decided that we were not going to ignore the market or try to change it by only making certain things. While we generally like dry wines more than sweet, the public was asking for certain things (including a sweet red). Instead of eliminating a certain portion of the public from being customers, why not cater to them? Less than one-third of our offerings are sweet, but they appeal to a large portion of the folks who visit our tasting room. We choose not to ignore the wine drinkers who want something sweeter, and they appreciate it and keep coming back."

Virginia has so much going for it in terms of boosting the wine industry, says Manley, such as its central location on the East Coast, the moderate climate, interest in the state's history, and support from the Commonwealth of Virginia and those in the tourism industry. "Our press has been great, but underneath it all, if we had lots of terrible wine being produced, none of this would be happening. It's a testament to the increased professionalism of our industry most of all. Not compromising quality for quantity is key to maintaining this trajectory."

Leaving West Wind, turn right and continue north on Rt. 52 until you see signs for I-81 north/I-77 south; get on the interstate toward Roanoke and Blacksburg. After crossing into Montgomery County, take Exit 109 south (Rt. 600/Tyler Rd.). In the town of Childress, turn right on Rt. 63 (Childress Rd.); you'll come to **Attimo Winery** in about a mile.

Attimo is a husband-wife collaboration. Rik and Melissa Obiso are originally from Sussex County, New Jersey, although Rik's family has winemaking roots in Sicily (*attimo* means "in the moment" in Italian), and both Rik and Melissa attended Virginia Tech in nearby Blacksburg. Little over a decade after marrying and leaving "Hokie Land," they were drawn back to the Blue Ridge Highlands, away from corporate America, to find a wholesome environment to raise a family.

Attimo is one of Virginia's newest wineries; the vines were planted in 2010 and the tasting room opened in July 2011. Wines range from dry varietals to semidry and sweeter blends, all with proprietary names. The labels are very visually evocative, combining photography with a conceptual name such as I Do (a semisweet blend of traminette and petit manseng). Other whites include a vidal blanc, a chardonnay, and a cabernet franc rosé. Reds include cabernet sauvignon, cabernet franc, and chambourcin. Sweeter wines are an apple and white-wine blend, and a raspberry and red-wine blend.

Returning to I-81, continue north. You can stop in Roanoke or Blacksburg for refreshment or lodging before continuing the tour. After crossing Rt. 43, you'll enter the Shenandoah Valley AVA.

The Shenandoah Valley

The Shenandoah Valley AVA may sound vaguely familiar to California wine drinkers; in fact, there is an AVA by that name in California as well. The Virginia AVA encompasses the watershed of the north and south forks of the Shenandoah River and their tributaries, as well as a section in the higher southern end that is classified as "Shenandoah Valley geologic." To the north it extends into the West Virginia panhandle, where the river joins the Potomac, and is bounded by the Allegheny and Appalachian mountains to the west and the Blue Ridge Mountains to the east.

Registered as an AVA in 1982, Virginia's Shenandoah Valley region is cooler and drier than the Piedmont because the Blue Ridge Mountains hold the more humid maritime air on the eastern side. Lower humidity helps keep fungal diseases down (rot-prone riesling, pinot noir, and grenache are all grown commercially in the valley), but the cooler mesoclimates mean occasional frosts and low winter temperatures, making site selection extremely important. Wines from the Valley are often brighter, with higher acidity, than those east of the Blue Ridge. The soils have a higher average pH than those of the Piedmont and are limestone dominated; two Virginia chardonnays from the same vintage, made by the same winemaker with the same yeasts, from fruit grown in the Piedmont and in the valley, will taste completely different. Today, the many limestone caves formed by the dissolving of limestone-based rock by rainwater over millennia attract thousands of visitors to the area. Luray Caverns are the largest.

The first Europeans to settle the Shenandoah Valley were predominantly Germans and Scots-Irish moving south from Pennsylvania.

The Frontier Culture Museum in Staunton demonstrates the different styles in which the European ethnicities built their houses when they settled the land and, like Colonial Williamsburg, it has period-dressed people performing tasks as frontier settlers would have done.

The Civil War had a major impact on the valley. Being protected by the Blue Ridge Mountains to the east, it offered a land full of prosperous farms to supply Confederate forces. In 1864, Union army leaders decided scorched-earth tactics would be applied strategically to help bring the Confederacy to its knees and the war to an end; the Shenandoah Valley was one of the targets.

General Grant finally found the nemesis of the valley in General Philip Sheridan. Although Confederate general Jubal Early caught two-thirds of Sheridan's troops by surprise at the Battle of Cedar Creek, Sheridan personally stood in the way of his retreating troops and by rallying them turned the tide of battle. Early was thereafter on the defensive, and the farms of the valley were torched to deprive the Confederates of badly needed provisions. Official Civil War records kept by Cornell University list the casualties of Sheridan's terrible damage to the valley as two thousand barns filled with grain and implements, seventy mills filled with wheat and flour, and "numerous head of livestock."

Frederick County around the city of Winchester was the site of seven major battles during the Civil War; the city was said to have changed hands over seventy times during the war (thirteen in one day) and was occupied by Union forces for five multimonth periods between 1862 and 1865. Today, Winchester is a happier place, and the center of Virginia's commercial apple industry; an annual Apple Blossom Festival is held in the spring. Winchester is also the where country-and-western singer Patsy Cline lived as a teenager.

Reaching Exit 205 on I-81 north at Raphine, take Rt. 606 one mile west and look for **Rockbridge Vineyard** on the right. Owned by Shepherd "Shep" Rouse and Jane Millott-Rouse, Rockbridge Vineyard is one of the oldest wineries in the valley, and Shep is one of the most respected and experienced winemakers in the state. He was previously the winemaker at Montdomaine Cellars and has consulted for other wineries. Originally from Williamsburg, Shep studied winemaking at the Geisenheim Institute in Germany, then moved to California and earned a master's degree in enology from UC Davis. In California, he made wine in the late 1970s at Carneros Creek, Schramsberg, and Chateau St. Jean wineries.

Shep purchased his farm in 1988 and planted five acres of vines. Now Rockbridge Vineyard offers a wide range of wines from vinifera, hybrid, and native varieties, and anyone who drinks wine will find a well-made product to enjoy here. The norton is one of the state's best and is priced to match top nortons at around $20, but all the wines are good quality and value for the money. In October 2011, a 2005 vintage touriga naçional, mature and wonderfully varietal in character, was being sold for $15, while the fun, sweet, concord-based Jeremiah's is popular with locals. A top-tier line called DeChiel—a family name—is used for the best vinifera labels and a Meritage, but the regular-label vinifera varietals are also consistently fine. Thanks to its valley location, the wines have excellent fruit-acid balance. Dechiel label standouts include reserve chardonnay, riesling, merlot, cabernet franc, meritage, and varietal touriga naçional.

Return to Interstate I-81 and drive north. When I-64 branches off I-81, take I-64 east toward Richmond/Charlottesville and leave by Exit 91 on Rt. 285 north, toward Fishersville. When you meet Rt. 250, turn left through Fishersville and after nearly a mile, just after the Food Lion, turn right on state Rt. 642 (Barren Ridge Rd.). Watch for **Barren Ridge Vineyards** after 1.5 miles on the left.

Barren Ridge is a fairly new boutique Virginia winery. Even though it doesn't have a mountaintop location, its modest elevation on a ridge affords impressive views to the east and west through the valley.

John and Shelby Higgs are the proprietors, and John is another valley winery owner whose property has been in the family; he lived here for a time when he was young, when it was his father's apple orchard. John became a chemical engineer and worked for Philip Morris as a plant manager in Richmond. He was assigned to Turkey and then western Europe, where the Higgses lived in the vineyards in Switzerland for five years. "We fell in love with the place and the wine culture that exists over there," says John. "We retired in Europe and finally made our way back to Richmond to our old home.

"Somewhere I got the brilliant idea that we could bring some of the best of Switzerland to the Shenandoah Valley and reclaim the family farmland and old apple-packing shed."

John notes that the climate in the Shenandoah Valley is semi-arid—due to its being sandwiched between the Allegheny and Blue Ridge mountains, which are only twenty miles apart—and has one of the most diverse ecological systems on earth. He says it's "one of the only places where the four f's—food, fuel, fiber, and feed—can be grown successfully in the same area."

As with other Shenandoah Valley wineries, the wines of Barren Ridge are noteworthy for freshness, delicacy, and finesse. One of the unique wines of Barren Ridge is their Harmony, a proprietary blend of chardonnay and aromatic varieties; the wine is delicately fruity but fresh. The label, featuring two amorous Canada geese in the snow, was designed by local celebrity artist P. Buckley Moss. Barren Ridge is the only winery she has designed labels for.

"Our winemaking philosophy is to let the terroir dictate the wine," says John. "Our goal is to produce wines that are pure and pristine in their ability to express our unique agricultural character. I would hope that sometime in the future there will be a style of wine called Shenandoah Valley."

He notes that there is a general interest across the United States in wines from the various regions. "Virginia wines are a great contrast to the wines the US has become accustomed to from California. Virginia wines tend to be more refined and delicate (that is, our best wines) and resemble more the traditional wines of Europe rather than the overripe and rich fruit bombs now coming from California. If I had to characterize the comments from our customers, it is that our wines have a sense of purity."

John likes the agricultural nature of the business but feels the winery could make a deeper contribution. "Our concept is that Barren Ridge should be a place where people can come to be transported in mind and body. We would like our quaint little winery to be a refuge from this world. We want people to breathe a sigh of relief by the time they are eight feet inside our door." He points out that there are no trinkets sold in the tasting room. "We are unabashedly and enthusiastically a part of the agritourism industry. This passion for the land and the fruits of this land is our mission, and we want to inspire as much of the general public with this love as we can. We believe that the more people have a physical and emotional connection to the land, the more well-rounded and fulfilled they will be. There is no better place to do that than in a vineyard."

Returning to Rt. 250, turn right instead of left and continue into Staunton (birthplace of President Woodrow Wilson), following signs for the Wharf District downtown to 44 Middlebrook Ave. John and Susan Kiers grew and sold quality wine grapes for twelve years before opening **Ox-Eye Vineyards** in 2010. Part of the operation is the tasting room in the Wharf District. They grow a range of cool-climate vinifera varieties including chardonnay, riesling, gewürztraminer, pinot noir, and cabernet franc, as well as the Cornell hybrid traminette. A specialty is lemberger, aka blaufränkisch, a red variety from Austria. Virginia wine industry veteran Brad McCarthy is the consulting winemaker; Kiers is both grower and winemaker. The wines are freshly cool-climate with bright fruit and minerality.

Leaving Staunton, follow signs to I-81 north and continue toward Harrisonburg, taking Exit 235 and Rt. 256 toward Weyers Cave. After about a mile, turn left on Rt. 276 (Keezletown Rd.) and continue for four miles until you reach Rt. 668 (Timber Ridge Rd.), in the hamlet of Cross Keys. Turn right and watch for the winery entrance on the left.

CrossKeys Vineyards has one of the most striking vistas in the state, which is saying a lot. The winery is sited on a plateau and is reminiscent of the Tuscan-style villas seen in California's North Coast counties. In the background, Massanutten Mountain rises dramatically, while to the east and west the Blue Ridge and Allegheny mountains frame the picture memorably. The vineyards were first planted in 2002, and the winery opened in 2008, winning acclaim for its estate-grown cabernet franc with a double gold medal in a national wine competition.

The vineyard has a sandy loam soil with shale that is well drained, and there are nice breezes over the property that dry off the vines. Occasionally they do get spring frosts, so they invested in frost machines to protect the planted acres.

Stephan Heyns, a South African with experience at the now-closed **Oakencroft Vineyard**, is the winemaker. "I like the fruit to express itself with as little interference as possible," he says. "In Virginia, the weather plays a big role in the ripening of fruit, and I try to change my style based on the growing season as well as the grape variety. Ideally, you want to have mature fruit when making wine, but if you have a frost or a rainy season, you need to be able to have a flexible style to make the best wine you can."

From CrossKeys Vineyard, return to Rt. 276 (Cross Keys Rd.) and turn right instead of left. Continue until the road intersects Rt. 33. You now have two routes to choose from: an eastern route between the Massanutten Mountain and the Blue Ridge, and a western route between Massanutten Mountain and the Alleghenies. For the eastern route, you will turn right on Rt. 33, then exit in Elkton for Rt. 340 north (more details to follow). For the moment, we'll focus on the western route, so turn left on Rt. 33, then take I-81 north to Exit 273 in Mt. Jackson. Turn left on Mt. Jackson Rd., then right on Rt. 614 (S. Middle Rd.), and left after less than a mile onto Rt. 703. The road zigzags for three miles to **Cave Ridge Vineyard**.

On the lower slopes of the Allegheny Mountains, on the western side of the valley, Cave Ridge is a welcome escape, especially on a hot summer day. The vineyards are meticulously maintained, and the wines are fresh, bright, and refreshing. Owner and winemaker Randy Phillips considers himself a winegrower, and his attention to vineyard management shows in the wines. Whites include a traminette, a riesling, regular and barrel-aged viognier, and a rosé. Reds include chambourcin, cabernet franc, a varietal syrah, and a reserve red called Fossil Hill Reserve (a cabernet franc–based Meritage blend).

Leaving Cave Spring, head southeast on Rt. 703 (Conicville Rd.) and take the first left onto Rt. 703 (Land Grant Rd.). Shortly after, take the first right onto Rt. 706 (Garlic Hollow Rd.). Proceed for 1.7 miles, turning left onto Rt. 707 (Headquarters Rd.) for 0.3 miles, then take the first right onto Rt. 706 (Stout Rd.). **Wolf Gap Vineyard and Winery** is at 123 Stout Rd.

Founded in 2004 by Willard and Diane Elledge, Wolf Gap is a fifty-acre estate. Reds dominate the product line, with varietal chambourcin, cabernet franc, cabernet sauvignon, and merlot; specialties are a fifty-fifty blend of traminette and viognier, a Mariage ("blend") of chambourcin and cabernet franc, and Chamerlot Reserve, a chambourcin-merlot blend. Reserve labels of cabernet franc and Mariage are also offered, along with blueberry wine and a semisweet rosé called Lobo Loco. Wolf Gap has won several awards in recent Governor's Cup competitions. The simple yet elegant patio can seat one hundred and fifty, and the winery hosts various events, including weddings.

To get to **Shenandoah Vineyards**, start out going northwest on Stout Rd., then turn left onto Headquarters Rd. In just under 2.5 miles, turn left onto S. Middle Rd., then almost three miles later turn left again, onto the Old Valley Pike/US 11. Follow US 11 for 1.7 miles to Edinburg, where you turn left onto Rt. 185 (Stoney Creek Blvd.). Take the first right after I-81 onto Rt. 686 (S. Ox Rd.), and go 1.5 miles.

Shenandoah Vineyards is the oldest vineyard and winery operating in the region and the third oldest in the state, having been founded in 1976 by Emma Randel. The winery/tasting room is located in a Civil War–era barn. Whites include chardonnay, riesling, and sauvignon blanc, but reds are the winery's strong suit. (Founder's Reserve Chardonnay is also consistently good.) Their specialty is Founder's Reserve Chambourcin, which is more full-bodied than most examples of the variety, benefiting from the addition of already-pressed cabernet sauvignon grape skins to the fermenting must for structure, color, and mid-palate tannin. Other reds include cabernet sauvignon and cabernet franc, several proprietary semisweet and sweet red blends, and a raspberry wine.

Next, continue north/east on Rt. 686 (S. Ox Rd.) for almost two miles, and turn right at Rt. 605 (Hoover Rd.). Half a mile later, turn left onto US 11 north (S. Main St.) and continue for five miles, then turn left onto Rt. 600 (Saumsville Rd.) for 1.3 miles. Turn right onto Rt. 642 (Swartz Rd.), and **North Mountain Vineyard and Winery** will be on the right.

The vineyard was planted in 1982, but some years ago the winery was sold. Now under new management, it has made significant strides. The winery makes a standard range of varietal reds and whites (chardonnay, riesling, vidal blanc, cabernet franc), a "claret" red Bordeaux blend, and a reserve cabernet franc, but its specialty is chambourcin—bright, zesty cherry fruit with some dimension and depth, and a consistent medal-winner. A chambourcin-based port (Mountain Midnight) is made in limited amounts and has also won an impressive number of medals.

Leaving North Mountain, turn right on Rt. 642/Swartz Rd., then right on state Rt. 655, then left on Rt. 642 again until you reach state Rt. 651; turn right and you'll intersect I-81 at Exit 291; turn left and resume your travels north. Soon the Massanutten Mountain will end abruptly and I-66 will join I-81. Continue north to Winchester, where you can linger and visit or get a bite to eat before taking Rt. 7 east. As you approach the Blue Ridge Mountains, you'll come to the last winery on this travelogue—**Veramar Vineyard**.

Founded in 2000, Veramar Vineyard is owned by James and Della Bogaty; son Justin is the winemaker and their two daughters, Tiffany and Ashley, also work in the business. The Bogaty family hails from the Italian Alps, where even today members of the family own and operate a small vineyard.

"Veramar Vineyard places great emphasis on its wines being superb and integral complements to food and the dining table in general," says James. He describes the style of their red wines as "fruity, beautiful bouquet, complex, dominated by black fruit. Luscious and velvety in-mouth feel. Long lingering finish." My impression was of reds with typical varietal character, but with both a freshness and depth of flavor that was consistent and appealing. While Veramar proudly declares itself to be "all about Old World style," the wines are also fresh, clean, and fruit-forward—the best of both worlds.

Veramar's 2008 norton won the "Best of Class" award in the 2011 New World International Wine Competition, where the wine stood out from the others as being elegant and balanced, with purity of fruit. I asked James if the wine had been blended with vinifera reds for more structure and balance; he said it was 100 percent norton and 100 percent estate fruit. Production is limited to between fifty and one hundred cases a year, and although the price is $50 a bottle (possibly the most expensive norton in the world), and sales are restricted to wine club members only, James says the wine sells out every year.

We can now explore the eastern route of the northern Shenandoah Valley. Returning to Rt. 33 after visiting CrossKeys Vineyard, take Rt. 33 east to Elkton, then exit to Rt. 340 north. This slow drive through the Page Valley will take you through towns such as Shenandoah, and you'll feel you've traveled back in time at least forty years. Watch for the main (express) Rt. 340 diverging from business Rt. 340 and take the latter toward Luray, turning right. When you come to the town of Stanley, Rt. 340 will fork to the left; take the right fork, Rt. 689 (Chapel Rd./Marksville Rd.). In half a mile, watch for the grape cluster sign and turn right at 1126 Marksville Rd.

Wisteria Farm and Vineyard is a very small, very inviting winery that still seems authentic and charming without being cutesy or inappropriately commercial. At the same time, it is a working farm with a flock of natural-colored Romney sheep as well as free-roaming chickens. In addition to their wines, they also sell wool products from their flock, including yarn and blankets. True to the winery's namesake, there are chairs and tables outside the tasting room under a trellis covered with wisteria vines.

The product line is weighted toward white wines, with both an oak- and steel-fermented chardonnay, pinot gris, seyval blanc, traminette, viognier, and late-harvest vidal blanc (Sweet Daisy), but I found the reds the most memorable. The merlot is richly fruity, with depth and complexity, and the norton is made in the same style. One added benefit at Wisteria is the option of ordering Mediterranean tapas to enjoy with the wine tasting.

Leaving Wisteria, return to Rt. 340 business north by turning left on Rt. 689, then in 0.4 miles turn right on Hawksbill Rd., which will merge with Rt. 340. Continue to the town of Luray, where the region's largest limestone caverns are a worthwhile diversion, especially in July or August. Continue north on Rt. 340 until you reach Rt. 649 at the traffic light; turn right and go five miles to the entrance of **Glen Manor Vineyards**, on the left [no large groups].

Glen Manor is owned and operated by Jeff White, who apprenticed with Jim Law at Linden Vineyards and whose sauvignon blanc grapes appeared for many years in Linden's vineyard-designate labels. The Glen Manor estate is 212 acres, of which 14.5 are planted to vineyards, and is recognized by Virginia as a Century Farm (owned and farmed by four generations of the same family for over a century). The estate is on the western flank of the Blue Ridge Mountains, five miles south of the entrance to the Skyline Drive, and features deep, well-drained soils. The first six acres of vines were planted in 1995 to sauvignon blanc, cabernet sauvignon, merlot, cabernet franc, and petit verdot. In 2006 and 2009, the vineyard was expanded in newly cleared areas at over one thousand feet in elevation and planted to the red Bordeaux varieties and petit manseng. The signature wines are sauvignon blanc and cabernet franc, both in very fresh, assertively varietal styles. White also grows merlot, cabernet sauvignon, and petit verdot, which are featured in two cabernet sauvignon–dominated blends: Hodder Hill (single vineyard) and Vin Rouge (also single vineyard but not labeled as such).

Returning to Rt. 340 north by Rt. 649, continue into Front Royal, where the entrance to the Skyline Drive will be on the right. Follow Rt. 340 by turning left. Proceeding through town, stay in the right lane to make a series of right-hand turns as you follow signs for I-66. After crossing the Shenandoah River, continue straight under I-66 on Rt. 340 until you reach Rt. 277; turn right on Rt. 340, crossing Rt. 50 and going through Boyce, until you meet Rt. 7 in Berryville. Turn right on Rt. 7 and continue out of Berryville. In a couple of miles, turn right onto Quarry Rd. Veramar Vineyard will be on the left.

Though we've reached the end of our journey, for the moment, you might want to continue east on Rt. 7 into Bluemont and beyond into Loudoun County to visit wineries not already mentioned.

RICHMOND ROOTS
FOR THE HOME TEAM

One of the reasons for the impressive growth of the Virginia wine industry and its reputation for fine wine quality is the support of state government in Richmond, as many industry members have pointed out. The Virginia Farm Winery Acts of the 1980s provided the model and funding mechanism, and former governor Mark Warner (a current US senator for Virginia) owns an operating vineyard and has described himself as a "proud supporter" of the industry. The current governor, Robert McDonnell, and First Lady Maureen McDonnell, however, have been equally ardent supporters of the Virginia wine industry, which is one of Virginia's most profitable sectors of agriculture. With the explosion of wineries has come a rise in winery tourism, bringing visitors who have a very positive impact on the rural economy.

At a seminar at the national Wine Bloggers Conference, held in 2011 in Charlottesville, Dave McIntyre, blogger and wine columnist for the *Washington Post*, pointed to the importance of state government providing funding for both marketing and research. "Thirty years ago people were talking about the winemaking potential of Maryland.

Today Virginia has two hundred wineries while Maryland has fifty, and Virginia now has an established wine reputation."

Annette Boyd, who heads the Virginia Wine Board Marketing Office (and has been involved in Virginia wine marketing for some twenty years), points out that "for every dollar that Virginia spends to attract visitors to attractions and wineries, the state received approximately five dollars back in tax revenues, and they see this return within ninety days of when the money is spent." In addition, dollars spent by visitors in wine country produce a similar "multiplier effect" in the local economy, and not just at wineries, but at restaurants, lodging establishments, and other traveler-oriented businesses.

The Virginia Wine Board Marketing Office's largest program is the October Virginia Wine Month. In 2010, over three hundred trade partners signed up, says Boyd. She also convinced industry leaders to successfully bid to host the 2011 Wine Bloggers Conference in Charlottesville, the first time the event has been held on the East Coast.

Many industry observers say that this is a golden time for the Virginia wine industry, and much of the credit is given to Drs. Bruce Zoecklein and Tony Wolf for their research and extension work, as well as Governor McDonnell and his wife, Secretary of Agriculture and Forestry Todd Haymore, and Annette Boyd.

When he ran for governor in 2009, McDonnell included campaign stops in wineries and farms across the commonwealth, and made the promotion of Virginia wine a signature piece of his "Jobs and Opportunities" agenda. In May 2010, Governor McDonnell traveled to the United Kingdom with Secretary Haymore, in conjuction with the London International Wine and Spirits Fair, to help promote Virginia wines there. Whole Foods now has a specific Virginia wines section at its four-story Kensingston High Street location.

In June 2011, McDonnell signed SB237/HB588, the Wine Promotion Fund, which requires the portion of the wine liter tax collected from the sale of wine produced by farm wineries to be deposited in a Virginia Wine Promotion Fund. This increased annual revenues for these programs from $580,000 per year to $1.35 million, at a time when funding for similar programs in other states was being threatened. In 2011, Virginia opened trade offices in Europe, Asia, and on the Indian subcontinent, further increasing opportunities for the export of Virginia wine.

First Lady Maureen McDonnell has become a visible public supporter of Virginia wine. In April 2010, she launched the First Lady's Initiatives Team Effort ("FLITE"), which will recognize programs, activities, organizations, and individuals embodying the ideal of creating "A Commonwealth of Opportunity" in their communities. One of these initiatives was "A Commonwealth of Opportunity for Economic Development, with a specific focus on the Virginia Wine, Film, and Tourism Industries."

Mrs. McDonnell points out that she and the governor support all Virginia agricultural products and are serving a great diversity of them at the executive mansion for public and private events. "We are particularly fond of Virginia wines since we traveled quite a bit when Governor McDonnell was in the military, stationed in Germany. We visited so many wineries around Europe that when we moved home we continued visiting wineries, only this time in our home state. We love what Virginia wineries are doing, and we are so proud of their great success."

Mrs. McDonnell prefers reds. "I am a big fan of cabernet franc," she says. "And I am really enjoying Virginia petit verdot as well as chambourcin, which is what we planted at the executive mansion. The Governor prefers our white wines, especially the viognier."

In March 2011, Mrs. McDonnell presided over the planting of chambourcin vines in the garden at the executive mansion in Richmond. "I wanted to celebrate the original 'Acte 12 of 1619' that required all men over the age of eighteen to plant ten vines each. When I started talking to wineries about the concept, I received an enthusiastic response. Many winery representatives have offered to help me plant, prune, and tend to the vines. It's been a very fun project, and I look forward to being able to harvest some fruit for wine in a year or two, in time for the two hundredth anniversary of the executive mansion."

Secretary of Agriculture and Forestry Todd Haymore—a tall, thin, friendly man with short, sandy hair—grew up on a tobacco farm. He explains that he didn't follow the Virginia wine industry until former governor Tim Kaine asked him to be commissioner of Virginia's Department of Agriculture and Consumer Services, and Haymore started meeting the leadership of the state wine industry and learned a lot about it from them. He told them that he had an MBA but didn't need it to see the industry's potential for growth. Shortly afterward—in 2007—he decided he would focus more on the wine industry. "I felt it was on the cusp of something great, and I thought state government could help be a catalyst for that."

Aside from being beneficial to other farms, he sees the Virginia grape and wine industry as helping preserve farmland and stimulating tourism, especially in rural areas. "Staycations are great for wineries," says Haymore. "You can get away but support the rural economies. The wineries are catalysts for growth, but also generate hospitality and tourism revenues; I see that for the future even more than today."

Secretary Haymore points out that even as a candidate, Governor McDonnell talked about agriculture—and especially the wine industry—being part of his economic development plan. "When the governor asked me to be his agriculture secretary, we started talking about priorities. And not just him, but the first lady as well. Soon after he was elected in 2009, all three of us decided that the wine industry would be a showpiece for Virginia agriculture. It has a ripple effect in the local economy: In the last two weeks, I've fielded calls from wineries looking for local farm products to serve at their wineries; we have directed them to Virginia farms and agribusinesses. Virginia wineries want to buy local and support their farm neighbors."

"Will we be the next California on the global wine scene?" asks Haymore. "Probably not; there's a huge difference in scale. But Virginia still has the opportunity to be a player on the national and international scene. The Governor said from the start that he wanted Virginia to be known as the East Coast center for wine and wine tourism." He points out that two-thirds of the US population is within a half day's drive of Virginia. "We also have all our history to amplify the appeal of Virginia as a destination. This can also impact overseas wine sales. The state of Virginia is a known entity outside the country; it's seen as the entry state to America because of our history—many foreigners know their American history from founders like Washington and Jefferson."

VIRGINIA WOMEN
OF THE VINE

The irony has often been noted that women buy most of the wine in the world, but the industry is largely run by men, much as women buy most of the food, yet until very recently celebrity chefs have been mostly men. Even more ironic is that women are more sensitive to aromas than men, which should make them natural sommeliers and winemakers.

While the wine industry's many facets, from vineyard to trade sales, remain largely in male hands, that is changing, and this is as true in Virginia as anywhere. This chapter looks at several successful women in the Virginia wine industry and shows that, despite a lopsided gender balance, women can and do make valuable contributions to it.

Lucie Morton: Viticulturist and Consultant

Lucie Morton is a Virginia native with an international reputation as a viticulturist, vineyard consultant, and researcher. Recently relocated to Charlottesville from Broad Run, Virginia, she has worked in

Virginia viticulture for the last forty years and has made a strong professional contribution not only to Virginia but to vineyards and wineries across the country. She is trained in ampelography (the science of visually identifying grape varieties by the characteristics of their leaves), and studied under the French authority Pierre Galet, with whom she wrote: *A Practical Ampelography: Grapevine Identification* along with Leon Adams.

Morton also authored *Winegrowing in Eastern America: An Illustrated Guide to Viniculture East of the Rockies*, has served on various Virginia agricultural and viticulture-related boards and committees since 1977, was a founding member of the International Council on Grapevine Trunk Diseases, was recognized by the American Wine Society with a National Award of Merit in 1994, and was declared Virginia Wine Industry Person of the Year in 1999. As if all this weren't enough, she was largely responsible for discovering a new fungal species, *Phaeoacremonium mortoniae*.

Morton has a straightforward, no-nonsense look (she also drives a Dodge Ram with the license plate "VITIRAM") but she can be fun-loving and is often frank and spontaneous in her assessment of wine quality.

She grew up on a farm on the Potomac River in King George County, and graduated from the University of Pennsylvania in 1972 with a degree in history. When I asked her how she became a viticulturist, the answer lasted about an hour and a half, and traced one of the most fascinating professional journeys I've ever heard. As with so many others with lives in the grape and wine industry, it all started with the question of what to do with the family farm. In the summer of 1972, her father asked her to look into the idea of planting wine grapes there. "He loved French wine"—her family has Huguenot heritage from the Bordeaux region—"and thought if they could grow grapes in the Gironde [Bordeaux], we could grow grapes along the Potomac." She points out that back then there were only fifty acres of concord grapes in the state; the large gallonage attributed to Virginia wine production belonged to then–Canandaigua Wine Company's Richard's Wild Irish Rose.

What sparked her father's interest, she explains, was hearing that William Schwerin from Alexandria, Kentucky, had written in something such as *Southern States* magazine about growing cabernet sauvignon on French hybrid rootstock in Kentucky and claimed he could get more money for them per acre than for any other crop he could grow in that state. Leon Adams, in his seminal *Wines of America* (1973 edition) confirmed that Schwerwin had sold several crops of cabernet sauvignon; the Ohio River Valley AVA has since emerged as a promising region for that grape. "Never mind that there were no wineries there then, but when Dad saw that, he figured there was a crop he could grow that would give him high value per acre and a farm deduction for some land he'd recently inherited: a hundred and thirty acres of woods, with thirty acres of open land sloping down to the Potomac on Rt. 118."

The other big influence for Morton's father was Philip Wagner, the Maryland-based champion of French hybrid grapes for eastern North America. Her father had given a copy of the first edition of Wagner's *American Wines and How to Make Them* ("the first practical American wine book after Prohibition was lifted") to his mother for Christmas in 1933, and she had planted concord grapes on an arbor on the farm. Forty years later, Morton and her dad went to visit Philip Wagner, and he autographed the book for them; Morton shows me the book with both her father's dedication and Wagner's signature.

After reviewing the land, Morton explains, they decided they really had only five acres where they could actually grow grapes. Since Philip Wagner was sold out of vines, she bought nine varieties of French hybrids from **Wiederkehr Wine Cellars**, in Arkansas: aurora, cascade, chambourcin, chancellor, baco noir, villard noir, villard blanc, chelois, and vidal blanc. "I planted them with a post-hole digger, an end-digger on a tractor my grandfather bought used in 1948, a brush hog, and a green hoe. I planted the vineyard knowing nothing, just being part of a merry band of industry amateurs. After I planted it, I told my father that nobody knew what they were doing, that everyone was getting their information from UC Davis or New York and didn't know whether hybrids or vinifera were the right choice in Virginia."

Morton had a deal with her father that if she acted as farm manager for a year, he would pay for the graduate school of her choice. She decided to go to Montpellier, in France (after UC Davis had insisted that, as a history major, she needed two years of prerequisites before getting into their viticulture program). Montpellier said she could come as an auditor, and if she could pass a faculty review board afterward, she could be accepted on the international program. This was a bigger deal than she realized; the audit was for a two-month crash course designed for final-year students about to get their agricultural engineering degrees.

She knew she had to improve her French, so she decided to work the harvest in Bordeaux to get fluent. One of her neighbors was good friends with Lilianede Rothschild, which got her an invitation to pick grapes at Château Lafite Rothschild for ten days. Her luck continued: The manager there, André Portet, called Montpellier and arranged to find her a room and get her student meal tickets. Another break was that they let her work the harvest just the first half of the day. "They gave me a Mobylette [a pedal-powered moped] and sent me around to visit other Bordeaux properties the second half of the day. I then showed up at Montpellier with no idea what to expect."

Morton explains that the Montpellier viticulture school was founded in 1881 in response to the phylloxera crisis; it was the center of R and D, tasked with coming up with a solution, and had a world-class grape collection that included vine species from all over the world (forty-eight different varieties within the *Vitis riparia* family, for example). They were the leaders in ampelography, and everyone who practices that science still trains in their research vineyard. "I found out that there were seven Frenchmen, one German boy, and me, and then five professors. In my class were people like the heir of the Bouchard family, from Bouchard Père & Fils, in Burgundy, and a few other progeny of prominent vineyard families." What the faculty review board had planned was to have the graduates go to a seven-month international course sponsored by the OIV (International Office of Vines and Wines) funded by the Marshall Plan. Montpellier asked her for only $75 tuition; room was only $30–$50 dollars a week. "I remember thinking, *America contributed to this and I'm benefiting*," she says.

The Montpellier program had not had either an American or a woman enrolled before. "I asked them why and they said, 'If you're working in the fields, you're with Arab immigrants, and it's a tough place to be, physically.' They didn't think a woman would even want to be in a rough physical environment driving tractors." But in her family, the women went to college and that was seen as perfectly normal. "I never felt growing up that there were different expectations for me just because I was a woman; I got along great with my dad and rode horses. At the University of Pennsylvania, I couldn't wait to get back to the farm. College taught me I really liked the country, not the city, or sitting behind a desk."

Morton recalls of her first days at Montpellier, "At first nobody talked to me. This was great; I had nothing to do but study. I looked at every viticulture book they had. I made a vow not to read English except for letters from home." She looked up in her French dictionary every single word she didn't know. "I was learning things in French that I didn't know in English." A couple of weeks into it, she saw that the ampelography course coming up was to be taught by Pierre Galet, the author of the book she was studying as a reference. "I asked him if he was the author of the book and he said, 'Oui, Mademoiselle,' obviously flattered, so I had him autograph the book." Morton explains he was delighted to have an American student, because his thesis was on American vine species.

She mentions some stereotyping she ran into: "They assumed

I wanted the sweet wine on field trips, because it wasn't until 1968 that dry wine overtook sweet wine consumption in America," but she didn't take it too seriously and wasn't sure if it was an American stereotype or sexism. She also says she often was the butt of jokes that the French made. "They'd say, 'Lucie is here to make Coca-Cola from *Vitis labrusca.*' They just couldn't get over how funny they thought that was."

The flip side of sexism was chivalry. "Galet's car was a Citroën, and looked like a phylloxera bug: wide in front and narrow in back. Galet always was gallant and made sure I sat in the front and the big French guys sat in the back crammed in, but I'd rather have been in the back since he drove like a bat out of hell." Also, on field trips the cooperatives took the students out to lunch; she got some very nice meals and was asked to sit at the head table, which forced her to be on her best behavior and maintain focus. "It was a good time to be a woman; the Europeans couldn't have been more polite."

The biggest challenge she faced, aside from speaking and studying in French, was to give a two-hour presentation to the class; she had to deliver the paper and then answer questions. "My presentation was on the American vine species and their crosses. Monsieur Galet came to my rescue. They had a world-class viticulture library where I could view American grape [leaves]. Philip Wagner put me in touch with John McGrew at USDA's research station in Beltsville [Maryland]. He said, 'Don't let them put you down because you're from the eastern US. Tell them that mechanical harvesting is being developed here, and we have more *Vitis* varieties than anywhere else.'"

Finally, the presentation came; she gave a two-hour lecture in French to an all-male, all-French audience. On top of that, "I had to present why American *Vitis* species were important, knowing that the founder of the Institute, Professor Jean Branas, was an anti-hybrid fanatic who helped get them all banned in France." She held her own, answered the questions, and got a passing grade, but nobody told her if she had qualified to be part of the international course. "I was terrified of Branas. Everyone was afraid of him; he was a very strict man," she says. By that time, her brother was living in Rome, and her boyfriend at the time was living in Beirut. "We wanted to meet in Rome, at my brother's house, but I didn't know what was happening after my studies. It all depended on Branas, who had told me at the beginning that I wasn't qualified."

The next-to-last day of class before Christmas break, she mustered the nerve to approach him and asked if she could continue her studies in the international course in Spain in the new year. "He said, 'Mademoiselle Morton, I've been meaning to ask you about your qualifications in natural sciences.' My heart was pounding. I said, 'Monsieur Branas, here's the situation. If I'd known I'd be talking to you here today, I'd have taken plant physiology, plant pathology . . .' I named every single biology course I could think of, but explained I last took biology in high school. Branas said, 'It's true you don't meet our qualifications, and the committee of international qualifications are very strict; I'll have to see if they'll make an exception in your case.' Well, of course, he was the head of the committee, and it was really his decision, but he never got back to me. I finally went up to him at the very end of the last day and asked him if he'd heard from them. He didn't even look at me and said, 'Oui, c'est OK.' The guys [others in the program], who were friends of mine by now, told me he was in earnest. The secretary confirmed it. I asked her how much it would cost, and she said, 'Nothing; you're part of our team now.'"

The coursework of the international studies program was amazing, she recounts. She learned about table grapes in Greece, and in Zaragoza, Spain, she was in a dormitory next to a monastery. "I got to know the professors because they always asked me out to dinner, but they wouldn't ask the guys." They were interested in America, too, and wanted to talk about it. Once, Professor Gärtel, who was head of the OIV and the Berkastel-Kues research station at the time, asked her what she thought about German wines. She said, "I know there are great German wines, but I've never had the chance to taste them." He threw down his card and told her she couldn't leave the program without tasting them and invited her to Germany for a week. "I remember thinking, *Where will I find the money?* People told me, 'You have to do this. Find the money.' So I did. When I got to Germany, one of the professors said they wanted to learn English and asked if I could teach them; it was only after I moved to their house and was sleeping on the couch that I found out that all expenses were paid in the program."

She recalls one professor taking her to an overlook of the Mosel and asking, If she could have a case of wine from any part of the vineyards, which would she choose? "I said, 'Well, that vineyard is wide spaced, probably on 5BB rootstock, with new clones. I'd rather have the closer-spaced older vines on that steep site.' He was very impressed, but the point is that by that time I had begun to view wine quality through the lens of the vineyard."

Morton and her colleagues would go into the vineyard and focus on what was happening empirically, from row and vine spacing to rootstock choices. "Growers would boast about their wines and how they were better than what someone down the road was doing, so we'd taste the wines and then make our own judgments, focusing on their viticultural practices." Meanwhile, at night she was researching her thesis on winegrowing in the eastern United States.

After all this intense coursework in five countries was over, she returned to her vineyard in King George, Virginia. "I didn't presume to know what was the right thing, since there was a lot of New World viticulture happening which I didn't really know, like the debate between hybrids versus vinifera, but at least I had a grasp on what questions to ask."

She had an early interest in ampelography as a practical way to identify incorrect varieties sent by grapevine nurseries, a common problem in those days (which still persists). "With ampelography, I learned that many people didn't know how to do that. Leon Adams [author of *The Wines of America*] said he'd been trying for years to find someone to do an ampelography book in English on American grapes and vines." The result was a three-author collaboration called *A Practical Ampelography*, written in English, by Galet, Morton, and Adams.

"I met all these great people in the American industry, like Hamilton Mowbray [the vinifera pioneer in Maryland] and Leon Adams, and Nelson Shaulis [the Cornell viticulture professor who invented the mechanical grape harvester and the divided grape canopy], because my professors were interested in America," and that was the focus of her thesis. She adds, "I'm still friends with some of my fellow students from 1973. The guys considered me a surrogate sister."

Beginning in the mid-1990s, Morton convinced her eastern clients to switch to closer vine spacing within the row, starting with Jon Wehner at Chatham Vineyards on the Eastern Shore. This has now become common practice. I asked Morton how her view of vine spacing and vineyard establishment had changed over time. "In Europe, where I was trained, there was an obvious association with small vines and better wine. Sites with less fertile soils were preferred, but in areas where summer rain caused the vines to grow beyond the limits of the trellis, training systems such as the lyre, pergola, etc., showed that canopy management on big trellises could yield interesting results. However, the trellises were expensive to install and maintain and difficult to adapt to mechanization. Wines from old vines were also highly valued, and more densely planted vineyards last longer."

Working in California in the 1980s with vineyards transitioning from what had been the standard eight-by-twelve-foot spacing to four-by-six-foot spacing gave her valuable firsthand confirmation that closer spacing could work. "By the time I began working again in the Mid-Atlantic area in the 1990s, it was clear to me that eastern vineyards would benefit from following the European model, if striving for critically acclaimed wines was a serious goal." Morton points out that vigor management is an aspect of sustainability which became a kind of obsession a decade ago ("I called it 'battling the vigor monster'"). When she converted Chatham Vineyards to cane pruning (eliminating the permanent horizontal cordons and replacing them with annual canes growing up from the trunk), "I did not expect the vigor to be any more or less of a problem than it was for other growers in the area. I also did not expect them to get higher yields, because I believe yields need to be controlled for wine quality."

Perhaps Morton's most fascinating professional adventure was discovering the cause of the mysterious "black goo" grapevine trunk disease that began in the early 1990s in California. "People having problems with young vine decline were blaming their choice of rootstock. For me this did not make sense, and I believed it was caused by a fungus related to Esca disease. This turned out to be true. The problem at the time was that the suspected fungus had many names: *Phialophora, Cephalosporium, Acremonium, Phaeoacremonium,* and now *Phaeomoniella.* To solve the mystery, I turned to an international group of scientists who later came together as the International Council on Grapevine Trunk Diseases, now with a website run out of UC Davis. It turned out that what I called black goo, Lionello Petri called Black Vein in 1912, and the disease is now officially called Petri disease. During this foray into the world of mycology, I isolated a fungus from a rootstock in Sonoma County and sent it to Dr. Pedro Crous in the Netherlands. It turned out to be an unnamed species of *Phaeoacremonium,* so he officially named it *Phaeoacremonium mortoniae.* This fungus is not, in fact, the black goo agent; it is a very common wood-rotting organism with microscopic spores that must have blown onto the rootstock at the time of field grafting."

It's quite a professional accomplishment for anyone to have a new species named after them, especially someone without a PhD. "Nothing would please me more than to have the opportunity (aka time) to pursue a PhD. The problem would be to pick which of the many things I'd like to delve into. Probably it would have to do with fungi and biocontols," says Morton.

I asked her what she thought was her most important contribution to eastern viticulture. "I guess my main contribution has been to believe in its promise and to help provide some insight into how people can realize that. The real credit belongs to those who actually tend the vineyards and do a good job overseeing the metamorphosis of their grapes into wine," she concludes.

Christine Iezzi, Regional Sales Manager, the Country Vintner

Another woman with a long professional history in the Virginia wine industry is Christine Iezzi of the Country Vintner, a wholesale distributor of fine wines. Iezzi, an energetic, articulate, and wine-passionate woman who lives south of Charlottesville, was influenced and inspired by Morton's example. Iezzi met Morton in 1977, when she was twelve; her father, Thomas Iezzi, planted a vineyard the next year, also in King George County, and Morton mentored him. They planted ten acres and supplied commercial wineries and home winemakers for many years. Thomas was one of the first grower representatives on the Virginia Winegrowers Advisory Board and was active in the American Wine Society.

Iezzi went with her father to visit the now-defunct Meredyth Vineyards when they were planting their vineyard in 1975. She also gave tours at Ingleside Plantation Vineyards in high school and college, and says, "I didn't realize wine was a 'man's world' until I got farther up, since Lucie was my role model."

Like Morton, Iezzi studied in France, as an exchange student in high school and then for a semester in college. She then took small tour groups through the wine regions. This is how she met Christian Moueix and was able to taste at the first growth châteaus as well as at Château Pétrus.

Iezzi's first job, right out of college, was as a secretary for the Country Vintner, and she has worked at the company a total of fifteen years. Although she's a regional sales manager today, she was formerly in charge of promoting Virginia wine in the company's entire territory, from Delaware through North Carolina, for five years. "Now Virginia wine is so much easier to sell, it doesn't need a dedicated brand manager," she said, laughing. For 2011, the Country Vintner's second-quarter sales figures for all of Virginia except the northern Virginia suburbs showed that among the top twenty on-premise brands, the most popular was White Hall Vineyards, with Jefferson Vineyards at number eighteen. "It's a testament to what we've worked on for so long" to have two Virginia brands in the state's top twenty of total brands, she says proudly.

I ask Iezzi how the status of Virginia wines has changed since she first started representing them. "Holy cow! It's a dramatic change!" she exclaims. "I used to have to force-feed Virginia wine to people. I had to do blind tastings to get people to accept them, but the quality and respect has gone up dramatically. I guarantee my sales reps that if they put Virginia wines on a list, they will get a reorder because of wine quality and consumer demand."

She adds that today there's less complaining about prices and more understanding, "like embracing the locavore idea completely and not forgetting about the wine. When I'm seeing guests at the Homestead [mountain resort] and other major destinations asking for Virginia wine, I feel that's a validation of the industry, so I feel it's my job to help promote them to the restaurants."

She's also very encouraged to see Virginia wines finding a ready market with a new generation. "Younger people are very open-minded for local wines, varieties, and blends, and share them with their friends. Having Gen X and Y be excited about local wines, that's what is making the difference" in the consumer market, she says.

To grow Virginia wine's market share in-state, Iezzi thinks the pressure needs to come from the consumers through the trade, but also feels that a lot of forward movement is hampered by the pricing wineries want, compared to what licensees are willing to pay. "By-the-glass programs really help in restaurants," she says. "Local consumers need to embrace it. Wineries need to target restaurant sales. We as an industry need to find ways of working with the wineries [to increase market share]; it involves everyone—consumers, local shops, and restaurants."

Iezzi explains that markets vary. In Charlottesville, for example, she can easily sell upscale Virginia wines to be poured by the glass in restaurants. "This market will pay the money because they trust that Virginia wine will be worth it, but not so much in other markets."

As the daughter of a longtime grape grower, it's not surprising to hear Iezzi say that understanding and fine-tuning viticulture "will be what makes us world-class," and that the maturing of Virginia's vineyards will help enable that development. She's also very encouraged by industry newcomers. "I love the new energy coming into the business," she says, and adds that, finally, newcomers such as Fox Meadow are buying land specifically for what works best for vineyards, not just planting a vineyard on random property they already own.

Has anyone in the trade had gender-based assumptions about Iezzi's wine qualifications? She stops and ponders the question for a couple of beats before answering. "Probably, at certain times, but once I start tasting and talking about wines, that stops." She thinks she got more negativity in the past, not because she was younger but because society has evolved. "You used to find more sexism in Europe, but once you work in the business, that changes." She points out that many people in the Virginia wine trade don't have world-trained wine palates. "Having that global view helps me identify what's best for my clients."

Another female viticulturist, Jeanette Smith of VineSmith, consulting in Loudoun County, echoes Iezzi's comments. She never really considered this industry to be a man's world: When she first started, Lucie Morton was the only vineyard consultant in Virginia. "Also, one of the first vineyards for which I worked—MJC Vineyards in Blacksburg—was managed by Joan Corr. She had more strength and mechanical ability than most men I know. With these women as role models, I have never felt out of place."

Kirsty Harmon, Winemaker, Blenheim Vineyards

Kirsty Harmon fits in with the straightforward and unpretentious sensibility of Blenheim Vineyards. She seems very natural and comfortable in the winemaker's uniform of jeans and a fleece vest, and whether giving an interview or pulling wine samples from barrels, there's not a hint of the dramatic flair that more theatrical winemakers might display—and she's a winemaker for a rock star. However, she does have a very engaging, playful manner when pouring her wines at public tastings, and a very different look when she (literally) lets her hair down.

Harmon's dark eyes are alert and quick, her even voice suggesting a slight accent (her mother is English), and in conversation she impresses you with a thoughtful but quick intelligence. Although she's a no-nonsense professional with a what-you-see-is-what-you-get deportment, she has a sense of humor that can catch you pleasantly off guard (she does an amazing, deadpan, accent-and-attitude impersonation of a French colleague in the region).

She admits that becoming a professional winemaker was an accidental path, although her professional background—working in yeast genetics—was very helpful when she turned to wine. Her parents were in the military; she grew up abroad and in northern Virginia, and her family settled in Albemarle County when she was thirteen (coincidentally, down the same road as the winery). After attending the University of Virginia, she decided to remain in the area. She started a side business as a wedding planner and worked on the wedding of socialite

Patricia Kluge and William Moses in 2000. Kluge took a liking to her, and as she was planning to open her winery at the time, she asked Harmon to build the facility for her.

Harmon had no real interest or experience in wine, but that changed when Kluge took her for a memorable meal at the famous French Laundry restaurant in Napa, where the wines included a meursault and an iconic Dalla Valle red. "That's when I realized, *oh, this is what it's all about.*"

Harmon readily acknowledges Gabriele Rausse as her winemaking mentor. He was the first person she met when addressing the Kluge winery design project, and he helped her learn the winemaking process when she began as Kluge's winemaker in 2000. "For me it was accidental," she says. "I got to do the work first, then got the love of it afterwards. Most people get the love of wine first."

She then went to work for Rausse at his small winery nearby. "He said, 'This is Virginia and you're a woman, so you should get a degree.'" She got her enology degree at UC Davis in 2005 and performed so well she won two scholarships, which took her to Burgundy and New Zealand for apprenticeships. "For me it was easier than for many of the other students who hadn't had the practical, hands-on experience I'd had with Gabriele. Doing the process backwards was the best method for me."

Dave Matthews's brother Peter is manager of the vineyard and winery estate. "He waved me over when I was walking the [Kluge] vineyard [which abuts the Blenheim property] in 2000; he showed me the winery, then called while I was in France eight years later to offer me the winemaking position. He wanted someone with a local background as well as solid winemaking credentials. He also knew my goal was always to come back and work in Virginia, but I didn't expect it would be on the same road as my family lives on," she said, laughing.

As most other Virginia winemakers do, she names the weather (especially high humidity and rain at harvest) as the biggest challenge.

Others she cites are dealing with vintage variation ("I'm a relatively new winemaker in this state") and trying to find new sources of high-quality grapes. "Some people see it as a negative that we don't grow all our own fruit, but Virginia has a variable climate and soil types; Albemarle County has fine terroir, but why should I only use that and ignore the rest of what the state has to offer?"

To demonstrate, she takes me to the cellar and pulls some wine samples from the just-finished 2010 vintage. The first, a viognier, is bursting with tangerine and apricot fruit, with a luscious viscosity. The fruit is locally grown. The next viognier tastes and feels more like a chardonnay—more green apple fruit, with crisp acidity and a mineral tinge. Same vintage, same grape, different vineyards and locations. Likewise, two samples of syrah from two different sites show differently—one bright and fresh, the other darkly brooding (both impressively elegant).

Harmon says that her signature style is "fruit-forward, approachable wines people can enjoy in their youth [the wine's, that is]. These are dry wines with good acidity, and they're meant to be food friendly, but you can taste that grapes were used to make the wine," she adds, perhaps delivering a subtle criticism of the more oaky, aggressive style that obscures the fruit in some wines. She's also a noninterventionist as much as possible, using just enough potassium metabisulfite for microbial stability and bentonite fining prefermentation, then trying to avoid adding anything else to the wine.

"In most vintages—with 2010 as an exception—we usually can't get the reds fully ripe. When that's the case, people could add tannins, chaptalize [add sugar to raise final alcohol level for balance], or use other manipulations; I want to avoid that as much as possible." Even with the very ripe 2010 vintage, her wines in the barrel taste remarkably consistent with her fresh and fruit-forward style, and she points out that the ripest lot of grapes was picked at only just over 14 percent potential alcohol. Apparently her style is winning fans; "We've doubled sales since 2009," she says. The 2008 vintage was her first at Blenheim.

She keeps in close contact with the tasting-room staff, even working the room herself on busy weekends, and she gets regular feedback from customers on her wines. "I try to stay as involved as I can" with the customers, she says, and describes her biggest satisfaction as "Just seeing smiling faces of customers; that's pretty big for me, that that happens on a regular basis. It makes me very happy."

Another large reward at this winery is being given trust and complete artistic freedom by the management. Some might assume that being a female winemaker in a winery owned by a male celebrity could invite a lack of personal or professional respect, but here the opposite is true. "Dave is very helpful and supportive. He just tells me to make the best wine I can without any strings attached, and whatever I need, they give me. Even though he's a rock star, Dave is laid-back, and so is the winery. It's working well for us. I don't know how I'd do if I were working somewhere that they told me to make a wine I didn't believe in."

Evidence of this creative freedom and Matthews's artistic influence can be seen in the just-released top-of-the-line Painted Red and Painted White wines from the 2009 vintage. These will always be blends, but due to vintage variation, Harmon won't know until harvest what grapes or ratios these blends will be, which keeps the whole concept fresh and intriguing.

When asked, she ponders whether there are stereotypical male and female wine styles. While she prefers a subtle, fruit-forward style, she wonders if this style would "be against the usual for what you'd expect" for a male winemaker, and characterizes the typical male style as "heavier, gutsier, more full-bodied."

Harmon acknowledges the simple fact that "there are many more male winemakers than female," but says she doesn't really think about it "until I'm standing in an elevator with a lot of other winemakers who are male." She adds: "There's nothing macho about hard work—it's just hard work."

She occasionally sees innocent gender preconceptions about her role. "Sometimes people waiting for cellar tours are surprised when they tell me they're waiting for the winemaker, not expecting it to be a woman. They're also surprised when they hear I've been at this for ten years."

The most overt sexism she's encountered in her work occurred during her apprenticeship, at Domaine Faiveley in Nuits-Saint-Georges, Burgundy. She was the first American recipient of the Chevaliers du Tastevin's prestigious scholarship, and "they asked me why I wanted to work in the cellar; didn't I want to be a secretary and work in an office instead?!"

There has been a superstition in Europe since medieval times about not allowing women in the wine cellar, which remains largely unexamined to this day. "In France, the male domination of the cellar work and gender stereotypes about work are much stronger than in the US. When I went to New Zealand, there was none of that; everyone is expected to work the same." She reflects, however, that the scholarships in both Burgundy and New Zealand "prepared me very well for this position."

In considering how the Virginia wine industry has evolved, Harmon declares that "there's been more progress in the last two years than in the previous eight," both in wine quality and in how the region is being perceived by consumers, the trade, and media. Looking to the future, she resists making specific predictions on trends in grape varieties and styles, but is confident that "we'll be seen as an important, significant wine region. Quality will be more consistent, and people will come to visit Virginia in part because of the wine, and it won't be seen as an odd curiosity or as a negative. I think the future is bright; Virginia is opening so many wineries that it will be difficult for it to remain ignored by the wine media." She refers to a recent *Wine Spectator* tasting which evaluated Virginia viogniers; critic James Molesworth wrote: "The group of wines I recently tasted was very consistent in quality, with the majority earning marks in the very good range (85 to 89 points on *Wine Spectator*'s 100-point scale)."

Although the Blenheim viognier 2009 was rated 87 points in this review, Harmon believes "it's not about ratings as much as exposure; it gets the public accepting the concept of Virginia wine as quality wine."

Amy Steers, Vineyard Manager, Well Hung Vineyard

You will likely find "Well Hung" either pretty clever or pretty tacky as a name for a vineyard, but we can all agree that the double meaning is hardly subtle. The label shows three pairs of male trousers beneath a grapevine trellis, with the clusters strategically placed. The kicker is that the middle set of legs belongs to co-owner William Steers, who in his "real" job is head of the Urology Department at the University of Virginia (the other legs belong to his two sons).

His wife, Amy, is the vineyard manager; her other two partners in the business are also women (Kathy Rash and Tracy Verkerke, the latter being the one who innocently suggested the name for the operation by commenting on how "well hung" the clusters looked on the vines). Far from causing a censorship issue with the mandatory label approval through the Tax and Trade Bureau, the all-women bureaucratic team reportedly put a "rush order" on the design, with their stamp of approval. Well Hung, possibly the smallest commercial vineyard in the state (one and a half acres), is planted close to the Steers' house in Ivy, west of Charlottesville. It is prominently visible from the house as the sun sets over the Blue Ridge Mountains in the background.

The vineyard looked meticulously groomed as I drove past it on my way to interview Amy Steers at the house on a hot June day in 2011. Steers is a tall, energetic, athletic woman with large brown eyes and an easy laugh. She and William planted their first chardonnay in 2000 (one hundred vines), then planted the rest in 2001. The vineyard is mostly chardonnay and cabernet franc, with small amounts of petit verdot and cabernet sauvignon.

Their first harvest, in 2003, was a poor, wet vintage. "We didn't have much fruit and basically harvested one ton," Steers recalls. In 2004, they brought in seventy-two lugs of chardonnay (each lug holds twenty-five pounds of fruit). Since then, the vineyard's yields have varied. "I had no idea what our yields should be, but when we hired Chris Hill as a consultant and learned about balancing the vines between fruit and canopy, yields got more even." Hill was hired in 2010, after a 2009 harvest so scant as to be nonexistent. Grape berry moth was the culprit, Steers explains. Hill then helped educate her on what to look for and how to address it.

Steers learned a lot of lessons the hard way. Initially she didn't net the vines, and the birds "cleaned up" the rows next to the woods. "Every single grape was gone from three rows out of eleven rows total," she recalls. And that was despite using flash tape and other bird scarers. In 2009, she finally netted the rows. She was told the first thing to install was an electric fence to repel the deer. "If they find out what's in the vineyard, they'll jump over anything to get in, but if they're trained to stay out first, like dogs, they'll train their offspring to avoid it."

Steers describes the details of vineyard labor by season: Spring is typically thirty hours per week, summer twenty to thirty hours per week, and she starts winter pruning after Christmas. "I love it when we have the first freeze in late fall," she says. "It means all the season's work is over."

In 2011, a record amount of rain fell between mid-April and mid-June, requiring "a huge amount of shoot thinning. Seventeen rows took about three hours per row, and I had to do each side separately due to huge vigor." When I interviewed her in early June, she said "I've already sprayed seven times. Last year, it was so dry in July I was doing fourteen days between sprays, but up to now I've been doing sprays in seven-day intervals." In fact, fungal diseases continued to cause growers across the state problems even through a dry 2011 summer, especially with a record rainy September.

Given the many hours of hard work in a hot, humid vineyard, why does she do it? Steers laughs and says, "my husband." But it's more than a hobby, and she loves it. "I come from a long line of farmers and love taking care of the crop."

When she and her husband planted the vineyard, they didn't know where it would lead. Since the vineyard is so small, they decided the most practical approach would be to use the custom-crush facilities at Virginia Wineworks, where Michael Shaps oversees the winemaking. They considered opening a tasting room to sell directly to the public, but after running the numbers decided instead to stay with wholesale distribution to the trade, although they do sell and ship wine from their website to states that permit it.

In 2010, they harvested 2.5 tons total or 5,000 pounds of grapes, which was a pretty good yield for them. Had they sold the grapes, they would have earned a gross total of $4,297, but chemical costs, equipment, and labor would have made the whole endeavor a financial wash if they hadn't turned the grapes into higher-value wine. They started with 220 cases of the 2008 vintage and are now producing 1,200 cases annually. "Custom crush allowed us to start without going into debt waiting for fruit to ripen," Steers explains. "Less than a year after bottling, we started making money on sales. Now the business is self-sustaining."

Well Hung is most known for its Burgundian-style crisp chardonnay, called Everyday, and their Loire Valley–like pure and fresh cabernet franc. They have expanded the product line since their first vintage in 2008; now they offer a very popular cabernet franc–based rosé, a Very Well Hung (oak style) chardonnay, a reserve red Bordeaux blend, and perhaps their most uniquely Virginia wine, "Verdot-Merlot," a blend of 85 percent petit verdot and 15 percent merlot. The wine is dark, with deep, brooding, wild berries and black cherry, violets, lavender, and coriander spice.

Aside from site selection, what's required for successful viticulture in Virginia? I asked. "Persistence. After our horrible '09 harvest, I thought, *I can't go through another year.* One of our friends said, 'Why don't you just pull out the vines and put in a putting green?' But then the spring comes and you get into it again. I used to get so nervous about what might happen with the weather and such. Each vintage is different, so it helps me appreciate how that harvest can be unique. I've gotten better about not worrying as much. You go to conferences and hear from other growers what they deal with and what their losses are, and it's so supportive and also a relief to know you're not alone."

Steers points out that David King, of King Family Vineyards, said it took him ten years to break even. "And they do polo matches, weddings, other events. They're in the entertainment business. I don't want that kind of lifestyle. Custom crush allows us not to pay for a tasting room or winery, and be able to just make wine and sell it."

Since they don't have a tasting room, Steers says they take advantage of the festival circuit to sell to the public. They've also made regular customers at the Charlottesville farmers market, another convenient sales channel. "I can't tell you how many people tell us at festivals, 'Oh, we'd like to put in some grapes,' and we tell them they won't make money. Just a tractor alone will cost fourteen thousand dollars. It takes a lot to make wine in Virginia, so I never complain about Virginia wine prices."

Debra Vascik, Winemaker, Valhalla Vineyards

Debra Vascik, winemaker and co-owner of Valhalla Vineyards, near Roanoke, recalls that when she and her husband were establishing their vineyard and winery, in the mid-1990s, she saw a lot of female winemakers in California and assumed it was an open profession. "In Virginia," Vascik recalls of that time, "it was an old boys network." However, she thinks things have changed dramatically. "Now, women are accepted and respected professionally, but in the midnineties, some people thought we were insane. Someone commented that I was just a 'bored housewife'; little did they know that I have a physical therapy practice and also act as the winery business manager." Today, she points out, there are all-women wineries in California, and women are generally more prominent in the wine world. Furthermore, scientific literature confirms that women have more taste buds on average than men, so why not use them professionally?

"I think what I love most about it," says Vascik, "is that it's farming, and the better fruit you can produce, the better wine you can produce. Every year is different; this isn't a cookbook industry. It keeps us in a constant learning curve. For anyone who wants a constant challenge, this is a great industry. I love it and have been happy. Jim and I have enjoyed being in the industry as a sideline to our medical professions; it's very uplifting."

Emily Hodson Pelton, Winemaker, Veritas Vineyard

The story of American wine is full of family feuds and sons storming out (or being thrown out) of the family winery only to strike out on their own and "show them" by starting their own winery and making their own style statement.

By contrast, at Veritas Vineyard Andrew and Patricia Hodson work harmoniously with their daughter, winemaker Emily Hodson Pelton. Father and daughter collaborate as winemakers, while Patricia was vineyard manager until 2011 when her brother Bill Tonkins took over. Not only are the Hodson parents unfailingly polite, they also share a sunny, warm disposition. They have realized their dream and embraced the life and work of Virginia winery owners. Perhaps because of their disposition or their good manners (or because, as a woman, Emily is unburdened by oedipal angst), the intergenerational strife so typical of the American wine industry is absent here.

Pelton earned her enology degree under Dr. Bruce Zoecklein at Virginia Tech, and her wines won critical acclaim from the start. She made national news in 2007 when she won the "Judges Choice" award (best of finalists) in the first National Women's Wine Competition for her 2005 Kenmar sweet traminette. In March 2010, Pelton was invited to pour the 2009 Veritas viognier at the State Department, where Secretary of State Hillary Clinton and guest speaker Michelle Obama presented the fourth International Women of Courage Awards to ten women from around the world.

Pelton is a strikingly attractive blonde in her midthirties, with an unhurried, calm manner and an engaging smile that is somehow both warm and cool. We relax on leather couches in front of the fire in the Veritas tasting room on a cold December morning. The winter sunlight spills in over the vineyards and Humpback Mountain through the floor-to-ceiling windows on either side of the chimney. While at ease with herself and others, Pelton is reflective and ponders my questions in a calm and deliberate way, which also seems to be her approach in the wine cellar. Like Kirsty Harmon, she, too describes herself as a minimalist, using as little intervention as possible in processing the wine.

As is often the case with the children of winery owners, she says she "had no thought" of getting training as a winemaker until after she had worked at the winery for a year and "was bitten by the wine bug." After seeing that California was green in the winter and brown in the summer (as well as seeing the housing prices in the North Coast), she decided it would be best to get her degree in Virginia. Having made wine for a decade, she says she'd like to "redo my education now; I think I could get so much more from it."

Working collaboratively with her father is great, says Pelton, because they have clearly defined and different roles, and "we need each other." Although as a physician he is well grounded in science, Andrew Hodson brings to the collaboration a lifetime of studying classic Old

World wine models and the relationships of blend components. Pelton's technical winemaking expertise complements her father's frame of reference, and they both work toward the same stylistic goal of Old World classicism, letting the fruit express vineyard terroir but ensuring the wine is sound, blended and finished with skill. While some wine-makers like to take all the credit, Pelton feels "lucky to have someone to work with and check me on my processes."

How does this play out in wine style? Alcohol levels are moderate, acidity is bright, and varietal fruit character is easily evident, while oak influence is minimal and in the background (except in the reserve reds). Although they make a Marlborough, New Zealand, style of sauvignon blanc as well as a more restrained Loire style (when crop size allows), Pelton explains that the musqué clone of sauvignon blanc, with its assertive passion fruit, convinced her to make a separate wine from it. Veritas's viognier is very bright and crisp, with delicate apricot fruit and impressive Old World minerality.

Veritas also makes a varietal petit verdot, interpreted and processed in an Old World way by blending lots harvested at different times and using different oak treatments to balance floral and spice elements for a final blend "styled on the Bordeaux model."

For Pelton, one of the big rewards of working in Virginia is "being part of the emerging locavore movement, which is such a fun, impor-tant market development." She also enjoys "cataloging the years with each individual vintage and its unique character," since they vary so much in Virginia. "As a winemaker, I feel so much more linked to the weather now; the wine, local stories or memories from that vintage; I get really focused on weather systems around harvest."

The rain and the quirks of weather variations with Virginia vin-tages are certainly a challenge. Despite the much-ballyhooed quality of the 2010 vintage, an isolated storm system blew up the Rockfish Valley in September and dumped four inches of rain in one day on her vines, right when the whites were ready for harvest. And the crop was already down significantly from a spring frost. "Every year I have to be ready for anything, from drought to hurricanes. Every year it's a different variety that suffers. Each vintage we have to anticipate problems in the vineyard, because I don't want to try to fix them in the cellar." While she had wanted all of her grapes to be estate grown, she discovered in the 2010 vintage that it's a good idea if they aren't all in the same place and vulnerable to the same weather (they're now leasing the mature Ivy Creek vineyard, about twelve miles away).

When asked how Virginia wine has changed in the last decade, her first response is "quality." She then points to the specialty grapes for Virginia—viognier, petit verdot, and petit manseng—which she feels are "starting to define Virginia" wine in the market (although chardonnay is still the most planted grape in the state by total acreage).

Pelton sees a difference between male and female winemaking styles. "I tend to be very hands-off, not aggressive," she says. "For example, if I think a wine needs a gram of acid addition, I'll add half a gram, then check it; I see my male winemaking colleagues adding a gram and a half to make sure the job gets done and the wine is definitely adjusted and stabilized. It takes me longer, but it fits my minimal approach."

The 2010 vintage was hot, and the grapes could finally ripen fully. But Pelton's approach was to pick as soon as the fruit was ripe, to avoid high alcohols and wines that would be uncharacteristic of the house style. "I was nervous about possibly picking too early; I know I picked long before most of my colleagues. I was worried, but Michael Shaps is our consultant, and after tasting my reds, he said they had more balance than many others he had tasted from the vintage, so now I'm thrilled."

When I ask Pelton what she sees for Virginia wine ten years from now, she exclaims spontaneously, "Ooh, I'm so excited!" It's not that quality will necessarily be better than it is now, she says, but "we'll be so high-profile that people will be flocking to this place to taste our wines. We'll be considered much more a part of the world wine market."

What changes does she see at Veritas? "I've planted malbec. I'd like to get more flavors and spice components for blending in my red Bordeaux wines. I just don't think cabernet sauvignon will do well for us here, but I want more than just cabernet franc and merlot." While she likes to add petit verdot strategically to other reds, and "customers love it when I do," there isn't enough of it to blend away too much of it from the varietal bottling. What about using carmenere—the grape that was confused with merlot in Chile and is now earning that country accolades—in her Bordeaux blends? She asks about its background, nods slowly in her careful and methodical way, and thoughtfully says she'll consider it.

PARADIGM SHIFT: GETTING RESPECT FROM THE AMERICAN WINE MEDIA

In 1976, the "Judgment of Paris"—arranged by veteran British wine retailer and writer Steven Spurrier—shook the wine world, when California chardonnays and cabernet sauvignons beat their French equivalents in a blind tasting by leading French judges. The California wine industry could finally be taken seriously. Still, through much of the 1980s, in major East Coast wine markets such as Washington, D.C., and New York, the wine regions most respected by critics and consumers remained France, Germany, and Italy. When American wine consumption began increasing again, in 1994, driven by baby boomers seeking out dry varietal wines, the California wine producers entered a golden age of ever-increasing sales, ever-increasing plantings and, until the 2008 recession, ever-increasing prices.

By the mid-1990s, California wine was as respected in the wine trade as French, German, and Italian wines had been in the 1980s. This was the result of a number of factors: huge production levels; an ideal climate for grapes, with predictable, ripe, and healthy crops; a lot less paperwork hassle than imported wines required and—thanks to Robert Mondavi—the near-universal branding of American wines with recognizable varietal names.

Unfortunately, the widespread success of "brand California" in the American market made it that much harder for wines from non–West Coast states to get respect, especially with highly variable wine quality in some regions. Vintages in the eastern states were not as dependable as on the West Coast, and states such as New York had to overcome the branding of the state name on Taylor and Great Western products, which were made from native American grapes. But the excuse most often given by major consumer wine media for not covering the regional wine scene was that local wines were either not in distribution or were produced in such small quantities as to be irrelevant to their readers.

The distribution issue has been a major hurdle for regional wineries; most distributors want big brands that sell themselves, and don't want to be in the hand-selling, wine-education business. Those that specialize in small-production wines want to carry high-prestige producers or appellations that, again, will essentially sell themselves.

While there is some merit to the argument that lack of availability makes regional wines less relevant to the average consumer, many in the regional wine scene suspected that there was more to the virtual boycotting of local wines by major consumer publications. Was there an attempt to laugh off or avoid reporting on the regional wine scene? Or could it be that the problem with regional wines outside California was that they simply weren't considered as glamorous as California or European wines, largely because their regions themselves weren't considered glamorous by the writers, publishers, and readers of these magazines?

Wine has increasingly been marketed as a symbol of a lifestyle involving travel to deluxe resort destinations such as California's Napa Valley or Italy or France (just look at the advertisements in consumer wine magazines or other lifestyle magazines where wine advertisements are featured). How could style-conscious publishers—or their writers, editors, and readers—believe that world-class wines were being made near Cleveland, Ohio; or in the conservative, unfashionable farm country of upstate New York and Pennsylvania; or in rural Michigan, Virginia, or Missouri? These places might appeal to sport fishermen or hunters, but not to publishers appealing to readers cultivating an image of themselves as stylish and glamorous. The first-tier baby boomers were the American wine consumers most likely to equate wine with glamour, and they were also the ones that major consumer wine and lifestyle publications targeted.

The creators of *The Muppet Movie* nailed this unexamined cultural bias about regional wine in the scene where Kermit the Frog takes Miss Piggy on a date to a fancy restaurant. After Kermit chooses a wine, Steve Martin, playing the overly obsequious and sarcastic wine steward, declares: "Sparkling muscatel, one of the finest wines of Idaho! Don't you want to smell the bottle cap?" Fittingly, both Idaho wines and Stelvin screw-cap closures are now firmly established as respectable.

Small regional wine producers' costs of production make it necessary for them to charge prices that are higher than the big brands in grocery stores, which are made from grapes that are a commodity crop farmed in low-cost dry climates on the West Coast or in the Southern Hemisphere. Both consumers and the mainstream wine press have until very recently been resistant to the idea that fine regional US wines could actually be worth the prices being charged for them.

In the last thirty years, there have been success stories for the regional wine industry in overcoming these biases. Washington State started branding itself as a reliable producer of affordable riesling, and when that became unfashionable in the 1980s and 1990s, they then branded themselves as a leading producer of the very fashionable merlot grape. Now that riesling has become fashionable again (mostly with Millennial generation drinkers), Washington State is again promoting riesling. Oregon established itself by producing top-notch pinot noir, then Dijon-clone chardonnay and pinot gris, but both those states still have the external respectability of the West Coast. How do major wine-producing states in the east, such as Virginia, brand themselves for consumers and the media? And more basically, how do they convince the media they are worth paying attention to?

Kevin Zraly is a major American wine authority. He was the head sommelier at the iconic Windows on the World restaurant, in the World Trade Center, from 1976 until its destruction on September 11, 2001. Zraly has been a role model for a generation of sommeliers and those learning about correct restaurant wine service. He wrote the *Windows on the World Complete Wine Course*, which is the top-selling book on wine.

Zraly says that Thomas Jefferson is one of his heroes, for his faith in the potential of American viticulture. Accordingly, he published a pocket-size *American Wine Guide*, reviewing the wines and statistics of every state in the Union. Since every state is now producing wine, reasoned Zraly, consumers should be able to find out about the wine scene in each of them (disclosure: this author was one of the regional editors).

The main thing that impresses Zraly about the Virginia wine scene is its rapid growth. In the 2006 edition, there were 108 wineries, and now there are almost double that number; he calls that an "amazing increase" in just five years. (By contrast, he says, Long Island's much-touted wine industry has not really grown during that time.) "Everyone asks me the same question," says Zraly. "What's the next state to watch for wine after the West Coast and New York? I'll say 'Virginia'; it's number five after those, not just for volume but quality."

Zraly feels Virginia wines don't get the attention they deserve from the trade and national wine media. He points out that even in his *Windows on the World Complete Wine Course*, he doesn't mention any brands (except select New York ones, since he's a New Yorker) that are not distributed nationally. He thinks if Virginia had something such as Oregon's pinot noir camp [designed for invited wine trade members], that could bring some national attention. "I think Virginia owns viognier, the way Tuscany owns sangiovese and Argentina owns malbec. I think viognier can be a very fine wine, and also a vehicle around which to build a wine reputation." In addition to viognier, he sees cabernet franc and norton as branding opportunities for Virginia.

Looking to the future, Zraly feels Oregon is a good model for Virginia to follow. "Oregon's wine industry is based on small family wineries, which is also the case in Virginia. Their wines have continued to improve, so I see only good things for Virginia in the future.

"I always say that there has to be a tradition around something to make its branding work. Virginia has it more even than California, thanks to Thomas Jefferson. The new wineries are continuing that; it's all going in a very positive direction." He also expects more wines from Virginia in a European style rather than in a West Coast style. "It's just a question of building an identity."

In July 2007, Bruce Schoenfeld, wine and spirits editor for *Travel + Leisure*, wrote an article titled "A Wine Lover's Guide: Five Regions to Visit Now." Along with Italy's Friuli and New Zealand's Central Otago, Schoenfeld listed Virginia among the five. It was the only North American region included. Schoenfeld started his section on Virginia by noting that "until recently, I'd felt that same dissonance about Virginian wine. The state had been trading on the grape-growing reputation of noted wine lover Thomas Jefferson for two hundred years without producing anything worthy of mention." Then a single bottle during a meal at a wine-centered restaurant convinced him that Virginia was ready for consideration. Virginia, he wrote, "should be on the must-visit list of any adventurous wine traveler."

The wine was Barboursville's 1999 nebbiolo, and the restaurant was Palladio at Barboursville Vineyards. Bruce described nebbiolo as "a fiercely difficult grape that I'd always assumed could be grown with success only in small, well-delineated pockets of Italy's Piedmont region. When Luca Paschina brought a bottle to the table . . . I snickered.

Nebbiolo from Virginia? That would be the punch line to a cruel joke." If there is a grape more notoriously difficult to produce anywhere in the world than pinot noir, it would be nebbiolo.

But as Schoenfeld points out, Paschina is from Alba, in the heart of nebbiolo's Piedmont homeland, and his confidence paid off. "The result is Virginia's best red wine—that deep, dusty, slightly tangy Nebbiolo—and a Cabernet Franc that isn't far behind."

For him, Barboursville was the highlight of Virginia's wine scene, but he explained that several small wineries near Dulles airport were "hot on its heels," foremost being Linden Vineyards. "I actually prefer Jim Law's 1999 Chardonnay from Hardscrabble to just about any California Chardonnay I've had in the past five years. What's more, it costs twenty-four dollars."

Robert Parker's influential *Wine Advocate* subscription newsletter has expanded its coverage to regional US wines. David Schildknecht covers America's eastern and midwestern wineries (as well as the wines of Germany, Austria, eastern Europe, Alsace, Burgundy, the Loire Valley, Languedoc-Roussillon, Champagne, New Zealand, and South Africa).

Tom Stevenson is a Briton and an authority on the wines of Champagne. He also publishes an annual *Wine Report* that manages to cover the entire wine-producing world, making use of regional specialists. Virginia is included in the "Atlantic Northeast" section, edited by Sandra Silfven. In 2007, Linden Vineyards made the Stevenson *Wine Report*'s list of the top ten wineries in the Atlantic Northeast region, and was the only one from Virginia on the list.

Doug Frost is one of only a handful of people in the world who hold certifications as both Master of Wine and Master Sommelier. He lives in Kansas City, Missouri, where he runs the Jefferson Cup Invitational Wine Competition and publishes beveragealcoholresource.com.

Reflecting on American wine media coverage of regional wine, Frost says "The rise of regional wine has helpfully coincided with the rise of wine blogging or other social avenues of wine conversation. The two large voices in winedom—the *Wine Advocate* and the *Wine Spectator*—are far less important than they were a few years ago." He explains that he doesn't think that people have rejected what those two magazines have to say about wine, but he thinks that the younger crowd has simply moved on to other media. "And the multiplicity of voices in the blogosphere adds to the sense that there are many wines to be tried, from grapes we've never heard about before and from places we didn't know had great wines."

Frost believes winery tourism is regional wine's greatest strength. "Day trips to wineries are very popular across all spectrums of age, race, educational background, and economic strata, and these winery visits spark a fascination with wine from anywhere, but particularly from those wineries that are nearby." Frost adds that winery visits "make people feel welcome outdoors, an experience that has diminished for most city dwellers. If only for these reasons, regional wine participation will grow and grow, perhaps to the detriment of wines from other places, but to the benefit of all local economies, I believe."

Deborah Parker Wong is a California-based member of the Circle of Wine Writers (CWW) who has written about Virginia producers a few times over the last couple of years for wine industry trade publications. In 2010, she judged in the Virginia Governor's Cup competition and was impressed with the viogniers and the Bordeaux varieties. "We make plenty of phenolic [coarse] viognier here in California, and I taste enough of them at wine competitions to keep my expectations quite low. I was pleasantly surprised by the overall quality and expression of the wines that were entered in the Governor's Cup."

While she believes Virginia wine isn't getting the attention it deserves on the West Coast, "You could say that for just about every other state besides Washington, Oregon, and New York.

"I'm intrigued by Virginia wines; their potential is apparent," she declares. To build a coherent regional identity, Parker Wong thinks

Virginia needs to "be itself" and differentiate in ways that appeal to emerging wine drinkers. "I don't really see serious wine culture being a good fit here. Virginia offers quality for value and fun, relaxed consumption habits: wine as a lifestyle versus wine as an intellectual pursuit." She also feels Millennial consumers respond to authenticity and believes they represent the future of the industry in Virginia. "Virginia has the opportunity to make wine fun, where it's too late for other regions to go that route. There is still so much stigma around wine. As I love to say: 'All you need to know is what you like.'"

Dave McIntyre writes the wine column for the *Washington Post*, but started as an online writer in 1999 and had his own blog before his print column began. He's one of the few wine writers in a major print medium who was online first. He has written frequently on the wines of Maryland and Virginia in both media.

McIntyre recalls tasting his first Virginia wine at Bell Wine & Spirits, on M Street in Washington, D.C., in 1988. "It was a 1985 cabernet sauvignon, and it tasted like it had marinated my college roommate's dirty socks. But my wife, Lily, and I were intrigued that wine was made around here, and we started visiting wineries, since we couldn't afford too many return trips to California, where we'd just 'discovered' wine." He says he realized Virginia had great potential when Gordon Murchie of the Vinifera Wine Growers Association asked him to judge the Virginia Governor's Cup one year in the early to mid-1990s. When McIntyre started writing regularly about wine in 1997, for Sidewalk.com, he included a few columns on local wines, and wrote some articles on Virginia and New York for WineToday.com around 2000. "Because it was an Internet publication, it was starved for copy and more amenable to articles about obscure wine regions. That may have been an early precursor for the Web's impact on regional wine today. By democratizing media, it also allowed wine industries that could not get noticed by the mainstream media to capture the imaginations of at least a sliver of the wine-drinking public," he says.

"Dave McIntyre's WineLine" was an e-mail newsletter (blogs hadn't been invented yet) that included articles on local wines. "I also got a few assignments for obscure magazines. The articles generally had a travel focus, on wine country rather than the wines, which were not widely available. Even in 2010, that was how I managed to write about Virginia and Maryland for *Wine Enthusiast*—in a piece mainly on Chesapeake Bay cuisine."

When he wrote for *Washingtonian* magazine in 2007–08, and then for the *Post* starting in October 2008, he kept his focus on the emerging local wine scene. He and Dallas-based wine writer Jeff Siegel created DrinkLocalWine.com in 2008, because "the mainstream media were ignoring local wines that bloggers were covering instead."

McIntyre says he's impressed not only by the sheer number of Virginia producers "but also the seriousness of their intentions. You still see rich doctors or entrepreneurs going for the lifestyle aspect, but increasingly new vineyards are being planted not because someone has land and loves wine, but because they have found a good site to grow wine grapes."

He finds younger consumers are more open to local wines. "The current generation, as America becomes a wine-drinking nation to some extent, is exploring at the same time as the industry is expanding and quality is improving." On the other hand, he thinks that for sustainable growth, "consumers still need to view Virginia wines as something to drink with dinner, and not just something to enjoy at festivals."

McIntyre walks a fine line as a writer dedicated to reporting on the Virginia-Maryland wine scene. "For a while, there was one idiot who kept complaining to the *Post* that I never wrote about local wines, but even he has shut up by now. Other letter writers who still don't think Virginia can make good wines have questioned my judgment, and even a few winemakers have said I may be too much of a cheerleader for Virginia."

As for the reluctance of major consumer wine publications to cover the regional wine scene, he thinks the situation is improving, but slowly. "James Molesworth has been chiding New York restaurants for not offering New York wines, but that's on his *Wine Spectator* blog—again, the Internet has infinite capacity. The magazines still have to write the same new vintage reports [for major regions] every year. But occasionally you see regional wines reviewed in *Wine Spectator* and *Wine Enthusiast*, and with improving ratings."

To be fair, in the early 2000s the *Wine Spectator* dedicated a cover story to the "Wines of America" and included wines from Virginia, New York, and the Midwest. However, this has not become an annual feature. Nevertheless, as Kirsty Harmon of Blenheim pointed out, Molesworth wrote a review of Virginia viogniers that had complimentary remarks for the consistent high quality of the entire category. In May 2010, another *Wine Spectator* writer, James Suckling, visited Boxwood and Chrysalis wineries near Middleburg and wrote online in "James Suckling Uncorked," "Last weekend was like discovering a new wine region in Italy or Europe. So fun."

McIntyre doesn't see the rapid growth rate of Virginia wineries continuing, but he feels the quality will continue to improve. "In ten years, we may no longer be debating cabernet franc versus petit verdot, but celebrating single-vineyard Bordeaux blends that show true terroir." He also points to pricing as a problem in today's market. "Too many prices seem driven by ego more than quality. There is still a lot of bad Virginia wine out there, and high prices are not conducive to Virginia wine being considered anything other than a special-occasion drink." To appreciate the value of wines such as Octagon, or Linden's Hardscrabble Chardonnay, or Boxwood's Topiary, Dave says, you need to taste them blind alongside other similarly priced wines from France and California.

DrinkLocalWine.com cofounder Jeff Siegel (aka "the Wine Curmudgeon") largely echoes McIntyre's comments on the evolution of Virginia wine, though he thinks the price criticism of Virginia wines is largely a cop-out and excuse. "The people doing the criticizing wouldn't buy the wine regardless."

Siegel is impressed with how progressive the Virginia industry is in keeping current with technology, and with the diversity and quality improvement in Virginia white wine. In ten years, he thinks, Virginia will be best known for its non-chardonnay whites, such as viognier and albariño.

In July 2011 Charlottesville hosted the fourth national Wine Bloggers Conference, and Jancis Robinson, MW, gave the keynote address. Her "Purple Pages" blog at jancisrobinson.com was established in 2000, and she is now one of the wine bloggers of longest standing. While blogging had been ignored by the mainstream media until recently, she now reports that her publishers now play up her website and blog. She also celebrates the leveling of the wine media playing field by bloggers; "to use a Marxist analogy, bloggers now control the means of production."

I interviewed major Virginia wine bloggers during the conference, whose comments will be available on beyondjeffersonsvines.com, who agreed that wine blogging has become more accepted by everyone including winery owners, and that Virginia wine had made almost universally favourable impressions with the attendees. These bloggers included: Frank Morgan of "Drink What YOU Like"; Paul Armstrong and Warren Richard of "Virginia Wine Time"; MJ and Dave of "Swirl, Sniff, Snark"; and Rick Collier and Nancy Bauer of "Virginia Wine in Your Pocket" (they designed the Virginia wine app). Dezel Quillen, another notable Virginia wine blogger of "My Vine Spot," was not able to attend the conference.

HOW THE BRITISH FEEL
ABOUT VIRGINIA WINE . . .
AND WHY IT MATTERS

The infrastructure of the international wine trade was built in the United Kingdom in the seventeenth and eighteenth centuries, and between the buying power of English consumers and their long-established wine-drinking habits, the UK's per-capita wine consumption is more than double that of the United States (20.72 liters versus 8.69 liters in 2009). While the United States is expected to become the largest wine market in the world in 2012, worth some $44 billion, the UK—with a population only one-fifth the size of the US—is still the world's largest market for imported wine, at just over 150 million cases worth $17.53 billion in 2009 (virtually all commercial wine in that country is imported).

Despite the global recession, wine consumption there increased during 2009, and the market is predicted to grow in value by double digits between 2010 and 2014. Also, the number of British consumers who pay more than $10 per bottle for an ordinary wine to accompany dinner is increasing, according to market research, so it's a discriminating and valuable market for wine-producing regions to cultivate. A majority of the world's most respected wine writers and industry authorities are also based in London, including Jancis Robinson, Michael Broadbent, Hugh Johnson, Andrew Jefford and Steven Spurrier.

Accordingly, for purposes of building a reputation in the international wine world, the UK—and especially London—is as Broadway is to musical theater: For a relatively unknown wine region, establishing a credible reputation there is vital. As we read on page 61, in 2007 the Virginia Wine Experience in London took sixty-four Virginia wines selected in a blind tasting to Vinopolis, the venue for many trade tastings. Wineries participating and pouring their wines for trade and media members included White Hall Vineyards, Williamsburg Winery, Pearmund Cellars, the Winery at La Grange, and Kluge Estate.

Tasters included Steven Spurrier, Hugh Johnson, Andrew Jefford, Stephen Brook (American specialist and columnist for *Decanter*), members of the London-based Circle of Wine Writers, and a few trade buyers, like Nick Room of Waitrose. When I asked Spurrier the next day what his impression was, he said, "What an eye-opener yesterday was! I saw Hugh Johnson later that evening, and he was as impressed as I was." Spurrier had visited Virginia about fifteen years ago, so his assessment of the wines as having gone from quirky to mainstream is noteworthy.

Oz Clarke, another leading British wine writer, wrote in his *Pocket Wine Book 2011*, "My most thrilling discovery in the USA this year has been the wine from vineyards spread around Washington, D.C., in particular those of Virginia, whose sumptuous, scented viogniers are world-class."

Jefford, in a piece for the *Financial Times,* cited as his favorites the Barboursville Malvaxia 2002, Kluge Estate New World Red 2002, Linden Cabernet Franc 2005, and the 2005 viogniers from Rappahannock Cellars, the Winery at La Grange, and White Hall Vineyards.

At about the same time, Christopher Parker, a Briton living in northern Virginia with professional experience in both wine importing-distribution and the high-tech world, was contemplating starting a business exporting Virginia wines to the UK. He heard about the Virginia Wine Experience in London and decided to follow up on its publicity beachhead. He connected with Judy Kornfeld, international trade specialist in the US Commercial Service, who obtained a grant from the Department of Commerce for $2,000 to be used for a virtual wine tasting. They arranged an Internet tasting between Breaux Vineyards and the prestigious Institute of Directors in London, called "An Evening in Virginia Wine Country." On September 30, 2008, London tasters were able to taste wines from nine wineries, meet the Virginia winemakers, and discuss their wines via the live webcast.

Parker describes his New Horizon Wines as a wine lifestyle company that combines import-export of high-quality wines with wine tourism and education, primarily focused on the introduction of Virginia wines into the UK market. He sees Virginia's wine brand as "a combination of wine, history, natural beauty, culinary arts (particularly locally sourced produce), and proximity to the nation's capital. Viognier, without doubt, is the signature grape creating the most interest. To find as many complex and interesting viogniers that have the core varietal characteristics is exciting. It was Michael Broadbent who commented, in his August 2009 *Decanter* article, that Barboursville Viognier Reserve 2004 'had the quality and flavor to match—even exceed—Rhône's finest Condrieu.' Praise indeed for Barboursville Vineyards and indicative of the quality and potential of viognier in Virginia. I also consider cabernet franc and petit verdot as signature grapes for Virginia."

In May 2009, Parker brought his client Virginia wineries (now including Barboursville Vineyards, Boxwood Winery, Breaux Vineyards, Keswick Vineyards, King Family Vineyards, Pearmund Cellars, Philip Carter Winery, Rappahannock Cellars, Veramar Vineyard, Veritas

Vineyard and Winery, White Hall Vineyards, and Williamsburg Winery) to the premier London International Wine and Spirits Fair (LIWSF). "We created an attractive visual display with a large panoramic picture of Barboursville Vineyards with the Blue Ridge Mountains on the horizon. On the first day of the fair, most people stopped at the stand because of the imagery. Expectations were low or nonexistent. They tasted the wines and word began to spread, about the viogniers in particular. By the second day we had people coming by the stand asking to taste the wines—they had heard there were terrific viogniers from Virginia! This was the first step in building awareness."

Throughout 2009 and leading up to the 2010 LIWSF, Parker presented wines to merchants, restaurants, and hotels in the UK. "There was a growing interest in Virginia wines and enthusiasm to learn more. We sent invitations to trade representatives to visit the stand [at the 2010 LIWSF]. Secretary of Agriculture Todd Haymore attended that year, showing the level of commitment and support from the Commonwealth of Virginia. Steven Spurrier and Oz Clarke again visited the stand, and Steven encouraged Monsieur Guigal, one of the most revered winemakers in the world, to visit with the winemakers to taste the viogniers. This was the highlight of the fair for the wine-makers. Once again, all of the wines were enthusiastically received, particularly the viogniers."

I asked Chris Parker if, based on the track record of New Horizon Wines over the last three years, he believed Virginia wines in the UK are more than just a passing trend and can gain a permanent place in that market. Demand is growing, he says, while noting that making a market is challenging and will not happen quickly. "I have taken the long-term view and believe, through a precise and focused effort, Virginia will be recognized globally as a significant wine producer, in much the same way New Zealand developed a global reputation over the last twenty to thirty years."

Interest in Virginia and the reputation of its wines had developed in opinion-making circles in the UK so much that by September 2010, the influential London-based Circle of Wine Writers made Virginia the destination for their annual weeklong wine region trip (this author is a member of the CWW and helped organize the trip). The idea for the trip developed from a conversation Chris Parker had with Steven Spurrier. Nine UK-based members and one Toronto-based member attended.

The week began near Dulles airport in Reston, and featured a circuit tour of northern Virginia wineries in Loudoun, Fauquier, and Rappahannock counties, then moved on to the Monticello AVA wine region. Following a tour of Monticello, which included a memorable lunch in the orchard next to Jefferson's replanted vines (see page x), the visitors took a bus to Williamsburg, where they toured the colonial restoration and Williamsburg Winery before returning home.

Jancis Robinson is editor of *The Oxford Companion to Wine* and columnist for the *Financial Times*. When she came to Virginia in July 2011 to give the keynote address at the 2011 Wine Bloggers Conference, she had time to visit some wineries, taste some wines, and write some impressions, which were published in her Purple Pages blog on September 14 and in the *Financial Times* on September 17. Aside from her many tasting notes, she focused on the new winery RdV, profiled on pages 1–8. Speaking of the winery's founder, Rutger de Vink, Robinson declares, "I sincerely believe his considerable efforts stand a good chance of putting the state definitively on the world wine map."

NEW DEVELOPMENTS
AND ANOTHER GLIMPSE
INTO THE FUTURE

Virginia has seen a practical doubling of the number of bonded wineries in the last four years. International critics have heaped high praise on the state's wines, and major medals in international competitions have been brought back to the Commonwealth. There's a growing professionalism among the international cadre of experienced winemakers who are fine-tuning Virginia's viticulture. There's also a growing awareness across the wine media that the industry is making serious wine—from world-class viognier to red Bordeaux blends (often led by cabernet franc and petit verdot rather than the more usual cabernet sauvignon), and unusual varieties such as albariño and petit manseng.

Medals and critical accolades are nice, but the most important praise is that Virginia wine sales continue to grow. In-state sales of Virginia wines increased nearly 7.5 percent from 2008 to 2009, despite the recession. That's twice the national average of increased consumption for wine of any kind. In fiscal year 2010, total Virginia wine sales were up 13 percent over the year before.

In October 2010, a feature-length documentary on Virginia wine—*Vintage: The Winemaker's Year*, by Silverthorn Films—premiered on public television stations in Virginia and across the nation. Instead of being a glitzy tourist promotional, the film is a frank, informative, detailed, and unromantic examination of the challenges and rewards of making wine in Virginia's climate. The documentary starts with dormant winter pruning in 2008 and follows the winemakers of the Monticello AVA throughout the season up to harvest and beyond. The film was shot mostly in vineyards, with an emphasis on showing the entire process, from grape and vine evolution to crush and winemaking. The film concludes with a wine tasting in February 2009 at the Virginia Wine Expo in Richmond.

Another measure of the professionalism of the Virginia wine industry is its attitude toward sustainability and the environment. New Kent Winery is perhaps the best representative of this trend (see page 66), but there are others: **North Gate Vineyard** in Loudoun County opened in 2011 with a gold-level LEED (Leadership in Energy and Environmental Design) certified tasting room; Cooper Vineyards, in Louisa, recently opened a redesigned tasting room with platinum LEED certification; **Sunset Hills Vineyard**, with the largest solar energy system in Loudoun County, bills itself as "turning sunshine into wine"; **DuCard Vineyards**, near Old Rag Mountain in Madison County, uses solar panels to generate all the electricity they use for their tasting room and, like many wineries, they used reclaimed hardwoods in the construction of their facility.

An activity at DuCard that is becoming increasingly popular at Virginia wineries near major hiking trails is "wiking," where people with an interest in both hiking and wine seek out wineries near hiking trails. DuCard lies at the eastern edge of the Shenandoah National Park, in the shadow of Old Rag Mountain and White Oak Canyon, with hiking access from the winery, and it participates with neighboring Sharp Rock Vineyards in the Foothills Scenic Wine Trail. DelFosse

Vineyards in Nelson County also touts its hiking trails and the many acres of forest on the property. In 2011, the seventy-fifth anniversary of the creation of the Shenandoah National Park and Skyline Drive by FDR, there was growing interest in combining visits to the park with visits to nearby wineries, as reported by John Hagarty, off-site events manager at Rappahannock Cellars, which is located near the Appalachian Trail. Hagarty wrote a piece on his blog (hagarty-on-wine.com) about hiking to wineries. Some lodging establishments near the park are promoting hiking and nearby wineries as joint attractions, and social groups, from the Wine & Hiking Club of Central Virginia to Outdoor Afro, are combining hiking and tasting at nearby wineries.

As Annette Boyd says, Virginia wines have reached an important turning point. Thanks to the reluctance of most wine distributors to take on regional US wines, gaining market share in the United States outside the state is still a major challenge, but thanks to the change in attitude across the spectrum of the wine media—from bloggers and leading English writers to the *Wine Spectator*—and the high quality of today's Virginia wines, that is more likely now than ever before.

"Grape quality is the most important feature governing wine quality," emphasizes Virginia's enologist, Dr. Bruce Zoecklein, who is now Emeritus Professor at Virginia Tech's Department of Food Science and Technology. In a 2011 newsletter, he reflected on the state of Virginia wine, essentially viewing the wine glass as both half full and half empty, to prevent industry members from becoming too complacent in a region where viticulture and subsequent wine quality are so naturally challenged.

Tom Payette is a consultant winemaker based in Rapidan, Virginia, with over twenty-five years of winemaking experience, including working under the esteemed Bordeaux enologist Jacques Boissenot. In 1999, Tom was declared "Winemaker of the Year" by *Vineyard & Winery Management* magazine, and was acknowledged in July 2011 with the Atlantic Seaboard Wine Association's Perpetual Wine Grape

Productivity Tray, an annual award recognizing a significant contribution to the Mid-Atlantic wine industry.

What impresses him most about Virginia wine today compared to ten years ago is "our ability to build on our [existing] knowledge. We are able to grow better and better grapes, and that is the key asset to fine wine. Better clones and better winegrower practices have combined and elevated us greatly." Payette believes Virginia "will be recognized for our wine quality foremost, and then for varietal strengths such as cabernet franc and viognier. I undoubtedly feel we compete with other wine-producing regions around the world, because we have balanced, well-made wines distinct to our region."

On a clear, crisp autumn day in early November 2011, I drive up through the normally closed gates of what Jefferson named Montalto, the larger, taller mountain (1,280 feet) to the southwest that dwarfs Monticello, twisting up the narrow, steep road to arrive at the summit, the dramatic remains of the geologic collision of the African and North American tectonic plates that formed the Appalachian Mountains some 480 million years ago. To the south is the placid lower Piedmont; to the west, the Blue Ridge Mountains, shining in the late afternoon sun; to the north, the city of Charlottesville.

I approach a cluster of about twenty people standing near a very large tractor with a twenty-foot hinged arm; several rows of neat parallel trenches are punctuated by galvanized steel posts. The occasion is the first planting of grapevines on Montalto, a collaborative effort between the Thomas Jefferson Foundation (which owns Montalto and Monticello), and Piedmont Virginia Community College, which will use the vineyard for vocational training for its Viticulture and Enology Workforce Services Training Program.

The group is of students from the program at PVCC, dressed for vineyard work and each with a shovel. Presiding over the planting, and the lesson in vineyard layout, are a pair we've met before; Oliver Asberger of Wine & Vine Care, and Gabrielle Rausse. If Virginia had a grand cru vineyard system, this would be in it. Thirty-five years after helping establish Barboursville Vineyards nearby and, through his grafting work, many other Virginia vineyards in the following decade, Rausse is helping the students ensure quality Virginia viticulture continues into the twenty-first century, on a world-class site originally owned by Jefferson himself. And the grape being planted? Pinot noir, one Jefferson appreciated while visiting Burgundy and had planted at his Monticello vineyard, and which Rausse points out can be made as a dry rosé, a sparkling blanc de noirs, or a fruity or complex oak-aged dry red wine. While the 2011 vintage was not nearly as fine as the 2010, Jefferson would be very proud to know that the famous red grape of Burgundy which he had enjoyed was being planted under expert guidance on a grand cru site he had owned in his lifetime, and that the patient science of viticulture would continue henceforth in Virginia.

ACKNOWLEDGMENTS

I'd like to thank the many members of the Virginia wine industry for their time and generosity, especially Lucie Morton for reviewing the viticulture chapter and Annette Boyd for her assistance arranging interviews with state officials on short notice and giving permission to reproduce the Wine Marketing Office's maps in this book.

ADDITIONAL INFORMATION

Current Virginia Wine Statistics

- Virginia ranks sixth among American states by volume of wine grapes produced (1.18 million gallons).
- There are about 200 operating farm wineries across the state.
- There are about 3,000 acres of wine-grape vineyards, with close to 90 percent bearing.
- Over 50 percent of Virginia wineries are located in the upper Piedmont, east of the Blue Ridge Mountains.
- The average price per ton for wine grapes in 2010 was $1,700.
- The Virginia grape and wine industry has a total economic impact of more than $362 million per year.
- Leading cultivars by acreage planted (2010): chardonnay (475); merlot (339); cabernet franc (316); merlot, cabernet sauvignon (263); vidal blanc and viognier, each (229).
- Leading cultivars by reputation: viognier, merlot, cabernet franc, chardonnay, petit verdot, cabernet sauvignon
- Major rootstocks: C3309, 101-14.

Virginia's Six American Viticultural Areas

- Monticello (most terroir significance)
- North Fork of Roanoke
- Northern Neck George Washington Birthplace
- Rocky Knob
- Shenandoah Valley (much promise and potential)
- Virginia's Eastern Shore

Highlights of Virginia Climate and Terroir

- Virginia's latitudes are between 36°32' N and 39°28' N, roughly analogous to the area between Carmel and Mendocino in California.
- Climate is temperate (Amerine and Winkler Growing Degree Days [GDD] 2600–3400°F, but typically near 3200°F) with some moderating maritime influence around the Chesapeake Bay.
- Rainfall (av. 42.7 in.) varies widely by location and growing season (west of the Blue Ridge is usually cooler and drier). The growing season is approximately 200 growing days, except in the far southwest and the Allegheny Highlands where it is shorter.
- Soils are sandy loam in the east, mixed clay acidic soils in the Piedmont, and limestone-dominated in the Shenandoah Valley.

Viticultural Challenges in Virginia

CLIMATIC
- High relative humidity and rainfall (especially late-season tropical storms) and resulting threat of fungal disease.
- Winter vine injury (varies by site and cultivar).
- Spring and fall frosts (varies by season and site).
- Summer drought.
- Hail; tornadoes; lightning strikes on vineyard trellis stakes, and, wires (rare and isolated, but still factors).

DISEASES

- Fungal diseases: Black rot, powdery mildew, downy mildew, botrytis bunch rot, phomopsis cane and leaf spot, anthracnose.
- Vine trunk diseases: "Black goo"/Esca, crown gall, eutypa dieback.
- Vine virus diseases: Leafroll virus, tomato and tobacco ringspot.
- Insect vector diseases: Grapevine yellows, Pierce's disease, a phytoplasma fatal to grapevines.

INSECT PESTS

- Phylloxera: A native North American aphid that preys on grapevine roots, killing own-rooted vinifera vines. After phylloxera devastated European vineyards in the late nineteenth century, European grape varieties began to be grafted onto resistant American rootstock (except in environments hostile to the insect).
- Grape root borer: An insect whose larvae feed on grapevine roots.
- Grape berry moth: The moth larva feeds on grapes; crop loss and fruit rot result.
- European red mite: This spider mite feeds on leaves, causing chlorosis.
- Climbing cutworms: These pests climb up tender shoots and gnaw them off close to new leaves.
- Grape flea beetle: Feeds on leaves but worst damage is with buds that are gouged out.
- Japanese beetles and green June beetle: Young vines with minimal foliage are particularly vulnerable to the depredations of these voracious invasive bugs, which can defoliate a young vineyard.

- Stinkbugs: A new pest nuisance which damages vines, and just a few can cause a strong corianderlike aroma in grape must. Research is ongoing on their effects on wine.

ANIMAL VINE THREATS

- Whitetail deer, raccoons, black bears: Deer are by far the most widespread large animal threat to Virginia viticulture, feeding on tender shoots and leaves in the early season, and on ripe grapes at harvest. A ten-foot-high deer fence is an economic necessity for a vineyard owner. Meanwhile, raccoons and black bears can tear up the vines while gobbling ripe grapes.
- Birds: The reproductive strategy of the vine is to attract animals to devour the ripe endosperm of the grape, and in the process germinate the seeds and also spread them. Birds and grapes have evolved in a symbiotic relationship, and the changing color of the ripening grapes from dull green to yellow and red cues the birds to hone in on them when ripe. Flocks of starlings and other birds can clean out a vineyard if precautions are not taken, and in Virginia wild turkeys are notorious for walking through a vineyard with their heads up, gobbling clusters of grapes as they go.

Vineyard Management Costs per Acre (2010)

- 250 hours of labor during the year @ $15 per hour = $3,750.
- Fungicides @ $500, materials @ $100, tractor use @ $50 per hour, total time @ 50 hours = $3,100.
- Machinery depreciation per season @ $400
- Establishment cost of one acre of vineyard (vines, trellis

wire, stakes, and posts) @ $15,000 (depreciating annually @ $750, assuming a 20-year life).

- Total cost per acre per year: $8,000

Rock Stephens on How to Be a Commercial Success as a Grower

1. Grow grapes where the demand is greater than the supply.

2. Grow grapes where the ratio of cost per ton sold to cost per ton to produce is the highest. (This does not necessarily mean the grape with the highest price per ton.)

3. Grow varieties that are matched to your terroir.

4. Pick a location that minimizes your production costs.

5. Develop a reputation for delivering quality grapes consistently.

6. Lay out your vineyard to minimize production costs. "For example, if you match your row spacing to the width of your mower, you will be able to mow it in one pass. If it is slightly wider, you would have to make an additional pass for each row, which would double your fuel and labor cost for mowing."

7. Stay on top of research and cutting-edge technologies. Be the "go-to person" whom other vineyards and wineries look to for advice.

8. Experiment, experiment, experiment. Be the grower who is the first to discover the next great varietal.

9. Mechanize wherever possible.

Tasting notes on select wineries can be found at www.beyondjeffersonsvines.com

INDEX